They are ignored and that suits them down to the ground because that way they can do what they want to do in their own quiet and crafty way.
           Michael de Larrabeiti, *The Borribles*

… knowledge comes only in lightning flashes. The text is the long roll of thunder that follows.
           Walter Benjamin, *The Arcades Project*

Gylphi Contemporary Writers: Critical Essays

Series Editor: Sarah Dillon

Gylphi Contemporary Writers: Critical Essays presents a new approach to the academic study of living authors. The titles in this series are devoted to contemporary British, Irish and American authors whose work is popularly and critically valued but on whom a significant body of academic work has yet to be established. Each of the titles in this series is developed out of the best contributions to an international conference on its author; represents the most intelligent and provocative material in current thinking about that author's work; and, suggests future avenues of thought, comparison and analysis. With each title prefaced by an author foreword, this series embraces the challenges of writing on living authors and provides the foundation stones for future critical work on significant contemporary writers.

Series Titles

David Mitchell: Critical Essays (2011)
Edited by Sarah Dillon. Foreword by David Mitchell.

Maggie Gee: Critical Essays (2015)
Edited by Sarah Dillon and Caroline Edwards. Foreword by Maggie Gee.

China Miéville: Critical Essays (2015)
Edited by Caroline Edwards and Tony Venezia. Foreword by China Miéville.

China Miéville
Critical Essays

A *Gylphi Limited* Book

First published in Great Britain in 2015
by Gylphi Limited

Copyright © Gylphi Limited, 2015

All rights reserved.

The moral rights of the editors have been asserted.

No part of this publication may be reproduced, stored in a retrieval system, or transmitted, in any form or by any means, without the prior permission in writing of the publisher, nor be otherwise circulated in any form or binding or cover other than that in which it is published and without a similar condition including this condition being imposed on the subsequent purchaser.

A CIP catalogue record for this book is available from the British Library.

ISBN 978-1-78024-027-5 (pbk)
ISBN 978-1-78024-028-2 (Kindle)
ISBN 978-1-78024-029-9 (EPUB)

Design and typesetting by Gylphi Limited. Printed by Amazon.

Cover image "Moth" by Anna Podedworna.

Gylphi Limited
Canterbury, UK

For Iain

For Judith and The Boys

China Miéville
Critical Essays

edited by
Caroline Edwards and Tony Venezia

Gylphi

Contents

Acknowledgements	xi
List of Abbreviations	xii
Preface to a Book not yet Written nor Disavowed *China Miéville*	xiii
1. UnIntroduction: China Miéville's Weird Universe *Caroline Edwards and Tony Venezia*	1
2. Ab-realism: Fractal Language and Social Change *Sherryl Vint*	39
3. 'Strange Tricks of Cartography': The Map(s) of *Perdido Street Station* *Raphael Zähringer*	61
4. Failing Better: *Iron Council*, Benjamin, Revolution *Dougal McNeill*	89
5. '*Blatantly* Coming Back': The Arbitrary Line between Here and There, Child and Adult, Fantasy and Real, London and UnLondon *Joe Sutliff Sanders*	119
6. Signatures of the Invisible: Reading Between *The City & The City* and Christopher Priest's *The Glamour* *Paul March-Russell*	139

7. 'You Should Be Teaching': Creative Writing
and Extramural Academics in *Perdido Street Station* and
Embassytown   159
Ben de Bruyn

8. *Iron Council*, Bas-Lag and Generic Expectations   185
Matthew Sangster

9. Between: International Law in *The City & the City*
and *Embassytown*   213
Anthony F. Lang, Jr.

10. Abnatural Resources: Collective Experience,
Community and Commonality from Embassytown to
New Crobuzon   239
Mark P. Williams

11. Afterweird: Konvolut n + 1: City/Slither   265
Roger Luckhurst

Notes on Contributors   285

Index   289

Acknowledgements

We would, above all, like to thank the contributors to this volume for their outstanding chapters, rigorous engagement with the editorial process, and ongoing patience as the volume went into production. Thanks also to the Centre for Contemporary Literature at Birkbeck, University of London and the University of Lincoln for their financial support of the 'Weird Council' conference at which several of these chapters were first presented as research papers. Our invited speakers Roger Luckhurst, Sherryl Vint, Joe Sutliff Sanders, John Rieder and Caroline Bassett were also instrumental in shaping the conversation around Miéville's writings and we thank them for their wisdom. Similarly, we would like to thank Damien Walter for his interest in 'Weird Council', which helped communicate our scholarly work to a wider audience. At Gylphi, we thank Anthony Levings for his generous support at the conference. Sarah Dillon is owed a special debt of gratitude for her vision and deft guidance, which helped steer the collection and made the editorial process an enjoyable one. Finally, we must thank China Miéville himself – for his astonishing fictions, his scholarly erudition, and his gracious engagement with the conference and this collection.

Caroline and Tony
July 2015

List of Abbreviations

Abbreviations of works cited by China Miéville.

Date of first publication is in parenthesis, followed by details of edition cited throughout (if different from original edition).

KR   Miéville, China (1998). *King Rat*. London: Pan Macmillan.

PSS   Miéville, China (2000). *Perdido Street Station*. London: Pan Macmillan.

TS   Miéville, China (2002). *The Scar*. London: Pan Macmillan.

IC   Miéville, China (2004). *Iron Council*. London: Pan Macmillan.

LFJ   Miéville, China (2005). *Looking for Jake and Other Stories*. London: Pan Macmillan.

BER   Miéville, China (2005). *Between Equal Rights: A Marxist Theory of International Law*. London: Pluto Press.

ULD   Miéville, China (2007). *Un Lun Dun*. London: Pan Macmillan.

CC   Miéville, China (2009). *The City & the City*. London: Pan Macmillan.

K   Miéville, China (2010). *Kraken*. London: Pan Macmillan.

E   Miéville, China (2011). *Embassytown*. London: Pan Macmillan.

R   Miéville, China (2012). *Railsea*. London: Pan Macmillan.

TME   Miéville, China (2015). *Three Moments of An Explosion: Stories*. London: Pan Macmillan.

Preface to a Book not yet Written nor Disavowed

China Miéville

Your intent had been to write a history and a philosophy of cast-out literature. Of the repudiated among books, of texts contraverted and disaffirmed by their authors.

What provoked the project was an aside, some mention in an essay subsequently mislaid. You paused midway through a brief history of vampire literature, fascinated at the claim – one you've been unable subsequently to confirm or deny – that it was Jane Gaskell herself who refused petitions to republish her precocious and rare second novel *The Shiny Narrow Grin*. And that she did so, as was at least insinuated, because she had come to disapprove of it. Considering the scope of her complex, caustic, unsettling works, you were curious as to what within its pages she might have taken moral or strategic objection to.

You sourced and read it with as much admiration as all her astonishing work evinces in you. What might have located it beyond the pale remained opaque.

Soon afterwards you read Octavia Butler's short shrift for her own *Survivor*. You felt guilty for how much you had enjoyed and found in the novel, and intrigued to read it again. It was pointed out to you that Jonathan Littell's Goncourt-winning tract of mythicized Nazism, *The Kindly Ones*, was not his first but his second novel, predated by almost two decades by the clunky, breathless, roguishly symptomatic Paris-set cyberpunk of *Bad Voltage*, for which he now expresses such offhand scorn. That J. G. Ballard refused to count *The Wind from Nowhere* among his work, effacing it as well as he could, denouncing it as 'hackwork'. Which it was, with the infelicities that would imply: but it was an ecstatic hackery, a hackstasy, that swept you up like the windblown debris of the hurricane it depicted, the apocalypse of an endlessly exhaling world.

You quickly realized that it is not only fiction the authors of which revoke its status. Auden renounced with bile what would become his own most-quoted piece, 'September 1, 1939'. The austere, demanding and latterly fashionable J. H. Prynne exiled from his own canon his first, 1962 collection, *Force of Circumstance*. So you pored over them both.

You began to outline the precise parameters of this negation, the qualifications for your nascent *Index Librorum Repudiatorum*. You are appropriately suspicious of authorial intent, but as organizing principle for this heuristic of disowned literature, the subjectivity of the writer/author-function is key. The line between distaste, or a changed mind, on one hand, and outright refutation on the other, must be carefully traced. Her apparent mild embarrassment of it notwithstanding, Jeanette Winterson does not disavow *Boating for Beginners*. Mike Dash may not list his engrossing history of the supernatural, *Borderlands*, on his website, but this is not necessarily quite disownership.

Nor can your list include books the authorship of which is denied out of political exigency, except insofar as such denial is also fundamentally sincere. In their performative self-criticisms, the Galileos and Pashukanises of history are primarily ventriloquizing the Vaticans and Politburos they have angered, and whether whispered, implied or merely sensible to the critic, their *eppur si muoves* remain stronger than the recantations.

Where a writer seems undriven by their lack of investment in any text, analysis is necessary to clarify its status. Though the title of his first, *No Sky*, greatly excited you, you came to judge Nigel Balchin's relation to his own unreprinted earlier work to be one of uninterest and neglect, rather than repudiation. In contrast, Christine Brooke-Rose's *The Language of Love* and *The Sycamore Tree* you inducted into your paracanon – though, uncertain, you avoid discussion of *The Dear Deceit* and *The Middlemen*.

There are many much clearer candidates. A writer may actively avoid all mention of such, as does Martin Amis of *Invasion of the Space Invaders*, an attic-banished child whose name he will not speak. They may proclaim the work negatively: it was his own damning of it that led you to Harold Bloom's novel *The Flight to Lucifer*, and you are glad that he could not, as he had wished, burn every copy. You read Nora Bloom's *Promise Me Tomorrow* against her own entreaties. You read Stephen King's *Rage* and Stephen King's essay on why he disowns *Rage*. You read Fleming's *The Spy who Loved Me* and Stanislaw Lem's *The Astronauts*. You sought other more successfully obscured obscurities.

If it is a subjective phenomenon from one optic, from another, repudiation is objective, or more accurately, social, being dependent on the fact of publication – which, given the history of the book, is overwhelmingly to say of the market. Commodification can be a mechanism by which the repudiation itself is actualized, as when an aghast Johann Beringer attempted to hide, by buying them, all copies of his *Lithographiæ Wirceburgensis*, with its pious, credulous faith in the unconvincing hoax fossils of his rivals; or when May Arkwright Hutton attempted to obscure her own earlier class fury at the treatment of miners in *The Coeur d' Alenes: or, A Tale of the Modern Inquisition in Idaho* by bulk-buying all copies she could – with the wealth she had latterly accumulated as a mine-owner.

More fundamentally, the investment of the (overwhelmingly monetized) mechanisms of publishing are ontologically necessary for the potentiality for repudiation in the first place. Without them, any crisis remains private. Burning his own poetry in 1868 surely bespeaks a colossal psychological drama for Gerard Manley Hopkins – but not, in your terms, a repudiation, the work being then publicly unknown. So with Virgil's deathbed desire to eradicate the *Aeneid*. His instructions to Max Brod to burn all his work have sometimes seen Kafka elevated to sainthood in this new canon, but however fervently or not the request was made, being of as-yet unpublished work, and even given its later publication, it is not, in your terms at least, disavowed.

As it is everyone's prerogative to change their mind, it was in nonfiction, so often predicated on argumentative positioning, that you might have expected to find the motherlode of denied literature. But the process of essayistic self-correction, the caveats and *mea culpas* and admissions of the merely wrong, is for the most part inadequately invested, lacking in the vigorous abjection necessary for true repudiation, whatever the theoretical *extremis*. There is clearly a Rubicon between Alastair MacIntyre's Marxist and his Thomist periods, but his attitude to the former appears to remain one of cordial respect, that distance notwithstanding.

Which is not to say that there are not exemplars of the tradition of authorially-despised within non-fiction. With sufficient vehemence, the repudiation of an author for their former work, such as that of Nathan Weinstock for *Zionism: False Messiah*, can inaugurate it into the *Salon des Abandonnés*. It is, though, mostly in the more mediated tenets of fiction and poetry that you find fecund grounds for your exploration.

———

You were not particularly surprised, on publishing a few tentative ruminations on this alter-genre, to start to receive obscure missives from one of the proliferative 'secret' societies competing in the niches of Modernity's psycho-ecology. Your correspondents urged you to join them.

They were very obviously in thrall to the usual species of vague and nebulous neo-Gnosticism. They tried to hook you with insinuations of insight, of an ultimate truth, and from their hints you instantly inferred what it was – that it is creation, the Word itself, that is the disavowed urtext, that we are the marginalia in a discard universe, an abandoned and repudiated thought experiment, and so forth. You did not respond: you remain agnostic on, and not very interested in, this thesis.

Yours was not a theological project any more than it was, any longer, a narrative one, no matter that a counterhistory of literature in its disowned castoffs remains necessary. When the missives arrived, you were already distracted, startled with a burgeoning understanding that demanded of you a different project than you had expected.

You were coming to understand that despite their innumerable differences and disparities, across all the epochs and languages in which they were written, whatever their absurdities, no matter their wrongnesses and, in many cases, their sheer badness, at base these texts share something. That their *having-been-repudiatness* is a superstructural expression of a fundamental *repudiatability*.

It is this shared quiddity that has become your subject. This quality of necessary disavowedness, a telos of refugee insight, of exile-tropism. And that shared, reviled substance, you have realized, the contours and content of which you struggle to articulate, you no longer need merely to note, but to tap.

What marks it out?

Some vision both vatic and stupid, that may be wrong and/or seemingly banal, but remains palpably indispensable. The vehemence of rejection is key, as with any repressed, and is why such ghosts return. In the spleen of the disinheriting parent is clear, uneasy overcompensation. In the sheer investment of the banishment dangerousness is imputed. These are dangerous texts.

You want to have written a dangerous text, too.

You are desperate to contribute to this lineage. To disown a book.

You set about evaluating candidates. You considered your own published work. One by one and with as unflinching an eye as you were able you reread them, listing their countless flaws. The idiocies, the mistakes and unending unworthinesses that comprised them. You forced yourself to stare at the basilisk fact of the degree to which your oeuvre so far was a pathetic pot-pourri of hip(ster) buzzwords and predictable tropes; of tortuous prose and un-killed darlings; of lazinesses and linguistic excess and inadequacies and indulgences; of political blindspots, constitutive fails; of corners cut and textures too smooth; of settling for adequacy, believing it good or worthy.

And yet, even in this unhappy satori, even in the welter of deep self-disgust it appropriately provoked, you could not quite bring yourself to find any of the texts worthless. There were, no matter how hard you hated, none, to your anguish, you could quite disavow.

The cowed relief this situation also provoked notwithstanding, this left you in severe crisis. Your desire for a repudiated text of your own refused to ebb. You spiralled into a depression out of which you were able to emerge only when you decided, finally, that there was one recourse open to you. You would have to write a text that you would later disown.

For a long time you pursued this strategy. Eventually, of course, you could no longer avoid acknowledging that this was a constitutively impossible task. There is no casting out that which is not within. You could not – no one could – commit to a work with a view to withdrawing that commitment. You cannot metabolize sincere fidelity with the intention of betraying it. You could only write texts in which you were not truly invested, the rejection of which would thus be their purpose, mere inevitable performance; or those in which you inadvertently believed and could not then disavow. You have scores of these failed failures.

In despair, you decided at last to turn your attention to groundwork: thus to write this preface. Necessarily abstract, as the text for which it opens is yet unborn, it seemed a useful way forward. Even, perhaps, generative of a method to inhabit a necessary, pre-emptively disinheriting cast of mind.

But key to your very project is the fact that the disavowed won't go quietly. That, in the opening formulation of Prynne's *Force of Circumstance*, 'locked rigid in the memory it lies'. The words deny their own denial, polysemically asserting that they are untrue, brittle, repressed – and going nowhere.

And you have come at last to understand that your own prefacing stance is predicated on that knowledge, on repudiatability as aspiration. Which pre-hobbles your own future efforts, and these words, this apologia, in an unexpected way.

If you should ever be successful in your efforts committedly to write a text you then committedly repudiate, and should this preface at last then find use, what it will introduce as disavowed will be a book in which, though not what you intend when you write it, you will find something unexpected, something worth finding. This very essay, in stating that what follows would better be repressed, will, like a traditional logic paradox, disprove its own predicates.

This preface, then, is pre-disavowed. Its imbrication with what may follow means it must ultimately disown the disowning it proclaims, in a metadisowning – one that is, however, simultaneously counterdisowned by the continuing rigour of its position, the truth of its claim that what it introduces is, as it must be, disowned. And, as instantly as it is pre-disavowed, these words must be pre-dis-disavowed again, in antiphase to its book, that you may come to write. And on and on.

You will have written two disavowed texts, and none.

———

There is no reason that such oscillation should ever end. Indeed it is the best and only success for which you can hope. But, or and, or and and but, this does not so much change as fractally recurve the terms of the project.

In attempting this prefigurative metatext – an observation platform which ineluctably alters the terms of what it hopes to observe – you permanently foreclose the possibility of any naive achieving of your hoped-for text. But what you open is, perhaps, another possibility. It may be that what you wait for is no longer literature to disavow, any more than that is what you currently write: nor, perhaps, is it literature to reavow again. Rather, it is precisely this osci-lit, this text that trembles between states of disavowal and reavowal, without ceasing.

As, at more occult and indeed disavowable level, do all books, avowed and disavowed and other.

This, then, is a preface to a book not yet written, a book you might never write, one which casts its potential and shadowless shadow across you and your snickering bluetooth keyboard forever.

This is a preface to a book not yet vowed.

1

UnIntroduction
China Miéville's Weird Universe

Caroline Edwards and Tony Venezia

I

What does it mean to 'unintroduce'? If we simply take an 'UnIntroduction' to perform the opposite, negating, function of an Introduction, it means *not* to bring to notice, *not* to acquaint, and *not* to present. But here lies the paradox: in not doing these things, the disavowal required of an antonymic UnIntroduction necessitates an Introduction in the first place. So let us both introduce and unintroduce.

This sort of taxonomic playfulness is inspired by the fictions of China Miéville. Since the publication of his first novel *King Rat* in 1998, Miéville has distinguished himself as one of the most exciting and inventive writers working in any genre in contemporary British fiction. He came to prominence with the first novel in his Bas-Lag series, *Perdido Street Station* (2000), which won him the Arthur C. Clarke Award and British Fantasy Award in 2001, as well as earning nominations for the prestigious Hugo and Nebula Awards. Part Victorian industrial pandemonium, part esoterically mapped unruliness, and replete with the most astonishing creatures, hybrids and non-human races, *Perdido Street Station* brought Miéville instant critical and popular success. The second novel in the Bas-Lag series, *The Scar* (2002), won the British Fantasy Award and the Locus Award for Best Fantasy Novel and Miéville was also the recipient of the Clarke Award in 2004 for the third Bas-Lag text, *Iron Council*. Subsequent honours have also been received for his 2007 young adult fiction, *Un Lun Dun*, which was awarded the Locus Award for Best Young Adult Book and *The City & The City* (2009), which won Miéville the Clarke award for an unprecedented third time, as well as the Hugo Award and the World Fantasy Award. In addition to popular success and critical acclaim, Miéville attracted academic attention early in his career, becoming considered an exemplary figure within the 'British Boom' of science fiction and fantasy (SF/F), which scholars argued saw the genre infused with a powerful new kind of inventiveness and purpose.[1] Along with writers like Ken MacLeod, Iain M. Banks, Justina Robson, Stephen Baxter, Gwyneth Jones, M. John Harrison and Nicola Griffith, British SF/F of the 1990s and early 2000s revitalized genre fiction.

The surrender to the weird

In the early- to mid-2000s, Miéville became aligned with the loose collection of writers who styled a 'New Weird' aesthetic.[2] H. P. Lovecraft's publication of 'The Call of Cthulhu' in 1928 in *Weird Tales* had defined the aesthetic strangeness of the literary Weird, with its unintelligible terrors and blank cosmic response to the pathetic vulnerability of man. Informed by the Weird tales of William Hope Hodgson, M. R. James, Clark Ashton Smith and Arthur Machen (whose works, taken together, form what is known as the 'Haute Weird' period between 1880–1940 [see Miéville, 2009b]), the New Weird sampled the sublime terror of these early pulp monsters, mixing it with an updated sensibility that had become fascinated with the monsters themselves, in addition to the supernatural terror they inspired. The New Weird was also informed by experimental New Wave science fiction of the late 1960s and early 1970s (inaugurated by writers like Samuel Delany, J. G. Ballard and Philip K. Dick) as well as new horror of the 1980s in influential texts such as Clive Barker's *Books of Blood* series (1984–5), in which horror began 'to focus on the monsters and grotesquery but not the "scare"' (VanderMeer, 2008: x). The epic sweep of Miéville's Bas-Lag trilogy has come to be considered as exemplary of the New Weird (although, it should be noted that by 2005 Miéville had distanced himself from the term).[3] As Jeff VanderMeer writes in *The New Weird* (2008), an anthologization of New Weird fiction he co-edited with Ann VanderMeer, *Perdido Street Station*, *The Scar* and *Iron Council* brought together 'pulp writing, visionary, surreal images, and literary influence to attract a wider audience' for contemporary fantasy (VanderMeer, 2008: xi–ii). The New Weird took as its precursor M. John Harrison's Viriconium series (1971–85), and prominent examples of the subgenre include: Jeff VanderMeer's own *City of Saints & Madmen* (2001–4) collection, which offers a journey through the teeming urban landscape of Ambergris with its mycological subterranean inhabitants and proliferating fungal spores; K. J. Bishop's *The Etched City* (2004); Paul Di Filippo's steampunk short stories; and Steph Swainston's *The Year of Our War* (2004). Common to these texts is a vertiginous sweep of genre-popping worlds that reconfigure our received understandings of literary boundaries – boundaries that are always-already problematic in terms of mapping critical frameworks onto texts that do not seek to fit within prescribed stylistic and aesthetic parameters. As Harrison put it, writing on a *Third Alternative* online thread, the writer of the New Weird seeks 'a liquefaction of boundaries' (Harrison cited in Luckhurst, 2005: 240).

    This liquefaction can be identified within a broader context of texts which hybridize several genres within the space of a single work. Gary K. Wolfe notes that such genre blurring has been called many things, among them nonrealist fiction, postmodern fantasy, transrealism, slipstream, postgrenre fiction, and New Wave fabulism (Wolfe, 2014:

66). Jeff VanderMeer describes the New Weird in more specific terms, as typified by 'texts combining transgressive body horror with urban science fiction' (VanderMeer, 2008: ix–x). Miéville's Bas-Lag teems with transgressive body horror: among the sentient races that populate the authoritarian metropole of New Crobuzon and its environs are humanoid cacti (Cactacae), beetle-people (Khepri), an exiled hominoid bird of prey (Garuda), a swamp-dwelling race of insectoid quadrupeds (Stiltspear), a stunted race of ugly flying creatures (Wyrmen) employed to carry messages, and a transdimensional-hopping giant spider known as the Weaver, who sutures the fabric of multiple realities and speaks in a gnomic, dream-like stream of consciousness that reads like incantatory prose poetry. But it is the Remade who most embody the grotesque forms associated with the New Weird's impulse towards body horror. Subjected to the city's punishment factories, criminals are 'remade' into new hybrid organic or mechanized cyborg forms – punitively compelled into extreme body modifications. These individuals are described in *Iron Council* as: 'ragged and variegated, their Remakings of steam-spitting iron and stolen animal flesh twitching like arcane tumours. Men and women with tusks or metal limbs, with tails, with gutta-percha pipework intestines dangling oil-black in the cave of bloodless open bellies' (*IC*, 20).[4]

The transgression of species boundaries in Miéville's body horror thus brings together the liquefaction of conventional genre categories with the hybridization of anatomical forms. Like the literary Weird, which Miéville argues functions as a 'placeholder for the unrepresentable' (Miéville, 2008: 111), the grotesque is also centrally concerned with the corruption of form: the corporeality of beings that subvert species taxonomies and inspire our disgust and abjection. This liminal zone of contact between self and monstrous Other, however, is also signified by transgressive behaviours such as friendship, desire and, even, love. In *Perdido Street Station*, the human protagonist Isaac der Grimnebulin is in love with the Khepri artist Lin, whose scarab head, mandibles, and chitinous physiognomy are described in sensuous detail: 'Lust came quickly. She held him back, opened her carapace and made him stroke her wings, which he did, with trembling fingers' (*PSS*, 171). As Joan Gordon (2003a: 459) suggests, such a bringing together of the monstrous and the romantic offers a 'normative grotesque' which closes the gap between the hybridized subject's traditionally monstrous position and a contemporary (or postmodern) sensibility of acceptance of the grotesque. In its mingling of inter-species attraction and repulsion, this 'illicit cross-affair' (*PSS*, 171) brings into focus Miéville's interest in examining species boundaries to wedge open a space in which to consider radically Other subjectivities and wholly alien ways of thinking.

This is further explored in his 2011 novel *Embassytown*. Set in a backwater colonial outpost on the planet Arieka, the novel charts the events that lead to a revolutionary crisis and civil war between different factions of the planet's ruling alien race, the Ariekei, and their human colonial subjects. The Ariekei (also known as 'the Hosts') are physically described as 'insect-horse-coral-fan things' (*E*, 141), which speak using two mouths and whose alien anatomy includes hooves, 'eye-corals' and 'giftwings'. The Ariekei depend upon interlocutors who can vocalize their double-voiced Language; this requires cloned human 'doppels' trained to think and speak as one entity in their ambassadorial role of communicating with these exotic Hosts. Despite their arresting physical presence, it is the Ariekei's use of Language which proves the most alien difference in the novel. In a pre-Saussurean turn, the words they use can only function as direct referents: their linguistic system thus prevents them from signifying anything, speaking metaphorically, lying, or describing events that have not already happened (like the rational equine society of Houyhnhnms in Jonathan Swift's *Gulliver's Travels* [1726]). In order to use similes, they have to enact the action described by the simile so that it becomes directly referential. The novel thus reflects upon the linguistic philosophies of Jacques Derrida, Paul Ricoeur and Ferdinand de Saussure and the alterity of the Ariekei opens up a broader consideration of colonial relations in which humans are subject to an arcane and virtually incomprehensible set of alien bureaucracies.

The politics of generic discontinuity

The liquefaction of generic frontiers in Miéville's writing takes place not just within the space of each single text as it challenges received literary conventions, but can also be identified across his works as a collection. As his career has developed to date, Miéville's fictional oeuvre has expanded and innovated, drawing into its own distinctive stylistic orbit a number of literary genres. He has experimented with fantasy, urban Gothic, and the Weird (particularly in *King Rat*, the Bas-Lag novels and his short fiction), post-apocalyptic fiction ('The Tain' and 'Looking for Jake', in *Looking for Jake and Other Stories*, and 'Watching God' in *Three Moments of an Explosion: Stories*), detective fiction and the police procedural (*Kraken*, *The City & The City*), bestial fable (*King Rat*), the Western (*Iron Council*), young adult fiction (*Un Lun Dun*, *Railsea*), science fiction and the space opera or planetary romance (*Embassytown*), and, more recently, he has reimagined the tradition of seafaring fiction (*Railsea* is a retelling of Melville's *Moby Dick*, and *The Scar* brings a tale of mysterious espionage onto a piratic floating ship-city). Even within any single text, Miéville's striking inventiveness weaves seamlessly between beloved genre staples and a philosophical interrogation of the alterity that such genres afford. As he has discussed in interview, Miéville freely admits that he finds 'that bleeding of genre edges completely compelling' (Miéville cited in Gordon, 2003b: 359).

This generic cross-fertilization can also be discerned in Miéville's comics scripting for DC Comics. Miéville wrote the story 'Snow Had Fallen' for *Hellblazer's* 250th issue (2008), and revived DC's series *Dial H for Hero* (2012–14). *Hellblazer* is a pre-eminent example of contemporary horror in comics. Its protagonist, John Constantine, was originally created by Alan Moore for the *Swamp Thing* series (1971–) and subsequently authored by others; a working-class occult detective, Constantine's cases have often been vehicles for social commentary. Writing for the series, Miéville joined the illustrious company of a long line of left-leaning writers who contributed to the comic such as Mike Carey, Jamie Delano, and Ian Rankin. *Dial H* had its roots in the sixties and underwent numerous revivals. Its premise is simple and attractive to any comic book reader: a mysterious dial enables ordinary people to become superheroes for brief periods, thus populating the Dial H world with protagonists who are effectively comic book fans transformed into their fantasies. Part of DC's 'New 52' continuity, Miéville's relaunch with artist Mateus Santolouco featured a sequence of outlandish heroes that bordered on the surreal. The skeletal, steampunkesque Boy Chimney, for instance, whose stovepipe hat is an actual chimney; or Captain Lachrymose, who parasitically draws strength from people's emotional breakdowns. Then there is the computational superhero Control-Alt-Delete who can reboot time; the snail-tank hybrid commando known as The Iron Snail; and The Rancid Ninja (thankfully, given descriptions of this character, he is never actually witnessed on the page). The protagonist, Nelson Jent, resembles a stereotypical 'comic book guy': overweight, unemployed, with dubious personal hygiene. Miéville can thus also be identified as belonging to a group of Anglo-American writers, including Michael Chabon and Jonathan Letham, that Roz Kaveney has identified as 'fanboy creators' whose work betrays the influence of comics and especially superhero comics 'derived from the favourite reading and viewing of their youth' (Kaveney, 2008: 202). Miéville's fanboy credentials were further enhanced when he co-authored a fantasy role-play game *Pathfinder Chronicles: A Guide to the River Kingdoms* (2010). In addition to these pop culture collaborations, Miéville provided the script for the experimental political short film *Deep State* (2012), directed by Karen Mirza and Brad Butler.[5]

Miéville's development of what Gary K. Wolfe (2011: 17) calls 'the post-genre fantastic' can be read as an explicitly political intervention.[6] The difficulty of his sophisticated engagement with divergent literary and generic forms – what has been referred to by Miéville scholars as 'generic overdetermination' (Birns, 2009: 208–9; Cooper, 2009: 213, 217) – thus uses genre to think through different political alternatives. As Carl Freedman (2008: 260) has suggested, in *King Rat* 'the generic discontinuity itself amounts to a political intervention of the highest importance'. Perhaps what is most impressive, or surprising, about Miéville's generic fluency is its resolutely old-fashioned commitment to the political impetus of science fiction's novum.[7] This reading invites us to reflect upon the role of fiction within the broader public sphere and to consider what it is that the contemporary literary imaginary may achieve, which such non-fictional discourses as philosophy and political debate are unable to articulate. In this regard, Miéville's novels offer a striking example of twenty-first-century literature's ability to imagine political alternatives at a time of crisis for leftist ideas within the political realm.

Miéville has stated that the two most significant influences on his life and his work are socialism and science fiction (Miéville cited in Gordon, 2003b: 360). Indeed, Miéville's political engagement is well documented and it is clearly visible in his novels.[8] The Bas-Lag texts, for instance, explore the issue of solidarity among different political, racial, or species groups: 'Cactus-women and -men; khepri with the two sputtering flails of the stingbox; raucous, frog-leaping vodyanoi. A llorgiss with three knives. Perhaps a dozen of mixed xenian races in startling solidarity' (*IC*, 357). The third Bas-Lag novel, *Iron Council* (2004), is arguably the most directly political. The novel is set during a period of political turmoil in the secondary world police state of Bas-Lag; its capital city, New Crobuzon, faces internal crisis as well as a war with the neighbouring city-state Tesh. The iron council is a perpetually moving renegade train, populated by revolutionaries from New Crobuzon who move through the desert ripping up and re-laying railtrack (echoing Christopher Priest's 1974 novel *The Inverted World*). In a gesture to the literary utopia, Miéville constructs a *eutopos* (good place) that is in no settled place (*outopos*): the 'promised place' (*IC*, 50), which affords 'a new life, a rolling democracy, Remade arcadia' (*IC*, 321), is neither fixed nor static but, quite literally, a moving process of collective struggle.

This understanding of utopia-as-process reveals Miéville's Marxist commitments. By aligning an assertion of the necessity of totalizing thinking with a post-structuralist appreciation of the fluidity of social, political, and ideational structures, Miéville's processual reading of political change yokes together the traditional and the contemporary in leftist political thought. As Christopher Palmer (2009: 225) has usefully demonstrated, the language of the contemporary left pervades Miéville's Bas-Lag novels, with their references to 'nomadic' cities (*TS*, 289), 'hybrid' cultures (*TS*, 306), the 'indeterminate' (*PSS*, 760), 'contingent and fleeting' (*IC*, 220) political formations, and the 'ragged, contingent democracy' (*TS*, 772) of a fluid process of negotiation and change. In *Iron Council*, which responds to the revival of leftist activist politics inaugurated by the protests against the World Trade Organization in Seattle in 2000, this 'dream of the commons' (*IC*, 560) brings together a twenty-first century resurgence of activism with Marx's vision of communism in *The German Ideology* (1845–6). As the golemicist Judah Low tells the Remade revolutionary Uzman:

> There must be a place beyond this. A place far enough. They won't follow you. You'll cross, right across the world. Where there's fruit and meat. Where the train can stop. You can hunt, fish, rear cattle – I don't know. You can read, and when you've read the books in the library car you should write others. You got to get there. (*IC*, 314)

Miéville's fiction is thus permeated with a commitment to Marxist dialectics, which theorizes the movement of historical and social change. Across his novels, we find numerous stagings of unionist and revolutionary political protest: underground subversive pamphleteers and guerilla fighters (*Perdido Street Station*); revolutionary struggles and civil wars (*Iron Council*, *Embassytown*); the 'primitive democracy' (*LFJ*, 244) afforded by the breakdown of established order in post-disaster scenarios ('The Tain'); or, the leitmotif of the Leninist question – 'What is to be done?' (*KR*, 24) – which Saul ponders in *King Rat*. As Sherryl Vint has written, in his fiction we encounter Miéville's conviction that fantasy can be 'something other than consolatory' (Vint, 2009: 198), and can overcome the long shadow of Tolkienesque conservatism that has plagued scholarship of the genre since Darko Suvin's privileging of science fiction as rational at the expense of irrationalist fantasy.[9]

Miéville's young adult fiction *Railsea* (2012), offers an interesting comparative text to *Iron Council*. The novel is a retelling of Herman Melville's iconic *Moby Dick* (1851), transposing Melville's seafaring narrative of the hunt for the great sperm whale into a quest for the ultimate 'moldywarpe' in an oceanic complex of railtracks. In a distant future, part-fantasy, part-dystopian projection, toxic ground pollution has rendered the earth unsafe to walk upon and great stretches of land between island city-states teem with a savage underground of myriad predators; colossal monsters descended from the small-scale garden animals and insects we know today (moles, rats, beetles, lizards, snakes, tortoises, owls, earwigs, centipedes, and so on). The novel's protagonists search for a mythical exit to the tangled railsea 'girderweb' (*R*, 213), chasing the dream of a single rail track that leads somewhere: 'An empty plain & single line' (*R*, 142). *Railsea* can be read as responding to the contingency of political struggle Miéville explored in *Iron Council*, in which the metaphor of the continually moving railtrack deconstructs linear notions of historical time as moving in a single direction of teleological progress. The 'contingent and fleeting' (*IC*, 285) track of *Iron Council* literalizes the non-synchronous movement of history and its moments of revolutionary possibility. The novel thus engages with a tradition of Marxist historiography which seeks to identify the historical moments in which revolutionary agency might disrupt capitalist development and strike out towards a new experience of time, and of political negotiation.[10] In *Railsea*, the historical train metaphor has severalized linear historical time into an 'endless spread of ties-&-iron … countless junctions, switches, possibilities in all directions' (*R*, 204). Contingency as literalized in the overwhelming snarl of unplanned, densely labyrinthine railtracks asks us to reflect upon the necessity of co-ordination, planning, and collective struggle within the political process. In this sense, *Iron Council* and *Railsea* examine the dialectical unfolding of material change as requiring both contingency, spontaneity and a continually evolving understanding of new political situations, as well as planning and strategic engagement between different actors and groups to achieve a broader alliance and solidarity that elevates local struggle onto the terrain of historical transformation.

II

Unto the breach

In his 2009 novel *The City & The City*, Miéville extends his earlier interest in the surreal aspects of the urban Gothic into a philosophically rich reworking of the police procedural. Drawing on Bruno Schulz's densely mythologized investigation of ontological uncertainty in his short story collection *The Cinnamon Shops* (*Sklepy Cynamonowe*, first published in Warsaw in 1934 and translated in English under the title of *The Street of Crocodiles* in 1963; Miéville cites Schulz in the novel's epigraph), the figure of the doppelgänger is stretched to encompass an entire neighbouring city. Set in a post-Soviet *Mitteleuropa*, the two cities of Beszel and Ul Qoma occupy the same geographical space but are rigidly separated under a regime of legally enforced and politically sanctioned apartheid. After a military confrontation referred to only as 'the Cleavage', the two cities are repudiated from acknowledging one another in a process called 'unseeing'. At the borderlands of the two cities, in a stretch of streets which belong to both, a 'crosshatching' of the map avoids prosecution: 'the lines and shades of division were there – total, alter, and crosshatched – but ostensibly subtle, distinctions of greyscale' (CC, 46). Any breach of the legal obligation to 'unsee' the other city results in an enforced process of 'Breach', which is described as overseen by a secret police: 'The Breach has no embassies, no army, no sights to see. The Breach has no currency. If you commit it it will envelop you' (CC, 248).

The all-encompassing Breach in *The City & The City* offers a culmination of one of Miéville's most sustained literary interests. Across his fictions, breach recurs as a way of naming the contact point between entities – whether physical, viscous, phylogenetic, conceptual, or ontological. The Collins Dictionary (Collins, n.p.) defines breach as etymologically encompassing the physical, the military, and the legal: in physical terms, breach is a crack, break or rupture, an obsolete word for a wound, the breaking of waves against the shore, and the moment when a whale parts the surface of the sea with its muscular upward thrust; in military terms it refers to the gap in a line of defence after an attacking party has battered its way through the enemy's fortifications (we might think, for example, of the most famous literary-militaristic breach as Henry rallies his troops in Act III of Shakespeare's *Henry V*, bellowing 'Once more unto the breach, dear friends') (3.1.1); and in legal terms breach describes the violation of an obligation or a legal severance.

This latter use of the term is of particular relevance to a consideration of China Miéville's fiction. Miéville's PhD in International Relations at the London School of Economics – subsequently published as *Between Equal Rights: A Marxist Theory of International Law* (2005) – offers a Marxist intervention into the field of critical legal studies. Drawing on the work of the Soviet legal scholar Evgeny Pashukanis, Miéville constructs 'a general outline of public international law from a commodity-form perspective' in order to assert that international legal frameworks are 'intimately bound up with capitalism and violence' (*BER*, 318, 319). As he concludes: 'A world structured around international law cannot but be one of imperialist violence. The chaotic and bloody world around us *is the rule of law*' (*BER*, 319, emphasis in original). Miéville's scholarly interest in international law can be traced in several of his novels. There are telling references, for example, to jurisprudence in *Perdido Street Station* and to maritime law in *The Scar* (as Miéville has noted in Gordon, 2003b: 356); in *Kraken*, strikers are '[p]ionioned under the law' and a policeman is memorably referred to as a 'law-worm' (*K*, 279); in *Embassytown*, local Bremen laws are variously invoked (concerning marital and guestworker status, religious law, arcane laws and provincial bylaws); in *Railsea* we are told that '[t]here were as many laws among the railsea lands as there were lands' (*R*, 120); and in the darkly appalling short story 'Säcken' we witness 'the end of the law' (*TME*, 165) as natural law is torn asunder by a mysterious curse.

The question of legal breach opens up an interesting analytical dimension to the category as it is used across Miéville's fiction. The image of a liquid meniscus at the point of fissuring as a solid object ruptures its surface recurs time and again in Miéville's novels and is a metonym for a broader philosophical point. In his fictions, breach is at once localized and particular: the fissuring of viscous liquids by a solid object signals breach ('The top of Isaac's head breached the lip of the hole' [*PSS*, 668–9], 'A mile below the lowest cloud, rock breaches water and the sea begins' [*TS*, 1]). In addition to numerous breaches of liquid surfaces such as the sea and the breach of military defences, Miéville also uses the term to consider the violation of a certain bond or covenant. Uther Doul, for instance, refers to the 'breach of Samheri and Kohnid laws' in *The Scar* (*TS*, 400), and Avice describes a geographical breach as pioneers fan out beyond the narrow confines of the eponymous colonial outpost in *Embassytown*: 'As our spies gusted out to search, we were breaching old agreements and habits of isolation' (*E*, 323). Miéville stretches the boundaries of legal breach to encompass not only specific juridical precedents, but also traditions or certain ways of doing things. Protocol is breached in *Kraken* (*K*, 277), as is political neutrality (*K*, 263, 338). Meanwhile, in even less distinct terms, faith is breached in *Perdido Street Station*, as Yagharek considers Isaac der Grimnebulin's final betrayal: '*What breach of faith, what cruelty*' (*PSS*, 860, emphasis in original). Similarly, linguistic breach occurs in *Embassytown* when the Ariekei split apart their non-signifying alien Language and start to incorporate symbolic references, metaphors and abstractions: 'They were signifying now – there, elision, slippage between word and referent, with which they could play. They had room to think new conceptions' (*E*, 363).

Miéville also explores literalized breaches, notably in *The Scar* (the oceanic breach of The Scar itself, an almighty 'crevice in the sea' that tilts the horizon and ruptures reality with puissant possibility [*TS*, 748]), *Iron Council* (the Cacotopic Stain, described as 'a rift through which split great masses of the feral cancerous force, Torque' [*IC*, 293]) and, most significantly, in *The City & The City* (where, as outlined above, Breach names the crime of forgetting to 'unsee' one's neighbours in the apartheid cities of Besźel and Ul Qoma). In addition to the physical, military and legal specificity of particular breaches, breach also suggests the profound ontological implications of boundary-crossing. In this sense, Miéville's interest in breach interrogates the existential and ideational parameters of what the French psychoanalyst Jacques Lacan famously termed the 'Real': that which exceeds conventional frames of understanding and which is experienced as a remainder, undermining stable definitional criteria (Eyres, 2012: 1–2; Moorcock, 2011: xi). In his 2008 essay 'M. R. James and the Quantum Vampire: Weird; Hauntological: Versus and/or and an/or or?', Miéville extends a philosophical reading of the literary Weird as that which refuses to cede to Manichean binaries of good or bad by extending what he calls a 'morally opaque tentacular' (Miéville, 2008: 111). In this sense, the Weird may be understood as the literary equivalent of breach: the moment when disparate and wholly incompatible entities are yoked together into a bastardized assemblage which cannot be reconciled into any form of union, but jostle uneasily. Such a breach transgresses taxonomies, linguistic parameters, species boundaries, and philosophical precepts. It seeks to name new conjunctions through a process of lexical articulation: as the narrator of Miéville's recent short story 'The Bastard Prompt' puts it: 'We need a new conjunction, a word that means "and" and "but" at the same time' (*TME*, 253). We have, of course, a number of conceptualizations which attempt to grapple with this kind of breach in literary discourse, and Miéville considers the irreducibly alien or Other, alterity, the Romantic Sublime, the Event as described by the contemporary French philosopher Alain Badiou, and the science fictional 'novum' – which, in an analogous manner to the functioning of the horror imaginary, the German utopian thinker Ernst Bloch describes as that which disturbs (Bloch, 1986: 432).

This is the central problematic with which Miéville's fictions are concerned – splicing together beings, forms and ideas into new, overlaid configurations without sliding into epistemological closure. As the striking new cover art from Crush Design released by Tor UK in 2011 for Miéville's novels demonstrates, the breach in our settled ontological sureties forces open a generative, fecund space of hybridized, grotesque forms. From the juxtaposition of a Victorian museum frontage with the tentacular underbelly of the kraken (*Kraken*), the conjugation of a ghostly ship, with main and mizzen course, topsails and jibs overlaid upon the back of a skeletal giant fish (*The Scar*); to the confluence of moth with dirigible (*Perdido Street Station*), sun disc with mysterious alien vessel (*Embassytown*), and the neat assemblage of upearthing mole with industrial machinic cogs (*Railsea*) – the new cover art lays emphasis on Miéville's dedication to a surrealist aesthetic. Such splicing distorts scale, hierarchy, and discretely autonomized areas of scholarly inquiry. We can trace this disjunctive collage aesthetic back to André Breton, who wrote in *Les Vases communicants* ['The Communicating Vessels'] (1933) that:

> To compare two objects as remote as possible from each other or, by any other method, to place them together in an abrupt and startling manner, remains the highest task to which poetry can aspire. (Richards, 1936: 123)[11]

This 'abrupt and startling' bringing into conjugation of remote objects or 'distant realities' (Breton, 1924/1972: 24) in Miéville's fiction is also informed by Walter Benjamin's reading of Surrealism. Benjamin was struck by the filmic montage aesthetic of moulding new conceptual forms that shock the viewer by ripping images and ideas out of context into arresting and unsettling associations. He modelled his own materialist 'dialectics at a standstill' (Benjamin, 2002: 10) – which actuates a new revolutionary historical consciousness through placing the past and the present in unexpected conjunction with one another – on Surrealism's use of montage. Where André Breton uncovered sur-reality by externalizing a Freudian dreamworld of unconscious interiority, in China Miéville's oeuvre to date we find the surreal located in an inescapably material world of fleshy, grotesque miscegenation. Miéville has discussed his interest in the surrealists, citing Max Ernst, Yves Tanguy, Hans Bellmer, and Paul Delvaux as influences on his own work (Miéville cited in Gordon, 2003b: 357). For Miéville, then, the fantastical and the avant-garde are aligned in their respective investigations of the otherness that such grotesque encounters afford. Indeed, in his Afterword to the collection he co-edited with Mark Bould, *Red Planets: Marxism and Science Fiction* (2009), Miéville argues that '[t]aking alterity as a starting point might allow us to trace structural relations between fantastic genres and the anti-realistic avant-garde' (Miéville, 2009a: 244). There is an intriguing connection here between Breton's 'Gothic Marxism' (Löwy, 2009: 22) with its revolutionary commitment to historical materialism, and what we might consider to be Miéville's own 'Gothic science fiction'. Although it names a seemingly oxymoronic term, Gothic SF undoes the distinction between SF as cognitive, and fantasy as irrational, that Darko Suvin established in his influential formalist reading of science fiction, *Metamorphoses of Science Fiction* (1979). Miéville's writing, both in fiction and criticism, offers a rebuke to Suvin, challenging the traditional instrumental Marxist reading that elevates SF above fantasy. A post-Suvinian reading of SF as entangled with the Gothic thus brings into dialogue the Gothic mode's relevance to the interrogation of monstrosity and otherness (Wasson and Alder, 2011: 3–5); something which Miéville's own fiction examines through its fluent melding of genres.

This blurring of categorical definitions – not just postmodern in the sense of the confusion between high and low cultures, but also, importantly between genre categories themselves – is a feature of much contemporary fiction and Miéville's writing is emblematic of this. Recent scholarly work on science fiction has reflected this, and the impact of Science and Technology Studies (STS), especially the work of Bruno Latour and Actor-Network Theory (ANT), has been influential here.[12] ANT is an ethnographic based approach which seeks to explain social order through the networks of connections between human agents, technologies and objects, with power being acquired through the extensiveness, stability, and durability of those connections (Latour, 2005). By overturning science's historical insistence on the separation of nature from culture, subject from object, and human from non-human, Latour agues that we should understand the interrelationship between the scientific and the social in terms of shifting, collective networks. This separation, or purification, of nature and culture into two distinct ontologies is part of the modern constitution which derives, according to Latour (1993), from the scientific revolutions of the seventeenth century: modernity works to categorize the world according to this binary, an act that is often violent, inflexible, and disciplining. This separation is doomed to failure as it is always already imperfect, resulting in 'the double creation of a social context and a nature that escapes that very context' (Latour, 1993: 16). Latour proposes that we have never been modern because of this failure of purification which obscures miscegenation and the intermixing of categories.

Thinking about ANT's impact on science fiction studies, and particularly the work of Miéville, reveals some intriguing connections. The rhizomatic topology of the network displaces any static topographies of margin and mainstream, high and low cultures. This is especially pertinent when considering the implosion of generic categories: 'if we read the history of SF as nonmodernist', Roger Luckhurst contends, 'it might appear that the genre has *never been modern* – that it was never a pure form and has produced little except "hybrid" writings' (Luckhurst, 2006: 13, emphasis in original; see also Luckhurst, 2005). The argument that SF, like the violent science/social binary, has never been modern thus offers an explicit disavowal of the purification of genres inaugurated by Darko Suvin's poetics of SF/F. Moreover, this sense of proliferating generic hybrids also helps us to read the work of much recent SF associated with the New Weird, as well as Miéville's fiction, which is often structured around both the blurring of generic boundaries and weird, hybrid creatures that resist easy categorization. As Luckhurst continues, the connection between Miéville and Latour is apt since '[the] clatter of adjectival over-determination is Miéville's principal strategy, and reads like one of Latour's lists of heterogeneous elements, combining human, animal, and machine' (Luckhurst, 2006: 13).

London's Overthrow

The fantastical remediation of Miéville's home city, London, recurs across his oeuvre to date. In the neo-Dickensian London of *King Rat* we are led through a new, subterranean part of the city as the protagonist Saul Garamond is inducted into a feudal rat underworld of internecine rivalry and warring gangs. This other London lies in the crevices between the mimetic, mapped reality of Miéville's readership, and a fantastical urban realm – 'tak[ing] place ten feet away, somewhere in another world' (*KR*, 213). The other world of the Rat King literalizes the poetic impulse to create another reality that is overlaid on the mundane topography of our daily lives. This fantastical literalization is, of course, common to children's literature and in *Un Lun Dun* Miéville examined another otherworldly incarnation of London. Although no less exuberant a setting than the 'chaos-fucked Victorian London' that New Crobuzon suggested (Miéville cited in Gordon, 2003b: 362), UnLondon is a simpler, somehow safer place. The quest narrative takes its young adolescent protagonists Zanna and Deeba on a journey through an inverted parallel city of monsters, magic, sentient objects and pleasingly erratic architecture. This 'abcity' is littered with the recycled detritus from the 'real' London and is described as the city's dream other. As a talking lectern announces: 'Abcities have existed at least as long as the cities ... Each dreams the other' (*ULD*, 109). Even with its malicious antagonist of sentient, deadly smog, the abcity imaginary of UnLondon is gleeful, charming, and populated with wonderfully inventive non-human characters (accompanied by Miéville's own pen and ink illustrations). However, in his short fiction we encounter a very different kind of London abcity. Miéville's 2005 collection, *Looking for Jake and Other Stories*, contains thirteen short stories and one novella, 'The Tain' (which was first published in 2002), several of which are set in London. Written in the second person (addressed to Jake), 'Looking for Jake' uncovers a post-apocalyptic north London after an unexplained 'quiet cataclysm' (*LFJ*, 7). Echoing William Morris's utopian *News From Nowhere* (1890), in which William Guest awakes in a future London, the narrator refers only to having 'woke up and found it like this' (*LFJ*, 14). After a societal collapse referred to as 'the fall' and 'an inexact apocalypse' (*LFJ*, 14, 9), new gangs have formed around Kilburn and a sense of profound difference is 'oozing out of the city's pores' (*LFJ*, 12).

The breakdown of social order that 'Looking for Jake' depicts is further explored in 'Go Between'. Morley is involved in a terrorist network of message-handling under the threat of mysterious and seemingly omniscient 'hidden agencies' (*LFJ*, 128). Since telephonic and digital communication cannot be trusted, messages are passed on scraps of paper inserted into ordinary objects that are moved around, Morley assumes, by an extensive secret organization of people like himself. He cannot be sure that atrocities broadcast on the news are not somehow connected to his own small involvement in this secret war, and the reader is left wondering to what extent his internal monologue is a result of narcissism or paranoia. Miéville returns to this juxtaposition of the ordinary, mimetic daily mundane with terrorism in 'An End to Hunger', in which videogames form the centerpiece of one cyberactivist's attempts to use 'guerilla software' (*LFJ*, 169) to bring down the government. Aykan's game is described as 'utterly extraordinary', 'an immersing piece of art': 'There was no "gameplay," only exploration, of the environment, of the conspiracies being unmasked' (*LFJ*, 168). Meanwhile, the dystopian future London of the short story ' 'Tis the Season' extrapolates a hyper-capitalist near-future in which Christmas is privatized by YuleCo., and anyone celebrating the festive holiday must pay a license for the proprietary decorations. The annual street party turns into a 'tinsel riot' (*LFJ*, 188) as protestors unable to afford the license fee clash with the police. This mixture of the fondly satiric and the dystopian takes a darker turn in Miéville's novella 'The Tain'.[13] Drawing on a rich tradition of apocalyptic London texts (including Richard Jefferies's gleeful devastation of the city in *After London; or, Wild England* [1885] and J. G. Ballard's 1962 ecocatastrophe *The Drowned World*), 'The Tain' features a violently transformed, post-apocalyptic London: a 'reconfigured city' of 'savage new communities' (*LFJ*, 282, 234), which has been taken over by a vampiric race of 'patchogues'. Living in another dimension, the patchogues were forced over the course of history to imitate humans in reflecting surfaces, a task which was substantially escalated as soon as mirrors were invented through the mixture of tin and quicksilver (which forms the tain, the tin membrane which transforms glass into a mirror). Over time, we are told by an unnamed patchogue narrator, these creatures learned to cross over the mirror-threshold into the human world, and a vanguard was sent to blend in as humans in preparation for the vampire revolution. Borrowing from Jorge Luis Borges's *The Book of Imaginary Beings* (in 'The Fauna of Mirrors' a league of 'mirror creatures' led by 'the Fish' break through the glass to invade the human world) (*LFJ*, 301), Miéville presents his reader with a host of 'pretend humans' or 'imago spies' (*LFJ*, 265) who have infiltrated London. After the deaths of millions, London's human survivors are scrabbling around the city's destroyed streets like rats, scavenging for subsistence, trying to avoid underground vampire nests, and pursued by resistance fighters, paramilitaries, and the grotesque imago 'detritus of reflection' of shattered facsimiles of human body parts that have become autonomous and move in feral abandon (grazing herds of hands, mindless scavenging teeth, and 'little clouds of colour-smeared lips like plump butterflies' eddying through the air [*LFJ*, 255]). The central character, Sholl, attempts to mediate with the vampire-patchogues and negotiate their 'alien psychology' (*LFJ*, 266), returning us to Miéville's interest in the question of a sentient intelligence that is unutterably other to human understanding. The weirdness of the imago shards and the vampiric patchogues is accompanied by the apocalyptic scenery of a destroyed London and its present atmosphere of open warfare. '[W]hat had been the Post Office Tower, then Telecom Tower', the novel's protagonist Sholl notices, 'was now something else altogether: a distorted beacon in the killing fields of central London' (*LFJ*, 237). Meanwhile, the science fictional short story 'Polynia' in Miéville's 2015 collection, *Three Moments of an Explosion*, presents an ambivalently catastrophized London. In the style of John Wyndham's *The Kraken Wakes* (1953), a number of aerial floating icebergs appear above the city, described as 'glowing things the size of cathedrals, looming above the skyline' (*TME*, 3); yet variously perceived by the narrator as threatening, exciting and, even, comforting.

While Miéville responds to the well-established apocalyptic tradition of London literature in these short stories from *Looking For Jake* and *Three Moments of an Explosion*, elsewhere his writing is concerned with another aspect of London literature: psychogeography. Originating in post-Second World War continental groups such as the Situationists, the term psychogeography was famously categorized with 'pleasing vagueness' by Guy Debord (1955/1981: 5) to indicate the affective intensities afforded by urban spaces. Debord described psychogeography as a 'renovated cartography' (1955/1981: 7) that could dismantle and recompose maps: by defamiliarizing the over-familiar, psychogeographers developed a refined bewilderment of the senses that forged new routes and passages in an attempt to unleash the emotional intensities of city environments. The *dérive* (or the purposeful drift as a form of willed disorientation), was both a new mobility as well as a new mode of appropriating and defacing already existing cartographic documents, through the collage mapping practices of *détournement*.[14]

Miéville's early writing in *King Rat* and the Bas-Lag trilogy established a recurrent spatial imaginary of London that responds to psychogeography's 'retrospective validation' (Coverley, 2006: 11) of a much longer tradition of visionary, Gothic London writing, including William Blake, Thomas De Quincey, Robert Louis Stevenson and Arthur Machen. This psychogeographical imaginary functions in two ways: first, to construct fantastical urban environments that resemble the 'real world' environments of the city; and, second, to offer a phantasmagorical doubling of contemporary London. The short story 'Reports of Certain Events in London' (2004), for instance, reimagines a malevolent topography of the capital's streets in which roads spontaneously appear and disappear, their status tracked and documented by a cabalistic group of urban explorers who resemble the London Psychogeographical Association (LPA). These 'Viae Ferae' (*LFJ*, 65) are liminal spaces that invade urban street grids, unstable passages that haunt the real, material places of the city. The story manages to rise above pastiche in its descriptions of the plausibly unreal. The Viae Ferae themselves recall both the hauntological *and* the weird: they are less an indication of a rupture or a break, than a recognition that, as with Lovecraft's alien Gods, they have *always* been with us. 'Reports of Certain Events in London' is presented as a compiled bundle of documents, including typed agendas and minutes from meetings of a secret society that monitors abnormal street activity, hand-written memos and letters, leaflets, reported sightings, tabulated chronologies, and the narrator's frame narrative. The scholarly narrator (a fictionalized version of the author) is a recurrent trope throughout Miéville's fiction, and recalls the narrators of weird and gothic fiction, the genealogists and antiquarians around which H. P. Lovecraft and M. R. James built their narratives. In a satirical gesture towards the London Psychogeographical Society, the secret group who issue these reports are themselves fractured with disagreement and their unbelievable descriptions deliberately recall the more outlandish pronouncements of the LPA; the reports themselves contain pseudo-marginalia that reveal the group's factionalism reminiscent of the sectarianism of post-New Left politics. The model of an alternative, magical London existing within the spaces of the everyday city is pushed to an extreme in the novel *Kraken* (2010). The improbable theft of a giant squid from the Natural History Museum reveals the capital to be subject to the whims of various secretive cults, each with their own agenda and shifting allegiances. A group called the Londonmancers offer another reimagining of the earnest *détournement* of contemporary psychogeographers, whose nostalgic preoccupation with ley-lines, Hawksmoor Churches and Jack the Ripper have lost much of the political radicalism of the earlier generation of Paris-based Situationists (Baker, 2003: 232). Digging up the pavement in an attempt to read the city's urban entrails, *Kraken*'s modern-day Londonmancers thus literalize, as well as satirize, the practice of 'taking a scalpel to the city and uncovering [its] dark truth' (Miéville cited in Manaugh, 2013: n.p.).

These texts reflect an ambivalent dialogue with psychogeography, and especially the literary tradition of London psychogeography. In his own London drift, *London's Overthrow* (2012), Miéville claims that psychogeography has degenerated into a 'local cliché. A lazy label for hip decay tourism' (Miéville, 2012: 58). The non-fictional *London's Overthrow* documents perambulatory meanderings through late night London in the autumn of 2011.[15] *London's Overthrow* borrows its title from Jonathan Martin's demotic pen and ink rendering of the city's prophetic apocalypse (c.1830),[16] and Miéville overlays this metaphorical eschatology onto the cityscape of contemporary post-riots London. Referencing the music of DJ/musician Burial and collaged cityscapes of urban activist Laura Oldfield Ford, as well as the ubiquitous Iain Sinclair, the pamphlet probes at the limits of psychogeography in its consideration of a post-millennial cityscape. Miéville takes his reader on a journey through the streets of contemporary London. Alive with youthful protest and revolt, the city strikes Miéville as 'pre-something' (Miéville, 2012: 14). The shimmering anticipation of a new order of political disenfranchisement and re-enfranchisement, unemployment and public sector cuts, tuition fees and 'sado-monetarism' (Miéville, 2012: 24), can be traced in a freshly radicalized youth movement and the increasingly hostile environment of a city in the grip of privatization, social cleansing and gentrification.[17] Miéville's political alignment with the youth movements of post-2011 London (specifically the Occupy LSX camp which occupied the square adjacent to St Paul's Cathedral from October 2011 to June 2012, and continues to be active in organizing anti-austerity protests) brings into focus his abiding interest in the city of London, socialist politics, and the process of radical activism. As he writes in an article on the literary Weird for the journal *Collapse*, 'with the advent of the neoliberal *There Is No Alternative*, the universe was an ineluctable, inhuman, implacable, Weird, place' (Miéville, 2008: 128, emphasis in original). Here, the Weird comes to signify our experience of capitalism in the twenty-first century. With the '*banlieueification*' (Miéville, 2012: 68, emphasis in original) of London as social inequality becomes ever more entrenched, our political lexicon appears inescapably Weird in the Lovecraftian sense: seemingly impossible, horrifyingly true, and cosmically uncaring. As *London's Overthrow* demonstrates, Miéville's political commitment to resisting privatization and defending public spaces via a creative engagement with the city at a local level (as exemplified in grime music, squatting, graffiti, allotment gardening, and local politics, as well as the practice of paying attention to these things) intersects with his own aesthetic praxis. Literary form meets content in the will to generic and stylistic experimentation, guided by the project of denaturalizing contemporary capitalist reality.

III

Miéville's importance as a contemporary writer lies not only in his astonishing fictions and his flair for narratorial and world-building complexity as well as pleasurable storytelling. As we have suggested, it lies also in his ability to pose broader questions of genre, philosophical reflection, and political imagining without compromising on story, plot, pace or characterization. The chapters in this collection respond to the extraordinary range of interests that have shaped Miéville's fiction to date. Sherryl Vint's chapter, 'Ab-Realism: Fractal Language and Social Change' offers an overview of Miéville's fiction via a persuasive reading of the political function of metaphor in his texts. Vint introduces the term 'ab-realism' to describe a narrative logic that both grasps the absurdities of capitalist 'realism' (the actuality of real life within contemporary capitalism), as well as constructing its own alternative 'realism' – a utopian imaginary that co-exists with our everyday lived experience. Drawing on Miéville's (2002) critique of capitalist realism, Vint argues that in his fiction Miéville is concerned to demonstrate the impoverishment of mimetic realism and demonstrate that the fantasy lies not in SF worlds but in capitalist 'reality' itself. Miéville's work, she argues, helps us to estrange the ostensibly naturalized realist literary genres and reveals that the everyday world of late capitalism that such fictions supposedly mirror are no less fantastical than science fiction and fantasy literature. Vint's reading of the ab-real suggests that Miéville's fiction does not present us with the opposite, or absence, of realism: rather, his narrative worlds encompass realism as well as those visions of alterity and possibilities for social transformation that challenge a restricted framework of conventional, capitalist realism. In emphasizing the gap between mimetic realism (and its ideological entanglement within capitalism) and the reality that we experience (as contingent, composed of innumerable strands of experience, and exploding the bounds of any singular narrative containment), Miéville's fiction thus reminds us of the contingency of experience and the ability to make, re-make and intervene in history.

Miéville's deconstruction of any fixed understanding of realism that does not already contain germinative alternatives is further explored in relation to the fluid, and frequently unreliable, maps found in Miéville's fiction. Raphael Zähringer's chapter '"Strange Tricks of Cartography": The Map(s) of *Perdido Street Station*' considers the function of such misleading maps in the first novel of Miéville's acclaimed Bas-Lag trilogy. Zähringer examines the reproduction of paratextual and intratextual maps within fantasy literature – noting such historical examples as Jonathan Swift's *Gulliver's Travels* (1726) and Robert Louis Stevenson's *Treasure Island* (1883) – and connects these with the medieval *mappa mundi*, which featured fantastical creatures decorating the edge of the known world within a cosmological hierarchy. Theoretical readings of the history of map-making reflect upon the double function of maps: first, as a means to inscribe power upon the landscape through an ordered topographical representation, and, second, to produce a cartographic object that requires craftsmanship and becomes fetishized for its artistry as well as the power it confers upon the map-user – leading to it becoming an object of lust. Miéville's map of the city of New Crobuzon forms a paratextual frame to *Perdido Street Station*. There are numerous missing street names and references to named passageways and buildings which do not appear in the paratextual map, reminding the reader of its imperfect and provisional representational status. However, as Zähringer argues, none of these maps offer official representations of the city, but are imperfect, hastily drawn and impermanent, (some are traced in mud or dirt), subjective, and subordinated to visceral experiences of the city.

Returning to the relationship between fantasy literature and political theory, Dougal McNeill's chapter 'Failing Better: *Iron Council*, Benjamin, Revolution', considers how both Fantasy and political theory share the task of imagining revolution – in *this* world, rather than in some secondary world or fantastical realm. McNeill argues that critical responses to *Iron Council* thus far have overlooked its indebtedness to the anti-capitalist movement, or *mouvement altermondialiste* (the movement for another globalization) from the turn of the twenty-first century. Miéville has admitted in interview that his Bas-Lag triology was a direct response to the post-Seattle, anti-capitalist movement (Miéville, 2008a: 70), and this resurgence of energy has returned leftist politics to a revitalized engagement with utopian dreaming that responds to the maligned tradition of revolutionary failures, and 'utopian', as opposed to 'scientific', socialism. Like Miéville, McNeill confronts the prevailing reading within SF studies of Fantasy as anti-political and often reactionary – what Miéville (2009a: 233) has referred to as the influential Suvinian 'paradigm'. Instead, he suggests that *Iron Council* offers what Nicholas Birns (2009: 203) defines as a 'heterodox rather than [an] orthodox' rehearsal of revolutionary uprising: messy and complex, it represents what McNeill calls 'a kind of realism-in-Fantasy', in which the novel stages a logical unfolding of the representational problems encountered in many revolutionary situations. McNeill names this strategy 'metaphorical *jamming*', which he describes as a baroque overload of images such that any unifying reading in terms of an allegory is thwarted – a philosophical gesture that keeps in mind Walter Benjamin's (1940: 256) insistence that 'nothing that has ever happened should be regarded as lost for history'.

Joe Sutliff Sanders similarly reflects upon the implications of Miéville's fiction for a reconsideration of the way in which we understand the relationship between SF and Fantasy literature, interrogating Miéville's contribution to children's literature in *Un Lun Dun*. His chapter, '"Blatantly Coming Back": The Arbitrary Line Between Here and There, Child and Adult, Fantasy and Real, London and UnLondon', argues that in questioning any rigid and ideologically enforced distinction between childhood and adulthood, Miéville's novel addresses the generic failures commonly found in masterpieces of children's fantasy. While invoking several clichés of the children's fantasy genre, *Un Lun Dun*'s story of the 'abcity' known as Unlondon rejects what Sarah Gilead (1991: 277) has called the 'return-to-reality' pattern in children's fantasy. Sanders argues that this is a problematic ideology common to the majority of texts in the genre, in which the child protagonist is ultimately forced to leave the magical world. This tragic sacrifice by the child hero – in which they must renounce their newly discovered realm of adventure and the power it confers on them to return to a life of school, rules and their parents' strictures – can be identified in influential texts and series, such as C. S. Lewis's *Narnia Chronicles* (1950–6), Philip Pullman's *His Dark Materials* (1995–2000) and Neil Gaiman's *The Graveyard Book* (2008). Sanders argues that the return-to-reality paradigm has problematic consequences concerning how we understand children's fantasy. Such endings suggest that fantasy is inferior to mimesis. Moreover, they enforce the expectation that as they mature child readers will graduate from escapist tales of fantasy towards the adult world of mimetic fiction; a move which mirrors the journey 'from magical to mundane' that the protagonists of classic children's fantasy are so often forced to endure. In rejecting the narrative logic of the child's return to reality after experiencing the exotic lands of fantasy, *Un Lun Dun* thus offers its readers a challenge to the conventions of children's fantasy. Sanders concludes that Miéville's rejection of the enforced separation between childhood and adulthood implied in the return-to-reality narrative also suggests a continuity with his other works of fiction, which similarly examine arbitrary lines of separation as well as the possible 'breaching' of such boundaries.

The question of 'breaching' arbitrary and punitively regulated boundaries is the subject of Paul March-Russell's chapter 'Signatures of the Invisible: Reading Between *The City & The City* and Christopher Priest's *The Glamour*'. The thematic tension of *The City & The City* hinges upon the co-existence of two cities, Besźel and Ul Qoma, existing within the same location but being entirely unseen by one another, with any breaches of this rule prompting punishment by a mysterious agency that polices the borderlines. March-Russell argues that the process of 'unseeing' in *The City & The City* echoes the means by which invisibility operates in *The Glamour* (1984), Christopher Priest's tale of doomed love between the 'partially' invisible Sue, the 'deeply invisible' Niall and the 'incipient, halfway' Richard Grey (Priest, 2005: 107, 109). In both texts, invisibility is explored outside of a rational-sceptical approach that would ascribe its power to any external agency (commonly associated in fantasy literature with the wearing of a magical token such as a ring or cloak). March-Russell examines a number of compelling historical points of reference that inform Miéville's use of invisibility as an instrument of state power, including the divided cities of Jerusalem, Berlin and the former Soviet Union. In tracing the intertextual associations of the trope of invisibility, he suggests that *The City & The City* may be read within the stylistic tradition of Modernists such as Conrad, Woolf and Faulkner, and the European literature of Franz Kafka, Bruno Schulz and Italo Calvino; as well as older folktales by Nikolai Gogol, the Brothers Grimm, and the literature of the Soviet period which literalizes the culture of disavowal. The networking of intertextual references to be found in Priest's and Miéville's engagement with the theme of invisibility thus invites readers to explore what March-Russell calls 'a plenitude of meaning' within the various allusions at work in each text. Such intertextuality, he concludes, is integral to both modernist and science fictional discourses. His strategy of absorbing numerous other sources thus gives rich texture to the intertextual density of Miéville's works, and may be read as informed by avant-garde literary experimentation. *The City & The City* can therefore be read not only as an explicitly political text that reflects upon sovereignty, the invisible effects of totalitarianism, and the constitution of national communities through processes of interdependence as well as disavowal, but also as the point at which Miéville's reimagined Weird aesthetic meets the modernist avant-garde.

Examining the importance of Miéville's connections with universities, Ben de Bruyn's chapter 'You Should Be Teaching: Creative Writing and Extramural Academics in *Perdido Street Station* and *Embassytown*', argues that critical responses to Miéville's fiction thus far have ignored the fact that they are all, to a greater or lesser extent, campus novels. Despite the richly-imagined Fantasy and alien settings of his fiction, de Bruyn argues that we can uncover an 'academic unconscious' in Miéville's novels which both represents, as well as systematically criticizes, university life. De Bruyn draws on Mark McGurl's influential study of the institutionalization of the creative writing programme within US higher educations in *The Program Era* (2009), in which McGurl argues that the emergence of 'programme fiction' in the post-Second World War period is informed by writers' absorption into the academy, particularly on creative writing programmes. De Bruyn suggests that using McGurl's historicization of late twentieth-century literary fiction to read Miéville has two consequences: first, it demonstrates the importance of the scattered references to universities, libraries and schools throughout Miéville's fiction; and, second, it reveals the importance of an alternative pedagogy of creativity which is central to Miéville's aesthetic practice. This 'extramural consciousness' plays itself out across a number of Miéville's texts in which teaching and learning at a distance from orthodox systems of education have demonstrable advantages. While universities frequently appear in his fiction as conservative, rigidly hierarchical bureaucracies, an alternative pedagogy of extramural research environments can be traced throughout Miéville's oeuvre. Such unorthodox modes of teaching and learning, concludes de Bruyn, constitute an important part of Miéville's aesthetic sensibility and reflect upon the historical gender and race biases of academic institutions.

In 'Iron Council, Bas-Lag and Generic Expectations' Matthew Sangster examines the readerly expectations of the trilogy: a publishing form that has come to be understood within fantasy literature as essential, since Tolkien's Lord of the Rings trilogy. Focusing his analysis on Miéville's Bas-Lag trilogy, Perdido Street Station (2000), The Scar (2002) and Iron Council (2004), Sangster argues that although these novels are resistant to many of the conventions of fantasy literature, the critical positioning of Miéville as a fantasy writer is informed by patterns of reading that have established certain readerly expectations within the genre. Sangster draws on the unprecedented datasets of reader responses to be found online at sites such as Goodreads, which recorded more than twenty-five million members in January 2014. Goodreads functions as a space of social performance, in which readers post their own reviews, advertise and discuss their tastes, and allocate star ratings for each of the books uploaded to the site. This collective body of opinion, as Sangster demonstrates, thus presents academic researchers with an unparalleled opportunity to harvest large datasets, since Goodreads records ratings details for each of the books on its site. Sangster offers comparative fantasy trilogies to analyse users' ratings for Miéville's Bas-Lag trilogy, including George R. R. Martin's epic fantasy series *A Song of Ice and Fire* (1996–), Stephanie Meyer's Twilight novels (2005–8), Robin Hobb's Farseer Trilogy (1995–7), Jeff VanderMeer's Ambergris books (2001–9), Neal Stephenson's Baroque cycle (2003–4), and Mervyn Peake's Titus books (1946–59). In particular, he considers how the departure in *Iron Council* from the fantasy conventions of Miéville's two previous Bas-Lag novels, has informed popular reception of the novel, encouraging readers to confound their own generic expectations.

Moving from the terrain of the literary to the legal, Anthony F. Lang, Jr.'s chapter, 'Between: International Law in *The City & The City* and *Embassytown*', examines Miéville's fiction in relation to the function of international law. As Lang demonstrates, international law was established to reflect the interests and practices of states within an international system that came into being during the period of imperialism. As both a novelist as well as a scholar of critical legal studies (CLS), Miéville's writing offers a unique opportunity to consider the operation of international law between the axis of apology (law reinforces pre-existing, unequal power dynamics) and utopia (international law aims to resolve conflict within a peaceful global order). Lang considers how *The City & The City* and *Embassytown* reveal the perversion of these two normative visions of international law, with the result that violence and injustice can outweigh peace and equality within the global system; echoing Karl Marx's famous phrase that 'between equal rights, force decides' (Marx, 1999: n.p.), which is the title of Miéville's 2005 monograph. In *The City & The City*, the law allows the two communities of Beszel and Ul Qoma to relate to one another in legal terms that arise not from legislature but from custom and the accretion of precedent, echoing the emergence of international law. *Embassytown* offers a contrasting legal perspective in which legal codes and protocols are established: although the breakdown of law by revolutionary violence reminds us both of the imperial context in which international law was founded, as well as its fragility in the modern world. Taken together, these two novels consider the challenges facing international law in the twenty-first century – its role within international affairs, the spectre of its imperial past, and its vulnerability in protecting states whose sovereignty is challenged.

Our final chapter returns us to Sherryl Vint's reading of Ab-realism at the beginning of this collection. In 'Abnatural Resources: Collective Experience, Community and Commonality from Embassytown to New Crobuzon', Mark P. Williams considers the interplay between the material and the immaterial in Miéville's novels. Drawing on his concept of the 'abnatural' (which Miéville derives from William Hope Hodgson's term 'ab-human', used to describe characters that are neither animal nor human), Williams explores the way in which fantasy functions in Miéville's novels to link the immaterial processes of social dreaming (as expressed in the utopian imagination) with the material practices of social and collective acts of creativity (such as making art or music). Referring to the theoretical framework established by Michael Hardt and Antonio Negri in *Empire* (2000), *Multitude* (2004) and *Commonwealth* (2009), Williams develops Miéville's theory of the abnatural into what he calls 'abnatural resources'. Abnatural resources bring together the immaterial and the material: for example, the strong correlation between music and community in *King Rat* reminds us of the material collective ties that underpin musical creativity as well as the immaterial experience such creativity affords in terms of those social, emotional, and affective experiences that lie outside of capitalist production. These social and aesthetic resources demonstrate how the *imagination* of alternatives can lead to collective political *transformation*, emphasizing cultural practices such as the production of art, fiction, music, and co-operative labour within the building of commonality (what Hardt and Negri term 'the multitude'). In offering 'abnatural resources', Williams concludes, Miéville's fiction reminds us of the power of collective cultural activities that operate outside of the nexus of commodity production and exchange.

Closing the collection is a satirical 'Afterweird' from Roger Luckhurst, titled 'Konvolut n + 1: City/Slither'. The explanatory note opening the chapter describes how a previously overlooked convolute (from the German term, *Konvolut*, meaning sheaf or dossier of notes) in the archive of Walter Benjamin's meticulously organized system of files and manuscripts has been uncovered. Hiding in fourth-dimensional space, the missing Konvolut was discovered through the application of 'abmathematics' and although the author cannot say with certainty that the Konvolut is not a forgery, it is nonetheless interesting to note the congruence of Benjamin's intellectual sources in the document with those of China Miéville. Assembled from a collection of notes, epigraphs and citations – from H. P. Lovecraft, Tennyson, Charles Howard Hinton and Rem Koolhaas to Bertolt Brecht, Bruno Schulz and Miéville's own works, among others – 'Konvolut n + 1' moves towards a set of working definitions ('Seven Weird Theses') of

Weird space, Junkspace and salvaging that can help us to appreciate a Miévillean reading of the city.

IV

Miéville's academic background, and the scholarly vocabulary that seeps into his novels, presents us with the challenge of undertaking a literary analysis of a writer who always seems to be two steps ahead of his critics. The chapters in this collection are developed out of a conference held at Senate House in London in September 2012, titled 'Weird Council', supported by Birkbeck, University of London, our publisher Gylphi, and the University of Lincoln. At the conference, academics experienced the uncanny sensation of delivering their papers in the presence of Miéville. We hope that this collection – and the conference which preceded it – does not echo the experience in *Embassytown* of Ariekei 'Celebrations of Language', which expose their human subjects to scholarly gatherings where, as Avice recalls, the Hosts would 'look at us, use and theorise us, without consensus' (*E*, 112–3). Rather, we would like to present the following chapters in the spirit of Captain Naphi's obsessive hunt in *Railsea* for her moldy-warpe, Mocker-Jack (a pursuit which is referred to as chasing her 'philosophy' or 'burrowing signifier' [*R*, 93]), which provides a metafictional apologue about the difficulties of categorization. Although '[h]umans', as Miéville's wily narrator informs us, 'like nothing more than to pigeonhole the events & phenomena that punctuate their lives' (*R*, 131), Mocker-Jack's evasive 'philosophy' thus 'resist[s] close reading' (*R*, 92), and cannot be parsed or conquered. The following chapters are intended to sketch out a number of ways to approach Miéville's generative fictions while acknowledging – as do the texts themselves – the impossibility of apprehending any final or settled position of critique. They both introduce and unintroduce a growing oeuvre, as well as suggesting the contours of future academic readings of Miéville's work. In the fluid breaching of these two activities lies a productive space in which readings can be suggested, tested, reconsidered, reaffirmed, and forged anew. We hope this collection affords such a dialectical space, and we thank China Miéville, all of our contributors, and Gylphi for their generosity and help in making this space possible.

Notes

1 For an informative reading of the British SF Boom, see Istvan Csicsery-Ronay's edited special issue of *Science Fiction Studies* (Csicsery-Ronay, 2003) on the subject. For critical scholarship on China Miéville's fiction see Sherryl Vint's (2009) special issue of *Extrapolation* which is dedicated to his work (at the time of publication in 2009, this included five novels and a short story collection). For other published readings of Miéville's fiction see also Farrell (2008), Rosenberg (2010), Maczynska (2010), Naimon (2011), Tranter (2012), Rankin (2013), Freedman (2013), Modestino (2013), Butler (2013), and Freedman (2015).

2 As Jeff VanderMeer notes, although the term 'New Weird' had been circulating for a number of years, M. John Harrison's thread on the *Third Alternative* public messaging boards in 2003 started a critical discussion about the term which marked a significant moment in the sub-genre's theorization (VanderMeer, 2008: ix).

3 By 2005, Miéville refuted the term New Weird as merely a marketing category, although it continued to be used by other writers, readers and critics (VanderMeer, 2008: xiii).

4 As critics have noted, Miéville's Remade offer a striking literalization of the biopolitical control of the individual body by the state and a violation of the body's sovereignty, reconfigured through a process of 'societal abjection' (Gordon, 2003a: 460; Newell, 2013: 501).

5 The film can be viewed online at: http://www.mirza-butler.net/index.php?/project/deep-state/ (consulted May 2014).

6 In considering what Wolfe identifies as the 'post-genre fantastic', Roger Luckhurst (2011: 23) has argued that a growing corpus of twenty-first century fictions are offering what he calls 'generic pile-ups': constructing increasingly complex fictional worlds that suture a sophisticated investigation of various generic traditions with a lucid awareness of their own hybridity as 'meta-critical commentar[y]'.

7 The novum (from the Latin, literally meaning 'the new') is a term that Darko Suvin develops in *Metamorphoses of Science Fiction* (1979) to identify those elements within works of SF that differentiate these texts from 'naturalistic' genres of fiction. Suvin borrows the term from Ernst Bloch

(1986: 432), who uses it to describe the presence of utopian potential or futurity within the 'now'. Suvin's examples of the novum include otherworldly or intergalactic settings, new technologies, and new forms of social organization that are substantially different from the world of the text's readership. The purpose of the novum, according to Suvin's (1979: 63–4, 81–2) political reading of SF, is to estrange its reader from their own lived reality and thereby reflect upon the political conditions of the 'real' world through the new perspective of the SF world; in this sense, the novum is a historical category.

8 For a discussion of Miéville's political involvement, which includes his work on the editorial board of the Marxist journal *Historical Materialism* and standing (unsuccessfully) for parliament as the Socialist Alliance candidate for Regent's Park and Kensington North in 2001, see Gordon (2003b).

9 Darko Suvin's influential definition of SF as 'the literature of cognitive estrangement' distinguishes SF as cognitive, rational and centrally preoccupied with scientific possibility, while fantasy (into which generic category he places also ghost stories, horror, Gothic and the Weird) is relegated to the position of 'anti-cognitive' which he describes as 'inimical to the empirical world and its laws' (Suvin, 1979: 8). Suvin's SF/F distinction has been substantially critiqued – most pertinently, for our discussion here, by Miéville himself who writes that Suvin's 'embedded condescension' to fantasy has stood as 'the major obstruction to theoretical progress in the field' (Miéville, 2009a: 232).

10 The image of railtrack as a metaphor for historical time and progress was so persuasive that it was even appropriated by communist thinkers and can be seen, for instance, in Georgi Plekhanov's assertion that the working class 'is seated in that historical train which at full speed takes us to our goal' (cited in Leslie, 2000: 174).

11 André Breton, *Les Vases communicants* (Paris: Gallimard, 1955), p. 148. The English translation is from I. A. Richards (1936: 123).

12 For informed discussions of SFS and its relationship to ANT, see Luckhurst (2006), Bould and Vint (2006), and Bould and Vint (2011).

13 Miéville's depiction of the protestors, we would argue, reveals a certain sympathy for the eclecticism of those innumerable groups that come together in protest marches. They are composed of a motley assemblage of Marxists, socialists, anarchists, a 'Gay Men's Radical Singing Chorus' (*LFJ*, 193) and radical pagans, all of whom tussle with one another but

eventually settle into a reasonably good-natured rendition of *Deck the Halls* interspersed with the *Communist Internationale*.

14 As with their practices of urban wandering which succeeded Surrealist *flâneurie*, *détournement* was a continuation of Dada and Surrealist practices of collage-as-juxtaposition.

15 *London's Overthrow* was published online at http://www.londonsoverthrow.org/ and subsequently as a booklet by Westbourne Press. All references are to the print version.

16 Jonathan Martin was the brother of the better-known Romantic painter and illustrator, John Martin. After attempting to set fire to York Minster in 1829, Jonathan Martin was incarcerated in Bedlam.

17 Following in Iain Sinclair's footsteps, Miéville mourns what has been lost in the contemporary privatization and redevelopment of the city: 'The unplanned London. Allotments; scrub; pokey businesses and local houses. Stratford animals, with the edgeland in which they thrived' (Miéville, 2012: 36-7).

Works Cited

Baker, Phil (2003) 'Secret City: Psychogeography and the End of London', in Joe Kerr and Andrew Gibson (eds) *London: From Punk to Blair*, pp. 323-3. London: Reaktion.

Benjamin, Walter (1940) 'Theses on the Philosophy of History', *Illuminations*, trans. Harry Zohn, pp. 255-66. London: Jonathan Cape.

Benjamin, Walter (2002) *The Arcades Project*, trans. Howard Eiland and Kevin McLaughlin. Cambridge, MA: The Belknap Press of Harvard University Press.

Birns, Nicholas (2009) 'From Cacotopias to Railroads: Rebellion and the Shaping of the Normal in the Bas-Lag Universe', *Extrapolation* 50(2): 200-11.

Bloch, Ernst (1986) *The Principle of Hope, Vol. 1*, trans. Neville Plaice, Stephen Plaice and Paul Knight. Cambridge, MA: The MIT Press.

Bould, Mark, and Sherryl Vint (2006) 'Learning from the Little Engines That Couldn't: Transported by Gernsback, Wells, and Latour', *Science Fiction Studies* 33(1): 129-48.

Bould, Mark, and Sherryl Vint (2011) *The Routledge Concise History of Science Fiction*. Abingdon: Routledge.

Breton, André (1924/1972) *Manifestoes of Surrealism*, trans. Helen R. Lane and Richard Seaver. Ann Arbor: University of Michigan Press.

Butler, Andrew M. (2013) 'The Tain and the Tain: China Miéville's Gift of Uncanny London', *CR: The New Centennial Review* 13(2): 133–53.

Collins Online Dictionary (consulted 28 May 2015), http://www.collinsdictionary.com/dictionary/english/breach

Cooper, Rich Paul (2009) 'Building Worlds: Dialectical Materialism as Method in China Miéville's Bas-Lag', *Extrapolation* 50(2): 212–23.

Coverley, Merlin (2006) *Psychogeography*. Harpenden: Penguin.

Csicsery-Ronay, Jr., Istvan (2003) 'Editorial Introduction: The British SF Boom', *Science Fiction Studies* 30(3): 353–4.

Debord, Guy (1955/1981) 'Introduction to a Critique of Urban Geography', in Ken Knabb (ed./trans.), *Situationist International Anthology*, pp. 5–7. Berkeley, California: Bureau of Public Secrets.

Debord, Guy and Gil Wolman (1956/2006) 'A User's Guide to Détournement', in Ken Knabb (ed./trans.), *Situationist International Anthology*, revised ed., pp. 14–21. Berkeley, CA: Bureau of Public Secrets.

Eyres, Tom (2012) *Lacan and the Concept of the 'Real'*. Basingstoke: Palgrave Macmillan.

Farrell, Henry (2008) 'Socialist Surrealism: China Miéville's New Crobuzon Novels', in *New Boundaries in Political Science Fiction*, ed. Donald M. Hassler and Clyde Wilcox, pp. 272–89. Columbia: University of South Carolina Press.

Freedman, Carl (2008) 'To the Perdido Street Station: The Representation of Revolution in China Miéville's *Iron Council*', in Donald M. Hassler and Clyde Wilcox (eds) *New Boundaries in Political Science Fiction*, pp. 259–71. Columbia: University of South Carolina Press.

Freedman, Carl (2009) 'Towards a Marxist Urban Sublime: Reading China Miéville's *King Rat*', *Extrapolation* 44(4): 395–408.

Freedman, Carl (2013) 'From Genre to Political Economy: Miéville's *The City & the City* and Uneven Development', *CR: The New Centennial Review* 13(2): 13–30.

Freedman, Carl (2015) *Art and Idea in the Novels of China Miéville*. Canterbury: Gylphi.

Gilead, Sarah (1991) 'Closure in Children's Fantasy Fiction', *PMLA* 106(2): 277–93.

Gordon, Joan (2003a) 'Hybridity, Heterotopia, and Mateship in China Miéville's *Perdido Street Station*', *Science Fiction Studies* 30(3): 456–76.

Gordon, Joan (2003b) 'Reveling in Genre: An Interview with China Miéville', *Science Fiction Studies* 30(3): 355–73.

Kaveney, Roz (2008) *Superheroes! Capes and Crusaders in Comics and Films*. London: I. B. Tauris.
Latour, Bruno (1993) *We have Never Been Modern*, trans. Catherine Porter. London: Harvester Wheatsheaf.
Latour, Bruno (2005) *Reassembling the Social: An Introduction to Actor–Network Theory*. Oxford: Oxford: University Press.
Leslie, Esther (2000) *Walter Benjamin: Overpowering Conformism*. London: Pluto.
Löwy, Michael (2009) *Morning Star: surrealism, marxism, anarchism, situationism, utopia*. Austin: University of Texas Press.
Luckhurst, Roger (2005) *Science Fiction*. Cambridge: Polity Press.
Luckhurst, Roger (2006) 'Bruno Latour's Scientifiction, Networks, Assemblages, and Tangled Object', *Science Fiction Studies* 33(1): 4–17.
Luckhurst, Roger (2011) 'In the Zone: Topologies of Genre Weirdness', in Sara Wasson and Emily Alder (eds) *Gothic Science Fiction, 1980–2010*, pp. 21–35. Liverpool: Liverpool University Press.
McGurl, Mark (2009) *The Program Era: Postwar Fiction and the Rise of Creative Writing*. Cambridge, MA: Harvard University Press.
Maczynska, Magdalena (2010) 'This Monstrous City: Urban Visionary Satire in the Fiction of Martin Amis, Will Self, China Miéville, and Maggie Gee', *Contemporary Literature* 51(1): 58–86.
Manaugh, Geoff (2013) 'Unsolving the City: An Interview with China Miéville', *BLDGBlog*, 18 February 2013 (consulted 29 May 2015), http://bldgblog.blogspot.co.uk/2011/03/unsolving-city-interview-with-china.html
Marx, Karl (1999) *Capital: A Critique of Political Economy*, Vol. 1, trans. Samuel Moore and Edward Aveling, ed. Frederick Engels. Marxist Internet Archive (consulted 20 October 2015), https://www.marxists.org/archive/marx/works/1867-c1/
Miéville, China (2002) 'Marxism and Fantasy: Editorial Introduction', *Historical Materialism* 10(4): 39–49.
Miéville, China (2008) 'M. R. James and the Quantum Vampire: Weird; Hauntological: Versus and/or and an/or or?', in R. Mackay (ed.) *Collapse IV*, pp. 105–28. Falmouth: Urbanomic.
Miéville, China (2009a) 'Cognition as Ideology: A Dialectic of SF Theory', in Mark Bould and China Miéville (eds) *Red Planets: Marxism and Science Fiction*, pp. 231–48. London: Pluto Press.
Miéville, China (2009b) 'Weird Fiction', in Mark Bould, Andrew M. Butler, Adam Roberts and Sherryl Vint (eds) *The Routledge Companion to Science Fiction*, pp. 510–15. New York: Routledge.

Miéville, China (2012) *London's Overthrow*. London: The Westbourne Press.
Modestino, Kevin (2013) 'Running High on Feeling: Emotional Ecologies in Sister Carrie, Robert Park, and China Miéville', *Studies in American Naturalism* 8(1): 52–78.
Moorcock, Michael (2011) 'Foreweird', in Ann and Jeff VanderMeer (eds) *The Weird: A Compendium of Strange and Dark Stories*, pp. xi–xiv. London: Corvus.
Naimon, David (2011) 'A Conversation with China Miéville', *The Missouri Review* 34(4): 52–66.
Newell, Jonathan (2013) 'Abject Cyborgs: Discursive Boundaries and the Remade in China Miéville's *Iron Council*', *Science Fiction Studies* 40(3): 496–509.
Palmer, Christopher (2009) 'Saving the City in China Miéville's Bas-Lag Novels', *Extrapolation* 50(2): 224–38.
Priest, Christopher (2005) *The Glamour*. London: Gollancz.
Rankin, Sandy (2013) 'A Sharp & Bladey Interpretation: The Fantastic as Marked Absence (or not) in China Miéville's *Railsea*', *Critical Insights: Contemporary Speculative Fiction*, ed. M. Keith Booker, pp. 152–68. Ipswich, MA: Grey House Publishing.
Richards, I.A. (1936) *The Philosophy of Rhetoric*. New York & London: Oxford University Press.
Rosenberg, Jordana (2010) '"The Future Historical Perspective": Miéville's Queer Durée', *GLQ: A Journal of Lesbian and Gay Studies* 16(1–2): 326–9.
Suvin, Darko (1979) *Metamorphoses of Science Fiction*. New Haven, CT: Yale University Press.
Tranter, Kirsten (2012) 'An Interview with China Miéville', *Contemporary Literature* 53(3): 417–36.
VanderMeer, Jeff (2008) 'The New Weird', in Ann and Jeff VanderMeer (eds) *The New Weird*, pp. ix–xviii. San Francisco: Tachyon.
Vint, Sherryl (2009) 'Introduction: Special Issue on China Miéville', *Extrapolation* 50(2): 197–9.
Wasson, Sara and Emily Alder (eds) (2011) *Gothic Science Fiction, 1980–2010*. Liverpool: Liverpool University Press.
Wolfe, Gary K. (2011) *Evaporating Genres: Essays on Fantastic Literature*. Middletown, CT: Wesleyan University Press.
Wolfe, Gary K. (2014) 'Literary Movements', in Rob Latham (ed.) *The Oxford Handbook of Science Fiction*, pp. 59–70. Oxford: Oxford University Press.

2

AB-REALISM
FRACTAL LANGUAGE AND SOCIAL CHANGE

Sherryl Vint

In *Do Metaphors Dream of Literal Sleep*, Seo-Young Chu (2010) argues for an understanding of SF that reverses Darko Suvin's position and challenges received wisdom about the relationship between SF and realism. 'Instead of conceptualizing science fiction as a nonmimetic discourse that achieves the effect of cognitive estrangement through "an imaginative framework"', she proposes to conceptualize the genre as 'a mimetic discourse whose objects of representation are nonimaginary yet cognitively estranging' (Chu, 2010: loc. 43–5). The importance of her distinction, she suggests, is that it allows us to understand the deep connection between the language of SF and that of lyric poetry, both defined by their capacity for intensely concentrated representation. The characteristic tropes of the genre, she continues, enable us to represent, and hence to understand, material experiences of modernity which are inherently cognitively estranging and hence resistant to representation within realism. SF overcomes this limitation through what she calls the 'science-fictioneme', that is 'a literalized figure of speech (or system of literalized figures of speech) through which a cognitively estranging referent becomes available for representation' (Chu, 2010: loc. 934–5).

On the surface, it might seem obvious to pair Chu's work with the fiction of China Miéville, especially *Embassytown* (2011), a book also deeply concerned with literalized figures of speech, the capacities of metaphor and the limitations of realism. Yet where Chu emphasizes continuity between SF and mimesis, Miéville's work points in the opposite direction: Chu links representation and understanding, implying that SF's power to represent what is counterfactual is a way to domesticate and process otherwise alienating experiences. She calls this SF's counterfigurative aspect, which displaces 'the ordinary attributes of figurative language – its weightlessness, virtuality, as-if-ness, dependence on cognitive labor – with the vivacity, solidity, persistence, and givenness that characterize the perceptible world of literal facts' (Chu, 2010: loc. 928–9). Miéville, by contrast, has long questioned not only the representative techniques of realism but also the givenness of this 'perceptible world of literal facts' it purports to mimic. As he argues in his 2002 introduction to the *Historical Materialism* symposium on Marxism and Fantasy, '"real" life under capitalism *is a fantasy*: "realism", narrowly defined, is therefore a "realistic" depiction of "an absurdity which is true", but no less absurd for that. Narrow "realism" is as partial and ideological as "reality" itself' (Miéville, 2002: 42, emphasis in original).

In his afterword to *Red Planets* (2009), 'Cognition as Ideology', Miéville, like Chu, interrogates the logic of Suvin's genre distinctions, in this case to question Suvin's preference for SF over fantasy. Working towards the observation that cognitive estrangement operates as '*something done with language by someone to someone*' (Miéville, 2009: 235, emphasis in original), Miéville concludes that the cognitive effect 'is a *persuasion*' produced by the '*charismatic authority*' of the text (Miéville, 2009: 238, emphasis in original). The persuasions of SF, fantasy and even realism all *do something* with language through distinct narrative logics, but none of these logics, he argues, is any more or less politically enabling – or any more or less ideological – than any other. He ends this essay with a call for more critical work on these many 'organizing principle[s] ... that structur[e] [the] temporo-moral ideology of narrative itself' (Miéville, 2009: 243), that is, for more work that explores the distinct ideological trajectories inherent in a particular genre's relationship to temporality. Miéville's fiction is itself a response to this call for further critical work, one that is organized according to a narrative logic I am calling ab-realism. Ab-realism is a narrative logic that simultaneously captures the absurdities of 'real' life under capitalism *and* points to the power of narrative to activate the utopian traces of another world that is possible and coexists with this one. In naming this tendency in Miéville's fiction ab-realism, I am following in the critical framework outlined by Miéville himself in his introduction to the special issue of *Historical Materialism* on *Marxism and Fantasy*. Resisting the dismissal of fantasy as a reactionary genre, in contrast to the critical potential ascribed to the *cognitive* estrangements of science fiction, Miéville (2002: 42) argues that what we take to be real within capitalism is itself fantastical. His work simultaneously denatures our experience of realist genres – and the everyday world of experience in late capitalism they supposedly mirror – and points out that this 'real' world is no less fantastical than are the worlds created by non-realist literary genres. While they share similar political commitments, then, Miéville's ab-realism engages the fantastical content of quotidian capitalism differently than does Mark Fisher in his term 'capitalist realism.' For Fisher (2009), capitalist realism is the world as seen by capital, an ideologically infused representation of this world that pretends to be mimetic reality even as it strives to convince us that this world as-seen-by-capital simply *is* the world, not one possible world among many. Miéville's ab-realism specifically targets the fragility and constructedness of this capitalist realism, refusing its pretence that the world-as-narrated is the same as the world-as-lived. Thus, Miéville's ab-realism conveys a deeper truth about the experience of the lived world than what can be conveyed by techniques of mimetic fidelity.

The power of narrative to transform social relations is everywhere evident in Miéville's fiction, not only in its political themes but also in the power of text-within-the text narratives. In *The Scar* (2002), for example, the persuasive effect of the counter-Hedrigall,[1] telling his first-hand tale of seeing the Armada destroyed, a tale – crucially – popularized by the respected Tanner Sack, turns the ship away from the Lovers' destructive plan. The novel refuses to resolve for us whether this Hedrigall is a 'real' nigh (a term used in *The Scar* to signify ghost-like traces of other realities) telling a 'true' tale or the original Hedrigall manipulating via a fiction: 'There were several possibilities', we are reminded, 'But it did not matter' (*TS*, 762); the power lies in the 'story, an awesome story, awesomely told' (*TS*, 764). This interest in the persuasive power of language to shape the experience of reality is repeated in tales of the Flexible Puppet Theatre in *Iron Council* (2004), whose plays of Jack Half-a-Prayer move from closed-down versions of a villain or a martyr toward more flexible options 'where the two little figures were not doomed or cursed with vision too pure to sustain or beaten by a world that did not deserve them, but were still fighting, still trying to win' (*IC*, 73).[2] The entire novel hinges on questions of narrative and belief: one of the novel's main protagonists, Judah Low, leaves the Iron Council to become its bard, as the revolution would accomplish less of lasting significance without an accompanying legend. At the same time, the Iron Council must be more than a legend for, as the Runagate knit-worker tells Ori, 'If there's no Iron Council, then we ain't never took power. But if there is, and there *is*, we did it before, we can do it again' (*IC*, 393, emphasis in original).

Perhaps the most compelling image of narrative complexity in Miéville's work is that of the railway line, central to both *Iron Council* and *Railsea* (2012). Refusing a vision of a fixed line leading inevitably to a single and given destination, *Iron Council* portrays instead a path always in the making, able to change its goal continually: 'Miles of track, reused, reused, it is the train's future and its present, and it emerges a fraction more scarred as history and is hauled up again and becomes another future' (*IC*, 285). Similarly in *Railsea* the tracks and lines proliferate, various switches and crossovers creating a nondeterministic system of rails. Further, this retelling of Herman Melville's 1851 classic, *Moby Dick*, is suffused with metafictional elements that continually remind us we are being told a story, and that narrative has a power to move us. Crucially, the obsessive object of the captain's pursuit is a literalized metaphor: a giant mole but also a 'philosophy', the term used in this world to refer to the prized giant moles, each of whom have specific names. The great white mole is referred to as Mocker-Jack, Mole of Many Meanings. 'You know how careful are philosophies', one shipmate comments on their struggle to track him, 'How meanings are evasive. They hate to be parsed' (*R*, 92).

In an interview with Stephen Shapiro, Miéville states that he is 'much happier with the notion of metaphor than allegory because metaphor is much more "fractally begetting" than one-to-one allegory' (Shapiro, 2008: 65). The polysemy of metaphor, its ability to enable multiple possibilities of thinking and signifying, is what distinguishes Miéville's use of literalized metaphor from the science-fictioneme defined by Chu. Rather than making concrete and hence understandable what exceeds representative realism, Miéville's literalized metaphors are evasive: they hate to be parsed. In the same interview, Miéville goes on to say:

> To literalize your metaphor does not mean that it stops being a metaphor, but it invigorates the metaphor because it embeds its referent within the totality of the text, with its own integrity and realism. ... The point of course, is not only that you could have both – [that is, the figurative, the monster *and* the thing it is 'really' about, realism] – the paradox is that genre *by its very literalism* invigorates both its metaphor and its 'internal' reality. (Shapiro, 2008: 65, emphasis in original)

Far from emphasizing the continuity between mimetic realism and SF mimesis, as does Chu, Miéville's ab-realism stresses instead the gap between mimetic realism and 'reality', which always exceeds both our representation and our understanding. This fractal metaphor allows us to perceive more possibilities in the social world and empowers us to change this reality by seeing it anew. As Lin, who sees with compound insect eyes, tells Isaac in *Perdido Street Station* (2000), his city – perceived through the parameters of his stereoscopic vision – is a much more constrained place than her own: '*You must process as one picture. What chaos! Tells you nothing, contradicts itself, changes its story.*

For me each tiny part has integrity, each fractionally different from the next, until all variation is accounted for, incrementally, rationally' (*PSS*, 16, emphasis in original). The difference between the world as Lin sees it and the world as Isaac sees it, given their divergent morphology and biological systems of vision, is one of the ways that the techniques of SF (through insect-hominid characters such as Lin) enables a fuller picture of the 'real' world than does mimetic realism. This difference in vision reminds us that how one sees the world, literally and metaphorically, is never merely mimetic of the world as it is.

The ab-real contains multitudes, contradicts itself, but is crucially structured according to a fractal logic, more than merely the deconstructive logic of both/and. That is, the ab-real requires a critical vision that can simultaneously encompass perspectives that linear logic would insist have to be resolved into ordered binaries, the rigid constraints of the either/or. The ab-real, by contrast, allows the latitude that from another point of view what appear to be contradictions from our limited perspective need not be resolved into larger and harmonious wholes.[3] The prefix 'ab' means 'away from' and so the ab-real flees from and refuses the givenness of realism, but without doing so in any particular orientation away from realism. It is not the opposite of realism – un-realism (the absence), a-realism (the contradiction), anti-realism, or the negation, non-realism. Instead, ab-realism multiplies our understanding of realism fractally, to include possibilities not dependent for their shape on their particular relation to the world as described by realism. There are many images of the ab-real in Miéville's fiction and they invigorate both the metaphors and readers' understanding of what they 'really' stand in for, because Miéville's ab-real metaphors partake equally of the 'ab' and of the 'real'.

In *Perdido Street Station*, it is the figure of 'crisis energy': Isaac's personal scientific discovery, which is generated by the simultaneous presence of more than one possibility. 'Potential energy's all about placing something in a situation where it's teetering, where it's about to change its state' (*PSS*, 169), as Isaac explains. Reality is always more than its givenness, he continues, '[t]hings turn themselves inside out by virtue of being things, understand?' (*PSS*, 170). The fullest image of the ab-real in this novel is the crisis engine that is powered by paradox: 'You tap the existing crisis energy in the water to hold it in a shape it fights against, so you put it in *more* crisis ... but then there's nowhere for the energy to go, so the crisis resolves itself by breaking down into its original form' (*PSS*, 170, ellipses and emphasis in original). The crisis engine works by acknowledging paradox and fractal possibility, and it produces, in the words of the novel, 'forces and energy that could *totally* change ... everything ...' (*PSS*, 170, ellipses and emphasis in original). This power of crisis energy is like the power of narrative as persuasion. Ab-realism is a narrative logic of language *doing something*, to use Miéville's language from *Red Planets*, to a reader's perception of reality. Just as crisis energy could change 'everything', so might the persuasive effect of ab-realism extend from remaking the world in its fictional representation to prompting the reader to see the world beyond the novel in a different way as well. Isaac describes his equations as trying 'to translate the ... uh ... *mundane*, into the crisis form' (*PSS*, 237, ellipses and emphasis in original), which is also a fitting description for ab-realism's relationship to mimetic realism: it makes visible multiplicity and tries to channel this energy into breaking down the original form, representing in a way that might change everything.

The combination of the Construct Council's consciousness (all rationality, formed from the artificial intelligence of the city's rubbish dump, configured into a hive mind) and that of the Weaver (a giant spider who exists on multiple dimensions, of which the city of New Crobuzon is merely one facet, and which cannot distinguish perception from dream) produces crisis energy because when these two patterns are combined they are 'simultaneously identical to and *radically divergent* from the original' (*PSS*, 633, emphasis in original). In this sense, the 'original' may be understood as the human mind whose experience of the world is never simply what Chu calls the 'perceptible world of literal facts' (Chu, 2010: loc. 929), but also encompasses abstract fantasies, disconnected from concrete materiality. The ab-real acknowledges that other possibilities, what the German utopian philosopher Ernst Bloch calls the utopian trace,[4] or Gilles Deleuze calls the virtual,[5] are not fantasies of an elsewhere or elsewhen, but are immanent possibilities of the material world. For Deleuze, the virtual is not opposed to the real but to the actual: the real exceeds the actual and contains multiple possibilities that might become actualized and change the givennness of so-called reality. Thus, the narrative logic of ab-realism is not the mystification Suvin associated with the fantasy genre he dismisses, seeing it as mere escapism from a political reality that needs to be grasped and resisted. At the same time, ab-realism also avoids the opposite response of the capitulation to charismatic authority that Miéville links to science fiction in his deconstruction of Suvin.

The ab-real in *Perdido Street Station* also structures the criminalized position of Yagharek, an exiled member of the bird-like garuda species from the Cymek Desert, whose crime of 'choice-theft' is described as a crime that 'steal[s] from the future as well as the present' because of the 'denied possibilities' (*PSS*, 693) that might have emerged from the un-chosen options of victims of choice-theft, from unactualized potentialities in the real. Humans would understand Yagharek's crime as rape: he forced someone to have sex against her will. Yet the person he assaulted, Kar-uchai, makes clear that their culture understands the crime differently and that this distinction matters to her. The point is not that he violated her sexually but that he took away her choice; he made 'concrete reality' (*PSS*, 692) a scenario in which she was abstracted as a thing in *his* story instead of being properly seen as a fellow community member empowered to make choices. This difference in how one frames the crime – and why it is a crime – points to the reciprocal relationship between fantasy and materiality in any reality – fictional or experiential – and the important consequences of divergent ways of constructing their truth. The ab-real similarly characterizes the Possible Sword belonging to Uther Doul, a highly trained bodyguard in *The Scar* who protects the leaders of the floating ship-city of Armada, as well as the possibility mining technique of the Ghosthead,[6] an ancient empire who ruled Bas-Lag over three thousand years before the events narrated in the novel. As Doul reminds the novel's protagonist Bellis Coldwine, she does not see the possible sword itself in what she takes to be reality, but only perceives the sword within one aspect of reality: the weapon's full reality is, rather, 'contextual' (*TS*, 479) and exceeds the actual in which she lives. The possible sword is also called a '*Might*-blade': 'It might; it might not. *Might* not meaning potency, but *potentiality*' (*TS*, 445, emphasis in original). Like Deleuze's notion of the virtual, Miéville's ab-real is shown here to be not a rethinking of merely epistemology but of ontology: that is, it is not merely a question of a different kind of knowledge about the world but of a different kind of world. When the Ghosthead crashed into the world of Bas-Lag from their other plane of existence, Uther Doul reminds Bellis, this force 'was violent enough to smash open the world – reality itself', fracturing the 'world's rules as well as its surface' (*TS*, 482). Yet their mantra was 'what we break we may reshape … We have found rich deposits of chance, and we will dig them out' (*TS*, 543). They had *scarred* the world, but as the novel so clearly shows us, scarring is a sign not of damage but of healing, of becoming something new, of actualizing other possibilities.[7] This Scar – near which nighs (the novel's word for the ghost-like traces of other realities) of un-actualized reals (that is, worlds which might as easily exist as our own but do not because different possibilities were actualized) become tangible – is 'teeming with the way things weren't and aren't but could be' (*TS*, 748). The Scar is a literalized metaphor for the persuasive power of narrative to actualize such possibilities.

In *Iron Council* golemetry is the science of the ab-real. As Judah describes the practice: 'Golemetry is interruption. Golemetry is matter made to view itself anew, given a command that organizes it, a task' (*IC*, 222). The living cannot be made golems because what is alive exercises its own agency and choices, makes its own possibilities, but the unalive:

> is inert because it *happens to lie just so*. We make it meaningful. We do not order it but point out the order that inheres unseen, always already there. This act of pointing is at least as much assertion and persuasion as observation. We see structure, and in pointing it out we see mechanisms and grasp them, and we twist. Because patterns are asserted not in stasis but in change. Golemetry is an *interruption*. It is a subordinating of the static *IS* to the active *AM*. (*IC*, 222, emphasis in original)

Golemetry, like the other images of change, is about making actual something that is materially present in the virtual. Reality is configured in a particular way because 'we make it meaningful'; thus, we have the power to make it mean otherwise. Further, *'Golemetry's an argument, an intervention'* and one can intervene *'in ideas or hopes'* (*IC*, 225, emphasis in original) as well as in clay. Like narrative, golemetry is a persuasion: a kind of pointing that enables us to see otherwise. Ab-realism is a narrative logic of pointing that asserts virtual possibilities beyond what mimetic realism, the 'real' world as seen by capitalist fantasy, has convinced us is the world we inevitably must see and inhabit.

When Judah creates the time golem at the end of *Iron Council*, he intervenes in the approach of revolution, preserving the power of the Council as both legend and material reality: drawing on Ernst Bloch's utopian formulation of the 'Not Yet', we might say that the Council is thus not-yet-arrived within the novel's present, but is nonetheless real and still coming.[8] As the novel's conclusion tells us: *'The Iron Council is not stopped it is* onrushing *it is* immanent *and we see it only in this one moment'* (*IC*, 613, emphasis in original). Like Uther Doul's Possible Sword in *The Scar*, it exceeds the reality we see in this one moment, is immanent – if not imminent – and as much a part of reality as is the defeat of the revolutionary New Crobuzon Collective by the Militia. Ab-realism is this power to represent simultaneously both mimetic reality and what is *away from* that image of a taken-for-granted, given reality presumed to be universal and neutral. It is the power of those who live and move in Breach, the omnipresent entity governing the two cities of Beszél and Ul Qoma in Miéville's 2009 novel *The City & The City*, which enforces a strict separation between the two cities and prevents citizens from acknowledging the presence of their neighbouring city. Perhaps more than any other of Miéville's fictions, this novel epitomizes the persuasive powers of language and narrative to enforce the ideological discipline of seeing and unseeing as convention demands. Miéville takes care to establish that the practices of Beszél and Ul Qoma are far more than just acts of denial or wilful effort. Tasked with investigating the murder of a young woman who, it transpires, has committed Breach, the police inspector Tyador Borlú notes more than once that he is not aware of certain things being in his 'grosstopical' vicinity (a neologism Miéville coins to describe things proximate in gross, physical space that are simultaneously in the 'other' country and hence impossible to simply move between) because they are not within his ideological world; although at times he sees what he is not meant to and must hastily unsee, at many others he seems literally *not to see* what for him is in a different country. And yet, as his Breach violation and the novel's conclusion affirm, he can choose to structure his reality differently: to live in a unified city rather than cross the border between two countries.

The novel literalizes the poststructural axiom that language and perception *make* the world we inhabit. And its conclusion epitomizes the fractal potential of ab-real metaphor in which the fantastical novum, in Suvin's sense, is more than simply a gateway to what the novel is 'really' about. Thus, near the end of the novel when Tyador tells us, 'I lifted my foot in Ul Qoma, put it down again in Besźel, where breakfast was' (CC, 253), the reader experiences this as an estranging act. The persuasive effect of the preceding pages is such that the act of physically walking in the city without acknowledging the split between the two countries now seems as transgressive to the reader as it seems to Tyador. The split works, we are told, because 'you don't blink. That's why unseeing and unsensing are so vital. No one can admit it doesn't work. So if you don't admit it, it does' (CC, 310). Living in the city *or* the city is like taking realism to be the sum of reality, seeing only what is authorized, ideologically, by one city or the other. When Tyador joins Breach in the end, he is told, 'No one knows if they're seeing you or unseeing you. Don't creep. You're not in neither: you're in both' (CC, 254). Living in 'both the city and the city' (CC, 312), the novel's final words, is living fractally, perceiving *both* the givenness of realism and the possibilities of the imminent ab-real.

In *Kraken* (2010) the ab-real is embodied in the living ink, whose magical power – like that of narrative – is contingent on persuasive effect. The novel accepts multiple apocalypses as predicted by many religions, and its crisis is constituted less by the fact that the *ends* of the world have come, than that these apocalyptic ends are being narrowed into a single thread. Early in the novel Moore, leader of a religious faction aligned with Kraken cultist Dane, informs the novel's protagonist, the Natural History Museum curator Billy Harrow, that: 'You can't *see* the future, there's no such thing. It's all bets. You'll never get the same answer from two seers. But that doesn't mean either of them's wrong' (*K*, 108); and that '[a]ny moment called *now* is always full of possibles' (*K*, 116, emphasis in original). Yet, as the Kraken awakes Fitch, a Kraken cultist, observes that: 'Everything's ending. ... And all the other maybes that should be there to fight it out are drying up, one by one' (*K*, 187). In the Christian tradition, the apocalyptic signifies both a violent end and a new beginning, typically the new and singular beginning of the Christian paradise re-established on earth. In Miéville's tale of multiple religions, the crisis is precisely this reduction of the ab-real in all its fractal multiplicity to the singularity of a vision of the world as seen by one religious tradition that presumes to have *the* truth, just as mimetic realism is commonly believed to represent *the* world, not a vision of the world from a particular and situated subjectivity. The thinning of the *ends* of the world to its end is described as 'that closed-down future' (*K*, 241). The novel is thus not about averting apocalypse but rather about keeping it open, and we are told in the conclusion, 'It was coming up to the end of the world again, of course – it always was' (*K*, 481).

Miéville here literalizes his theory of metaphor, creating a world in which religion is simultaneously figurative and concrete. When his giant squid specimen is stolen from the Natural History Museum, Billy at first thinks this is the work of a deluded cult, but is chastised by Moore: 'Mad beliefs like that, eh? Must be some *metaphor*, right? Must mean something else? ... What an awfully arrogant thing. What if faiths are exactly what they are? And mean exactly what they say?' (*K*, 99, emphasis in original). Magic is literally true in this world, but its literal truth depends upon its persuasive ability as metaphor. Vardy, the senior Fundamentalist and Sect-Related Crime Unit detective, criticizes his younger colleague's cynical dismissal of those who have faith:

> You should consider the possibility that faith might be a way of thinking *more* rigorously than the woolly bullshit of most atheists. It's

not an intellectual mistake. ... It's a way of thinking about all sorts of other things, as well as itself. The Virgin birth's a way of thinking about women and about love. The ark is a far more bloody logical way of thinking of *animal husbandry* than the delightful ad hoc thuggery we've instituted. Creationism's a way a thinking *I am not worthless* at a time when people were being told and shown they were. (*K*, 242, emphases in original)

By making its metaphors living, material realities for both its adherents and this way of thinking – giving equal ontological weight to both the metaphor and the thing it 'really' stands in for – faith is a more rigorous way of grasping what animates our social world.

Understanding the power of faith – the power of metaphor and narrative – enables the materialist insight that reality is shaped by contingent human choice and belief and that we, like the Ghosthead, can remake it. Billy realizes that ink has the power to reshape worlds, that the giant squid's ink lets you *be* otherwise: 'The very writing on the wall. The logbook, the instructions by which the world worked. Commandments' (*K*, 402). This living ink and the invention of print culture meant that '[t]raditions could be created, lies made more tenacious. History written down sped up, travelled at the speed of ink' (*K*, 402). At first it seems that the godly ink itself is what contains this power to shape historical narratives, but Billy learns that the real power lies in what one can *do with* language, with narrative as *persuasion*. He discovers the cult's interest in him is not, as he thought, because he was the keeper of the giant squid; instead, the cult is interested in him because his joking tale about being the first person born by IVF has been given life by the belief of the bottle cult. As he feels the world about to be rewritten by the villain who has appropriated the squid's ink, Billy has an etymological epiphany: '*This is a fiasco*. He might almost have laughed at that strange formulation. It was the catastrophe, the disaster, the, the word was weirdly tenacious in his head, *fiasco*. He opened his eyes. That word meant bottle. *It's all metaphor*, Billy remembered. *It's persuasion*' (*K*, 460, emphases in original).

Grasping this power of metaphor, Billy renames the powerful entity, re-metaphorizes and hence re-positions it within a network of context and meaning. 'It's not a kraken', he announces, pointing at the god, and continues: 'It's not a kraken and it's not a squid' (*K*, 460). Both terms, kraken and squid, place the material entity within webs of meaning that are animated by distinct beliefs: each of these networks grants a power that Billy cannot control. Yet he can reassert control by labelling the entity a specimen, more specifically *his* specimen, that 'didn't exist until [he] curated it' and that has been 'written up' (*K*, 460). Disaster is averted because 'the universe had heard Billy, and he had been persuasive' (*K*, 461). Metaphor, like faith, is thus shown to be a way 'of thinking about all sorts of other things, as well as itself' (*K*, 242), and this way of thinking, if deployed to persuasive effect, can enact change. Crucially, Billy's power to change the world emerges because he recognizes the role of his own contingent choices in making meaning and a world animated by belief. History – reality – is *made by human choice*, not by impersonal supra-entities or forces such as fate.

Miéville's most extensive exploration of literalized metaphor occurs, of course, in *Embassytown*: here as well as literalizing metaphors to create the world of the novel, he creates a world that is inhabited by a species for whom figurative language is necessarily literal. These aliens, the Ariekei, speak Language, a semiotic system premised on the reversal of Saussure's assertion that 'in language there are only differences' (Saussure, 2011: 120). In Language, with the capital L, words *are* the things to which they point and the only way to make something speakable is to make it exist, materially. Avice, a human girl who grows up near the Ariekei, is made a simile in her childhood: the Ariekei want to speak a concept of 'making do' and thus Avice becomes 'the girl who ate what was given to her'. In order for the Ariekei to be able to convey the idea embodied by this phrase, Avice must literally undergo an experience of 'eating what is given to her' so that she may thereafter serve as the material antecedent for this word in the Ariekei Language. Avice is a simile, not a metaphor: she performs the action of eating what was given to her, and *then* the Ariekei can speak the concept of 'making do' by saying that something is *like* 'the girl who ate what was given to her': her material action makes thinking the idea possible. As Avice narrates, for the Ariekei 'each word is a funnel. Where to us each word means something, to the Hosts, each is an opening. A door, through which the thought of that referent, the thought itself that reached for that word, can be seen' (*E*, 55). Language – with the capital L – is thus without polysemy: each word can mean one thing and one thing alone, since meaning derives not from a system of differences *à la* Saussure, but from the one-to-one correspondence of original thing/thought and word.

The absence of polysemy means a closed-down world and a closed-down future. As Avice's boyfriend Scile, a researcher into Ariekei Language, explains, for the Ariekei there are 'no what-ifs ... Everything in Language is a truth claim. So they need the similes to compare things to, to make true things that aren't there yet, that they need to say' (*E*, 56). This narrowness of language is like the narrowness of mimetic realism: it can describe and refer only to what is, not what might be. A further idiosyncrasy of Language is that the Ariekei speak with two mouths simultaneously. Unaugmented humans cannot speak this dual-articulated Language, and so the inhabitants of Embassytown develop a system of training 'Ambassadors', in which two individuals are schooled to turn themselves into perfect mirrors of one another. In this way, an almost Siamese pair of humans can speak with two mouths using a voice that purportedly comes from a single mind: so fused have they become in appearance, behaviour and – it is claimed – thought. The Ambassadors are the embodiment of a naive conception of the relationship between mimetic realism and reality: each difference that occurs between them is carefully pruned away to restore an appearance of singular identity. The amount of work that Ambassadors regularly enact to maintain this appearance of one-to-one correspondence suggests – as does the function of unseeing in *The City & The City* – the ideological work required to reduce the complexity of the world as it actually exists to the perceptions and representations authorized by realism.

Ariekei society is changed when a rebel works to introduce other figurative tropes into their culture, to move *away from* the one-to-one correspondence of simile to the fractal potentiality of metaphor. As Scile explains to Avice: 'to go from "I'm like the rock" to "I am the rock". See? Same comparative term, but different. Not a comparison anymore' (*E*, 141). They desire to make Language say something new, because they realize that in saying something new they open the door to being something new. The key is the capacity for contradiction, for more than one thing, simultaneously, to be real and true. Most Ariekei are resistant to the change and Scile sees the loss of Language as a Fall from innocence, as introducing the capacity to lie into Ariekei culture. But metaphor is a complex kind of lying: it states things that are untrue by the standards of mimetic realism – being *like* a rock can be true, *being* a rock can only ever be figurative, or a lie – and yet metaphor is an 'enabling not-truth' (*E*, 291) because 'insisting on a certain might-be, changed what was'; thus the ability to speak in metaphor is a way 'to lie to insist on a truth' (*E*, 292). The alien Ariekei prove physically incapable of directly speaking a lie and thus cannot deploy their simile-words in ways that make them simultaneously true and untrue: they cannot say they both are and *are not* like, for example, the girl who ate what was given to her. The rebels discover in the pronoun 'that', however, a way to escape such rigidity: as Avice explains, 'Polysemy or ambiguity were impossible and with them most tropes that made other languages languages at all. But thatness faces every way: it's flexible because it's empty, a universal equivalent. That always means and not that other, too' (*E*, 295).

We should recall that in *Iron Council* golemetry was described as a kind of pointing to 'the order that inheres unseen, always already there ... [that] is at least as much assertion and persuasion as observation' (*IC*, 222). The 'Thatness' at the heart of the new language invented by the rebel Ariekei, colloquially called the Absurd, who insist on speaking in this referential way in language unmapped to material antecedent, similarly is about persuasion and change, about 'thinking of the world differently. Not referring: signifying' (*E*, 296). They rely on body language to supplement the spoken word and 'inven[t] pointing. With the point they'd conceived a *that*. They'd given the gag of the body, the outthrust limb, power to refer. That *that* was the key. From it had followed other soundless words' (*E*, 295, emphasis in original). Crucially, the Ariekei who participate in this 'semiotic revolution' (*E*, 295) can use language to lie, but equally important is the fact that this semiotic shift opens up the possibility for better communication with humans since this new language is one humans might share while Language was always impossible for humans. These Ariekei can speak contradictory things simultaneously using their two mouths, and this script – translated into English – is shown in the typography of *Embassytown* as a fraction equation in which the two terms can never cancel one another out. This is expressed most strongly in how the word metaphor is translated into this new language. The typographical convention is to put the words from each mouth over the top of one another so that the text can convey that they are spoken simultaneously. Sometimes both mouths say the same thing, such as Spanish Dancer's question to Avice as they prepare to discuss terms with the Embassytown council:

$$\frac{\text{You are ready?}}{\text{You are ready?}} \ (E, 330)$$

The Ariekei language is written this way in 'English' but with the words stacked on top on one another to convey the name in Ariekei. Yet even when the two alien mouths say the same thing, the implication is that they can say them with slightly different inflections, capturing the complexity of a world in which some statements are 'as much a truth as a lie' (*E*, 330). And this is how Spanish Dancer translates the word metaphor into the double-mouthed language. It is not:

$$\frac{\text{metaphor}}{\text{metaphor}}$$

but rather:

$$\frac{\text{lie that truths}}{\text{lie that truths}}$$

or, more succinctly:

$$\frac{\text{truthing}}{\text{lie.}} \ (E, 335)$$

These aliens can thus be read as speaking in the ab-real: metaphor is a 'truthing lie', the novel concludes, 'a lie that truths' (*E*, 336). Through the use of SF tropes that insist simultaneously and equally on the 'realist' referent and the SF trope, Miéville's ab-real becomes a way of using the persuasive power of narrative to see and *make* the world otherwise. For the new Ariekei:

> The said was now not-as-it-is. What they spoke now weren't things or moments anymore but the thoughts of them, pointings-at; meaning no longer a flat facet of essence; signs ripped from what they signed. It took the lie to do that. With that spiral of assertion-abnegation came quiddities, and the Ariekei became themselves. They were worldsick, as meanings yawed. Anything was anything, now. Their minds were sudden merchants: metaphor, like money, equalised the incommensurable. They could be mythologers now: they'd never had monsters, but now the world was all chimeras, each metaphor a splicing. (*E*, 312)

This is the fractal power of metaphor. As the mysterious police consultant Vardy tells Billy at the end of *Kraken*: 'It's all a matter of persuasion, as perhaps by now you know. It's *all* a matter of making an argument' (*K*, 468, emphasis in original). The ab-real is a way of making an argument about metaphor as a rigorous way of thinking. It makes an argument about more fully seeing our social world beyond its ideological construction in mimetic realism, a literary mode that works to reinforce the ideal that the world as narrated by bourgeois realism is simply a neutral reflection of the world itself, not the world as understood and experienced through the class values of those who invented and popularized this literary form. In Miéville's fiction, ab-realism is a way of using this power to intervene in our understanding of the social world and our opportunities for action in it: the fiction writer as golem maker.[9] By persuading others to believe in a new narrative of the squid, Billy activates the apocalypse as revelatory as well as destructive. It is an ending, but also 'a fiery rebooting. Uploading new worldware' (*K*, 469). In his introduction to the *Historical Materialism* symposium on Marxism and Fantasy, Miéville quotes from Antonio Gramsci's *Prison Notebooks* (1929–35) the claim that '[p]ossibility is not reality: but it is in itself a reality' (Miéville, 2002: 45). This reality of the possible is the narrative logic of the ab-real.

Notes

1 Hedrigall is one of the crew of the Armada that is the main setting for *The Scar*. One of the conceits of the novel is that there is an area of the world in which various other possible worlds bleed into one another. After a certain battle, it is unclear whether the character – believed lost – has returned or if another version of him from another possibility has come to the Armada instead. I favour the latter interpretation.

2 Jack Half-a Prayer is a Remade criminal who becomes a folk hero among the dispossessed of New Crobuzon. The Remade are bio-engineered people who are punished with body modification by the judiciary. Such modifications are sometimes used to reshape their bodies for labour but are often merely whimsical and macabre instances of 'poetic' justice. Their collective movement rebrands them the fReemade. Jack is a sort of Robin Hood figure of resistance.

3 There are obvious affinities here between Miéville's ab-realism and Haraway's cyborg figuration. Haraway (1991: 149) calls her manifesto an ironic myth and explains that 'Irony is about contradictions that do not resolve into larger wholes, even dialectically, about the tension of holding incompatible things together because both or all are necessary and true.'

4 Bloch (1986) argues that there is a utopian trace of longing for a better world that often appears in disguised and muted ways. This is the trace of desire for unalienated existence, something found in the utopian not-yet of the future and sometimes projected backward in nostalgia for a past that never was. Yet even reactionary cultural forms reveal this trace of a desire for things to be otherwise.

5 Deleuze (2007) distinguishes between the virtual and the actual, not the virtual and the material. For Deleuze, similar to the idea of the possibility sword in Miéville's *The Scar*, multiple possibilities for reality and subjectivity exist simultaneously, but only some are actualized into material experience. Crucially, for Deleuze, being actualized means being more material but does not mean being more *real* than those possibilities that remain virtual.

6 The Ghosthead are mysterious and powerful – and gone. There are rumours that they could mine possibility but there is no clear knowledge of, nor way to reproduce, this power, if indeed they ever really had it.

7 The most important example here is the Lovers, who cut one another, leaving patterns of scars on their bodies, as part of their courtship. Their

fusion as a couple marks a new way forward for both, escaping the limitations of their tribal destinies. On a more metaphorical level, Bellis feels emotionally scarred by her exile on the Armada (and is physically scarred by the flogging she endures), but she is also transformed into a person capable of wider political consciousness and commitments through these experiences. As well, some of the Remade, scarred by the justice system, find these wounds healing in the salt water of the ocean and further that the bodies meant to be punishment become instead a tool that helps them sustain their alternative ocean community.

8 See Bloch (1986), who writes that: 'A central task in this part is the *discovery and unmistakable notation of the "Not-Yet-Conscious"*. That is: a relatively still Unconscious disposed toward its other side, forwards rather than backwards. Towards the side of something new that is dawning up, that has never been conscious before, not, for example, something forgotten, something rememberable that has been, something that has sunk into the subconscious in repressed or archaic fashion' (Bloch, 1986, *Vol. 1*: 11, emphasis in original).

9 Here I am referring back to the passage from *Iron Council* quoted earlier which describes Judah's work as golem maker in terms very similar to the role of a fiction writer whose work seeks to change our vision of the world. For example, 'Golemetry is interruption. Golemetry is matter made to view itself anew, given a command that organizes it, a task' (*IC*, 222); and 'Golemetry is an *interruption*. It is a subordinating of the static *IS* to the active *AM*' (*IC*, 221, emphasis in original).

Works Cited

Bloch, Ernst (1986) *The Principle of Hope, Vols 1–3*, trans. Neville Plaice, Stephen Plaice and Paul Knight. Cambridge, MA: MIT Press.

Chu, Seo-Young (2010) *Do Metaphors Dream of Literal Sleep: A Science-Fictional Theory of Representation*. Cambridge, MA: Harvard University Press. Kindle edition.

Deleuze, Gilles (1994) *Difference and Repetition*, trans. Paul Patton. New York: Columbia University Press.

Deleuze, Gilles (2007) 'The Actual and the Virtual' in *Dealogues II*, trans. Eliot Ross Albert, pp. 148–52. New York: Columbia University Press.

Fisher, Mark (2009) *Capitalism Realism: Is There No Alternative?* Ropley: O Books.

Gramsci, Antonio (1929–35/1992–2007) *Prison Notebooks, Vols. 1–3*, ed. and trans. Joseph A. Buttigieg. New York: Columbia University Press.

Haraway, Donna (1991) 'A Cyborg Manifesto: Science Technology, and Socialist-Feminism in the Late Twentieth Century', in *Simians, Cyborgs and Women: The Reinvention of Nature*, pp. 149–81. New York: Routledge.

Miéville, China (2002) 'Symposium: Marxism and Fantasy: Editorial Introduction', *Historical Materialism* 10(4): 39–49.

Miéville, China (2009) 'Afterword: Cognition as Ideology: A Dialectic of SF Theory', in Mark Bould and China Miéville (eds) *Red Planets*, pp. 231–48. London: Pluto.

Saussure, Ferdinand de (2011) *Course in General Linguistics*, trans. Wade Baskin, ed. Perry Meisel and Haun Saussy. New York: Columbia University Press.

Shapiro, Steven (2008) 'Gothic Politics: A Discussion with China Miéville', *Gothic Studies* 10(1): 61–70.

3

'Strange Tricks of Cartography'
The Map(s) of *Perdido Street Station*

Raphael Zähringer

It is customary in contemporary fantasy fiction to provide the reader with a map printed at the beginning of the novel as a means of orientation. Since the storyworld is usually a world of its own with few or even no similarities to our world, the map supports the reader in several ways: it may help him/her to better imagine the storyworld, to get a feeling for its geography, and to track the movements of the novel's characters from place to place. Irrespective of whether they refer to our 'real' world or to an imagined topography, maps are generally considered to be helpful in terms of orientation and imagination; to be artefacts of precision and preservation. China Miéville's highly acclaimed second novel and the first instalment in his Bas-Lag trilogy, *Perdido Street Station* (2000), presents itself as a meditation on maps, luring the reader into a game of recognition and misrecognition as well as offering a sustained exploration of spatial imagination itself. As we are told in the description of the city of New Crobuzon's historic 'torque' storm (a meteorological phenomenon that devastated the city): there are 'strange tricks of cartography' going on (*PSS*, 231). In the following analysis, I will draw on Michel de Certeau's reading of urban space in *The Practice of Everyday Life* (1980/1984) to show how Miéville's novel plays with space – specifically, the triad of map, the territory it refers to, and the map user – in order to examine the force field of lust and power inherent to maps and cartography, understood as inherently textual artefacts and human products (Stockhammer, 2007: 69).

Tour and *Map*, Lust and Power

In his model of looking at the world (and especially the city) in *The Practice of Everyday Life*, de Certeau links space and language. He treats walking and the production of linguistic utterances as analogous performances that both relate to spatial organization. Language, according to de Certeau, is in itself highly spatial. For example, deictic elements, i.e. words and phrases such as 'you', 'here', or 'tomorrow', which rely on contextual information in order to convey meaning, help speakers to locate themselves and others in time and space. Thus, reports, stories, and speech acts in general are considered to be 'spatial trajectories' that are essential for everyday life (de Certeau, 1980/1984: 115). He then distinguishes between two different ways of approaching (city) space: firstly, one can assume the position of an observer, or voyeur, who looks at the city from high above. Distance and passivity allow the voyeur to see the city as a text, 'to read it, to be a solar Eye, looking down like a god' (de Certeau, 1980/1984: 92). However, the voyeur who is reading the city is merely reading a 'facsimile' of the urban landscape, what de Certeau calls a 'theoretical (that is, visual) simulacrum' (de Certeau, 1980/1984: 92, 93). In the very act of detaching himself/herself from the city down there, the voyeur thus puts himself/herself into a position that leads to a 'misunderstanding of practices' (de Certeau, 1980/1984: 93). De Certeau's counter-concept to the position of the voyeur is that of the perspective experienced by the person at street level walking through the city. Instead of being passive observers, walkers actively experience the city and, in the act of walking, literally create the city space. This apprehension of city space, however, is limited insofar as walkers are unable to read the text they are creating precisely because they do not inhabit the observer's position and so lack the requisite aerial perspective to view the city within its spatial context; additionally, at ground level they can be observed themselves (Huck, 2010: 37). Walking should therefore be read as an appropriation of the topographic system, a spatial realization of place and, at the same time, a matter of relation between disjunct positions. Furthermore, according to de Certeau walking belongs to a sphere that he calls *tour*, in which space is created through 'a discursive series of operations' (de Certeau, 1980/1984: 119). The opposing perspective to *tour* is that of the *map*: belonging to the voyeur, this represents a way of seeing rather than a mode of movement (as in the example of walking), and allows the voyeur to construct a distanced 'knowledge of the order of places' on a 'tableau' – which de Certeau describes as a 'plane projection totalizing observations' (de Certeau, 1984: 119). Together, these bipolar phenomena offer an interplay of proximity and distance which reminds us of the overall discourse on objectivity in cartography,[1] and on closer inspection we can see that our original understanding of the distanced position from outside (or, in de Certeau's sense, from above) a map becomes complicated: '[i]n a somewhat paradoxical way the observer has to be part and not part of the observed world, and the simultaneity of these mutually exclusive positions makes this stance fragile' (Huck, 2010: 47).

Now, what does literature have to do with maps? First, linking maps and literature as human products is a comparatively old phenomenon, as a brief glance at the history of cartography can show (Schneider, 2006). The medieval European *mappae mundi*, for instance, were highly narrative, incorporating text that ranged from the description of beasts and fantastic creatures to biblical history. In general, maps can be understood as some kind of text in the sense that they are humanly constructed artefacts (Stockhammer, 2007: 53). Secondly, literary texts might refer to maps within the storyworld itself, or even provide maps of the literary text's territory within the paratextual framework: either at the request of the author (as in the map drawn by Robert Louis Stevenson, which accompanied his 1883 adventure novel, *Treasure Island*), or as a supplement added later by a publisher or editor (as in Jonathan Swift's 1726 satirical travelogue, *Gulliver's Travels*).[2] In both cases, the maps function as paratextual devices in the sense that Gérard Genette defines, i.e. as 'framing elements' (Genette, 1997: 18; Pavlik, 2010: 28) accompanying the novel text. Both maps that are incorporated within the novel text, as well as those that accompany the text as paratexts, encourage the reader to reflect on the power of the map as a narrative device, and on literature's own relation to this power. By doing so, such literature offers us maps which oscillate between functioning as artefacts of power (Gabaude and Maleval, 2013: 140) and as aesthetic artefacts of lust (Stockhammer, 2007: 69). The power of maps refers to the power which can be exerted on somebody or something with maps (Harley, 1989: 12); one might, for example, draw a borderline on a map, which will then influence the real-world territory in question. Lust, on the other hand, refers to the notion of a map as a work of art: the map is treated as an outstanding piece of craftsmanship which gives pleasure to the viewer or owner, which adorns one's living-room, or which one reads with delight while tracing its roads with a fingertip and imagining the places the map refers to. Featuring both a printed map of the city where the story's action takes place, as well as many additional maps within the storyworld, Miéville's *Perdido Street Station* offers us an exemplary case for considering this interplay between topographical power and cartographic lust.

For the Reader: the Extra-textual Map

Right before the prelude in which the exiled member of the bird-like garudan species, Yagharek, enters the city for the first time, Miéville provides his readers with a double-paged map of New Crobuzon with a scale and a wind rose (Figure 1).

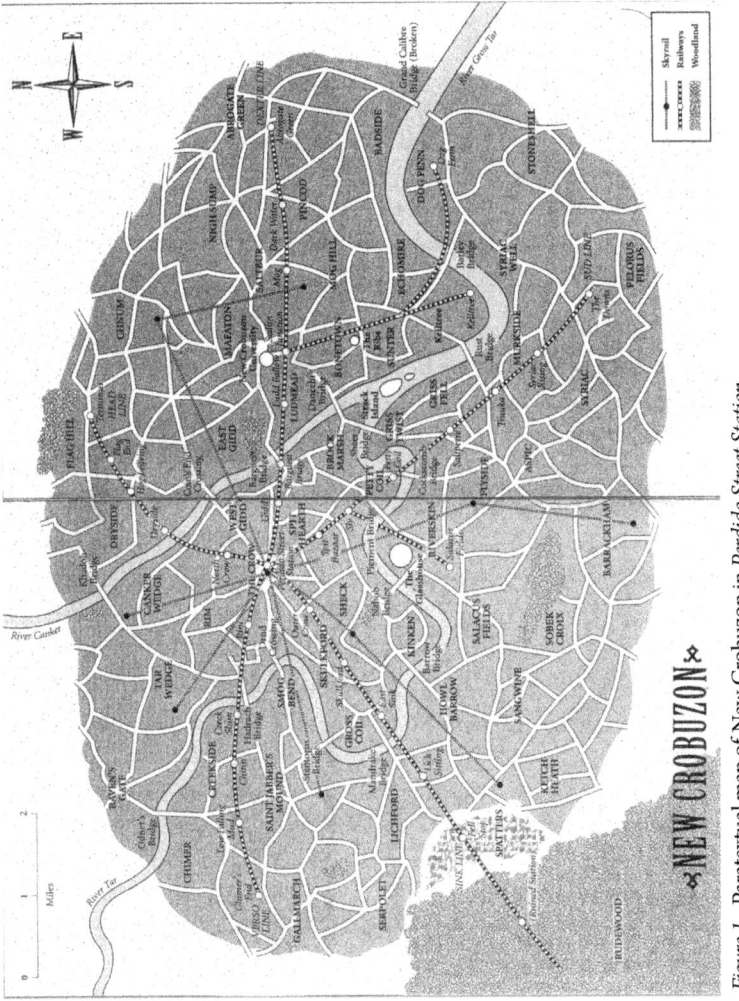

Figure 1. Paratextual map of New Crobuzon in *Perdido Street Station*

We are given the names of the city's quarters and its network of railways and skyrails with all of their stops indicated and the city's bridges and rivers are also named. Compared to early examples of literary maps,[3] this map of New Crobuzon is very sophisticated. In an interview with Joan Gordon (2003), Miéville explained how maps inform his world-building:

> [To write a novel] I start with maps, histories, time lines, things like that. I spend a lot of time working on stuff that may or may not actually find its way into the novel, but I know a lot more about the world than makes it into the stories. That's the "RPG" [role-playing game] factor: it's about systematizing the world. (Miéville cited in Gordon, 2003: 257)

Thus, Miéville's imagining of the Bas-Lag storyworld is much bigger and more intricate than the reader actually encounters within the novel itself. Exceeding the parameters of narrative constraint, Miéville's act of cartographic production is therefore an act of systematization, as well as elaboration, of a single image that I would like to suggest can be read as playing with the notion of controlling the story space. As Stockhammer (2007: 63) argues: 'all those maps support the spatial imagination of the represented area and ensure "total control" over it. They enable the author to invent coherent results by means of their "correct" localization and they enable the reader to verify these results' (my translation; cf. Bulson, 2007: 20). Here, we can see that the role of the map producer is of high importance. A map is not as objective as one might think, since the appearance of the map is always shaped by an authorial process of creation and selection (Schneider, 2006: 8). The fact that as a writer Miéville is in control of his fictional world's space, however, does not mean that his readers are able to exert a similar level of imaginative control. As we will see, the focalization of *Perdido Street Station* reveals that Miéville is playing with the reader, as well as the novel's characters, in terms of spatial control and verification. In the following analysis, I would like to argue that *Perdido Street Station* is not only the novelistic expression of a fictional world that happens to have a map, but is itself a meditation on mapping and imagining space.

Although the streets themselves are not named, the map of New Crobuzon is a useful extra-literary tool for readers to follow the novel's characters as they move from quarter to quarter, since *Perdido Street Station* involves a high degree of movement through its urban space – be it by public transport or on foot. At the beginning of the novel, Yagharek offers the reader an introduction to this space as he enters New Crobuzon. With his wings sawed off his back, the birdman approaches the city on a small boat steered by an unnamed man. After several italicized passages describing Yagharek's personal impressions, the man relays some information concerning where they are exactly, in topographical terms. In combination with Yagharek's perception, the description of his arrival can be read as corresponding to the paratextual map, as names and urban sites are detailed:

> *The river twists and turns to face the city.* [...] *The man murmurs to me, tells me where we are. I do not turn to him.* This is Raven's Gate, *this brutalized warren around us. The rotten buildings lean against each other, exhausted.* [...] *A train whistles as it crosses the river before us on raised tracks.* [...] *I am in* Smog Bend, *he tells me, and I make myself look away as he points my direction so he will not know I am lost* [...]. *A little to the south two great pillars rise from the river. The gates to the Old City* [...]. *Behind them, a low bridge (*Drud Crossing, *he says).* (PSS, 1–3, emphasis in original)

By using the map, the reader can ascertain that Yagharek enters the city on the River Tar in the northwest of New Crobuzon: the twist of the river mentioned in the text clearly suggests this. The river flows through Raven's Gate, passes the Verso Line railway that runs across the water, and leads to Smog Bend with Drud Crossing to the left. Although both Yagharek and the reader are strangers to New Crobuzon, the reader has the advantage of cross-referencing these named locations against the paratextual map, which he or she can use to view the city's topography from de Certeau's voyeur's perspective – that is to say, from a perspective that is both distanced and uninvolved. At a first glance, we might think that Miéville includes the map as a helpful tool that unambiguously establishes the realism of this fictional place. But the closer we look, the more we get the impression that Miéville's map – just as the map of an actually existing place (Dünne, 2013: 238) – functions only as a 'symbolised image' (Wood, 2003: 17): a model that does not show everything and is less helpful than we expect it to be. Although the reader has the advantage of being able to adopt a voyeur's perspective (if he or she chooses to consult the map), s/he is not really superior to Yagharek in terms of understanding this fantastical terrain. The map seems to help to a certain extent, but it does not provide all the information that we would require in order to comprehend New Crobuzon's intricate landscape. Not only are some street names missing, as I have already mentioned, but there are also innumerable alleys and passageways referenced within the narrative that the reader cannot locate on the paratextual map, not to speak of named individual buildings. The map therefore reminds us of its own imperfectly representational status: it serves as a neat, but ultimately non-realistic, representation for Miéville's reader. As Bulson puts it: '[S]patial representations are products of a particular time and place always partial and incomplete' (Bulson, 2007: 39).

In addition to Yagharek's first journey into New Crobuzon, many more detailed descriptions of walks can be found in *Perdido Street Station*.[4] Miéville creates numerous occasions where the reader is invited to treat the map as more than just a paratextual decoration. We are reminded here of de Certeau's account on the relationship between *tour* and *map*, and the important distinction between walker and voyeur. Dorothea Löbbermann considers these two opposing figures in de Certeau's thinking in comparison with two opposing groups whose traversal of the city space reveals their transient status – tourists and vagrants (Löbbermann, 2005: 263). According to Löbbermann, the tourist assumes the position of the voyeur. To him/her, all places of interest in a city (whether museums, castles, famous squares, bridges, or statues) are of equal importance, while all other (ordinary) places are ignored. In this way the unfamiliar is domesticated by the tourist and the world that is created through his/her perspective is one that seems to defer completely to his/her wishes to see what s/he wants to see. Tourists thus produce pleasure-oriented fictions of cities by revelling in the cities' superficial lust: city maps and travel guides enable them to apprehend the city. However, the tourist is only a producer of particular fictions of the city – s/he knows that s/he is only moving at the level of surface. According to Löbbermann's reading, the tourist is thus continually trying to catch a glimpse behind the scenes to discern the 'true' face of the city – which is the world inhabited by the vagrants (Löbbermann, 2005: 266). In so doing, the tourist hardly ever strays from the established routes of main roads and city guides (Löbbermann, 2005: 268). Löbbermann's reformulation of de Certeau's *tour-map* dichotomy is useful for our reading of *Perdido Street Station*, since Miéville arguably places his reader in the same position as the tourist. Obliged to refer to a map that shows only the biggest streets and with only a rough idea of New Crobuzon's quarters, the reader quickly comes to realize that a map as a paratextual device is just one of the textual components that constitute the storyworld's topography in a novel, which sometimes works in opposition to the narrative itself:

> Texts are never able to tell as much as maps do implicitly. Even if every road on a map with all its turns and curves were described in great detail in an itinerary – one would only need to travel in the opposite direction or make a different turn at a junction as it is described in the itinerary, and one would have found a new narrative that is potentially there already. [...] Never, on the other hand, can texts tell as few as maps do explicitly. The geographic map of Ptolemaic kind is, according to a helpful distinction of Lotman, exemplary for a text without a *syuzhet* where nothing happens – until a directional line is drawn that denotes a rudimentary action, such as the course of a ship. (Stockhammer, 2007: 76, my translation)

The map, as such, does not tell any story because its static visual composition cannot depict action, but it is potentially charged with an endless number of possible stories as Stockhammer indicates, provided that the reader can put it to use. Or, to frame this problem in hypothetical terms: if Löbbermann's tourist or Miéville's reader was given this map of New Crobuzon and dropped off in some run-down alley of the city, s/he would be completely lost, stranded with a map that would be absolutely useless. In *Perdido Street Station*, then, power and control over both maps and the city space itself are primarily attributed to the author or map producer.

One might add that the etymological connotations of the place names on Miéville's map of New Crobuzon seem to contribute to the map's implicit narrativity. On their own, they do not tell a story either, but like the map-as-artefact they share in the potential narrativity inherent to the map. New Crobuzon's characteristics – grim, dark, faecal, dirty, industrial, full of crime – are touched upon in the names of many of its quarters: Spatters, Tar Wedge, Smog Bend, Skulkford, Raven's Gate, Bonetown, Canker Wedge, Lichford, Spit Hearth, Badside, Nigh Sump, to name but a few.[5] These names therefore appear to refute Stockhammer's argument that as physical objects or artefacts, maps in themselves do not tell any story; rather, New Crobuzon's allusive place names constitute what J. B. Harley calls a desocialization of the territory they represent: 'They foster the notion of a socially empty space' (Harley, 2001: 81). Miéville seems to be aware of the map's tendency towards desocialization and arguably incorporates the sociality of New Crobuzon's space through his implementation of functionalist 'telling names' (i.e. place names which reveal their purpose or characterize their bearers [Nünning and Nünning, 2007: 196]) and, more importantly, by offering detailed descriptions of the quarters and their specific characteristics within the narrative itself, so that map and novel complement one another. In considering New Crobuzon's locations via the notion of speaking names, we can also identify a connection with one of Ute Schneider's crucial points (Schneider, 2006: 9): that is to say, the names convey extra information about the place or quarter to which they refer. Thus, Miéville demonstrates that paratextual maps need not be as socially empty as one might expect them to be. In this way, just from the richly suggestive names alone, the reader learns about the various quarters of New Crobuzon, which greatly differ from each other in terms of population, architecture, atmosphere, history and the arrangement of their streets and passageways. Still, the question remains to what extent Miéville actually uses the map as a helpful tool for the reader so that s/he can verify the fictional area and thus help to imagine the represented fictional area in question (Stockhammer, 2007: 63). We are given the names of each of New Crobuzon's quarters on the map, but do they really help us to visualize these spaces when we read such names within a simplified, abstract cartographic representation?[6] Similarly, does it help us if we notice that this sketched map of New Crobuzon – particularly in terms of its meandering rivers, waterways and islets – resembles our own London? My argument is that Miéville deliberately lures the reader into the world of New Crobuzon, setting his story within an alternative space whose cartographic similarities to London hint at a possible allegorical tale – which it is not. An assumed connection between the two cities is, therefore, misleading. The fact that *Perdido Street Station* includes a paratextual map does not necessarily mean that this map refers to an actually existing area. On the contrary, according to the Swedish writer Per Olov Enquist the act of drawing and examining maps of fictional areas affords a much greater pleasure than constructing or looking at maps of the 'real world', and should therefore be considered an act of sheer lust (Stockhammer, 2007: 66ff.). In this sense, a map of London – or knowledge about the real city – is just as useless to Miéville's reader in his/her quest to understand New Crobuzon as the novel's printed map of the city would be to the characters of *Perdido Street Station*.[7]

Let us return to our earlier discussion of Dorothea Löbbermann and the question of transient urban figures. Löbbermann associates vagrants with de Certeau's conceptualization of the walker. Vagrants, in her formulation, lack the ability (affluence, access, leisure time etc.) to view the city as a whole; rather, they see behind the scenes as they translate and appropriate the city space according to their specific needs – food and shelter, for example (Löbbermann, 2005: 266). If we search for an equivalent vagrant figure in *Perdido Street Station*, we might consider Yagharek as a character whose outsider status within the city can be read as enacting precisely this vagrancy, as he learns how to survive in New Crobuzon as a stranger. Obtaining food, finding a warm place to sleep, and experiencing other people's disgust and ignorance are pressing issues facing Yagharek; issues that also confront the vagrant.[8] Similarly, after their first encounter with the militia, the whole group accompanying Isaac is forced to lead a similar life. As Yagharek's thoughts narrate, at the end of chapter LI: '*We move by night. We are fearful of the milita and of Motley's men.* [...] *We watch carefully for sudden movements and suspicious glances. We cannot trust our neighbours. We must live in a hinterland of half darkness, isolated and solipsistic. We steal what we need* [...] (*PSS*, 768, emphasis in original).

For the Characters: Intra-textual Maps

In addition to the extra-textual map intended for the reader, there are also many maps contained within the story of *Perdido Street Station* itself, which shed more light on our reading of the force field of the lust and power that are inherently inscribed within the act of mapping space. Before travelling to the ganglord Motley's place for the first time, the khepri artist Lin (one of a race of humanoid beetles) is given a map in order to find her way. After exiting the cab her map, the narrative informs us, 'directed her to a nameless alley on the south side of the Ribs. She wound her way to a quiet street where she found the black-painted buildings she had been told to seek' (*PSS*, 32). This brief description of Lin's map reveals a general attitude towards their city, which is shared by New Crobuzon's citizens. Even if you have been born and raised in the city, it seems, you cannot always find your way. New Crobuzon is large and confusing enough that each of its characters quickly becomes lost as soon as they move away from lines of public transport or significant landmarks – they are unable to assume the position of de Certeau's voyeur. Although the city's larger streets are given names, we are very much reminded in the novel of the importance of practices of orientation. Analogously, in the Japanese cities documented in Roland Barthes's *Empire of Signs* (1970), streets are not even named. As Barthes observes: 'There is of course a written address, but it has only a postal value, it refers to a plan [...], knowledge of which is accessible to the postman, not the visitor' (Barthes, 1970/2000: 33). As with the disoriented characters traversing New Crobuzon in *Perdido Street Station,* Barthes considers the confusion encountered by the visitor to Tokyo, who must 'figure out the address by a (written or printed) schema of orientation, a kind of geographical summary which situates the domicile starting from a known landmark; a train station, for instance' (Barthes, 1970/2000: 33). In short: Tokyo's inhabitants draw their own personalized map of their neighbourhood.

In New Crobuzon, as we can see in Lin's case, the loss of orientation encountered when attempting to traverse the city affects not only strangers and visitors, but also locals. Lin's perspective, however, becomes significantly altered as soon as she visits Motley's hideout, placing her in the reverse position of the stranger to his neighbourhood, rather than the local inhabitant. During his sittings for Lin's commissioned sculpture Motley keeps on talking about mob crime, a sphere unknown to Lin and one which she despises: 'Every conversation he had with her wherein he disclosed some hidden details of New Crobuzon's underworld lore, she was embroiled in something she was eager to avoid. *I'm nothing but a visitor*, she wanted to sign frantically. *Don't give me a streetmap!*' (*PSS*, 112, emphasis in original). Ironically enough, the map she had been given in order to find Motley in the first place was Lin's streetmap into this underworld and, as the novel progresses, it will become clear that there is no way out for her after her first arrival at Motley's. Getting involved with the underworld means that one cannot simply walk away from it again.

In addition to Lin, many other characters make use of maps in *Perdido Street Station*, or produce maps themselves. The journalist and editor of the underground *Runagate Rampant* newspaper, Derkhan, checks 'the directions she had been given [...] in the note' on her way to the psychic medium, or 'communicatrix' (*PSS*, 316) and confers with the A. I. Construct Council 'over a scribbled map' (*PSS*, 598); Lemuel Pigeon, Isaac's underground middle-man, 'scribble[s] designs [of the Glasshouse] in the dust' (*PSS*, 486); adventurers and rogues are said to be repeatedly hired for 'useful services: research, cartography and the like' (*PSS*, 492); the workers of the Construct Council are 'all equipped with maps, torches, guns and strict instructions' as they enter the undercity sewers (*PSS*, 614); Isaac draws a rough sketch of the city on a piece of paper: 'a jagged sideways Y for the two rivers, little crosses for Griss Twist, The Crow, and scribbles delineating Brock Marsh and Spit Hearth in between' (*PSS*, 584); and even creatures of the night and mutants '*crawl from sewers into cold flat starlight and whisper shyly to each other, drawing maps and messages in the faecal mud*' (*PSS*, 58, emphasis in original).

Thus, we encounter numerous characters in the novels who are concerned with maps. It is striking that none of these maps are official representations of the city space. Instead, they are quickly scribbled down in accordance with the particular subjective requirements of the user and, taken together, question the map's function as a tool of power. Again, Barthes's analysis of Japanese culture in *Empire of Signs* can help us to interpret the significance of these many maps in the novel. Barthes describes the remarkable skills of the Japanese city's inhabitants and how they:

> excel in these impromptu drawings, where we see being sketched, right on the scrap of paper, a street, an apartment house [...], making the exchange of addresses into a delicate communication in which a life of the body, an art of the graphic gesture recurs: it is always enjoyable to watch someone write, all the more so to watch someone draw [...]; the fabrication of the address greatly prevailed over the address itself, and, fascinated, I could have hoped it would take hours to give me that address. (Barthes, 1970/2000: 34–5)

In *Perdido Street Station*, however, such 'impromptu drawings' are far from being aesthetically pleasing. They are quickly scribbled on scraps of paper, or drawn into dust or mud and are thus subordinated to the level of a visceral experience of the city – instead of being clean and well-structured they are spontaneous, dirty engravings carved into the city's skin. They are not meant to last for eternity or, even, to store the information they contain for any length of time. Rather, these maps reveal to the reader that in New Crobuzon's labyrinth of roads the primary concern is not to record the topography permanently, which raises the question: is the city too confusing and liable to change for anyone to gain power over it by means of measurement? This is reaffirmed by the fact that within *Perdido Street Station* institutional attempts at mapping, and thus controlling, the city all fail.[9] Take, for instance, the city 'meteoromancers', whose task is to map the weather forecast (*PSS*, 205). The government's attempt to render in cartographic form the nocturnal forays of the city's 'slake-moths' (giant moth-like monsters who prey on the dreams of New Crobuzon's citizens and threaten the city's very survival) is also futile. As Eliza Stem-Fulcher, Mayor Rudgutter's assistant, says: 'We're plotting a map of the nightmare hotspots, see if we can't see some pattern, track the moths in some way' (*PSS*, 408). The government is thus unable to map the hunting moths. Another depiction in which the moths roam the city sky is striking in its reference to the history of cartography: 'From all the way across the city, from the four compass points, they converged in a frenzy of flapping, four starving exultant powerful bodies, descending to feed' (*PSS*, 637). The four compass points locate the slake-moths at the city's margins and therefore at the margins of New Crobuzon's map – or even, arguably, outside the map. This extra-cartographic position reminds us of the marginalization of stories and pictures in the history of map drawing (Schneider, 2006: 33–4). Ute Schneider highlights this marginalization by comparing two maps: the medieval Ebstorf map (a good example of the *mappae mundi* I discussed earlier) from 1284, drawn by Gervase of Ebstorf, and Hartmann Schedel's map of the world, reproduced in his *Nuremberg Chronicle* (1493; Figure 2).

Whereas Ebstorfer's 1284 map depicts and locates fantastic creatures such as the birdmen on the edge of the world, but still visible within the map, these creatures are placed outside the mapped world, appearing to the left, in Schedel's more recent 1493 map. In later maps, the fantastic creatures disappear completely as narrative elements within the *mappa mundi*. From the fifteenth century, maps start to lose their narrativity, increasingly erasing their own illustrative and descriptive value, and limiting themselves to the representation of topographical characteristics (de Certeau, 1984: 120–1). The rich, illustrative woodcuts of fantastic creatures whose presence in the historical maps of the *mappa mundi* indicated the world's position within a cosmological hierarchy, thus gradually move from the map, to its margins and, finally, are relegated beyond the map completely. By contrast, the slake-moths in Miéville's *Perdido Street Station* move into the map of New Crobuzon. Coming into the city from outside its borders, and with an unknown origin,[10] they can be identified as functioning in a comparable manner to the mythical creatures in Hart-

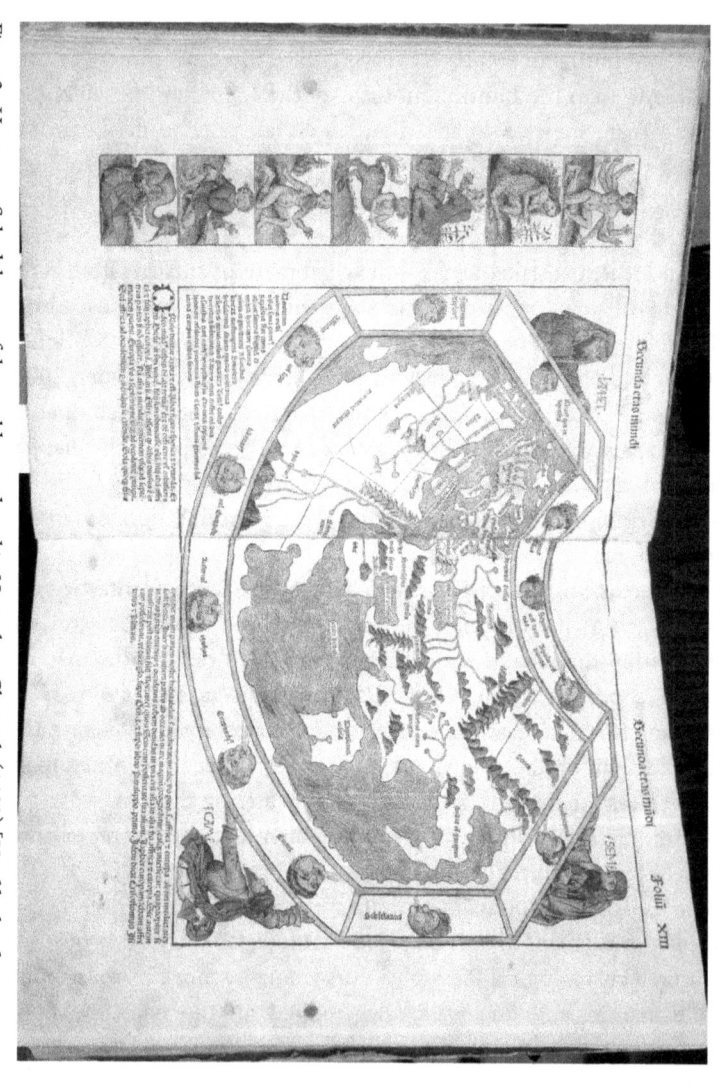

Figure 2. Hartmann Schedel, map of the world reproduced in *Nuremberg Chronicle* (1493) [Used by kind permission of Bryn Mawr College Special Collections]

mann Schedel's 1493 map of the world in the *Nuremberg Chronicle* (Schneider, 2006: 32–3). However, we should note that their movement is reversed: they re-import both a fantastic element that remains partly unexplainable and a story element which heavily influences the overall narrative.

Another creature stands out in the novel in terms of its use of maps: the Weaver, a supernatural and powerful entity beyond human understanding. At first, it seems not to be concerned with maps at all. Then, in a later passage, it comes close to the act of map production: 'The Weaver was tracing its index finger through the water on the roof, leaving a trail of scorched dry stone, drawing patterns and pictures of flowers, whispering to itself' (*PSS*, 639). It produces a trace, a trail, a drawing that could pass as a map – but this 'map' consists only of patterns and pictures, and thus has no value in terms of aiding orientation within the city (to non-Weavers, at least). The trail seems to conform to what I identified earlier as an 'artefact of lust'. If we look at the way in which the Weaver treats space and planes of existence on a larger scale, namely as elements within an all-encompassing, multi-planar aesthetic web, this makes a lot of sense. It does not need to draw a map of the city onto the city's surface, or skin, because the Weaver possesses the greatest map of all: the 'world weave' or 'worldweb', a map of all reality in the shape of a vast web (*PSS*, 336). Miéville's reader is afforded an impression of this map as the Weaver saves Isaac, Yagharek, and their companions from the New Crobuzon militia, and the group experiences moving through the world weave:

> [T]he dancing mad god moved along powerful threads of force. [...] I glimpsed at the reality through which the dancing mad god was treading. [...] Spread across the emptiness, streaming away from us with cavernous perspective in all directions and dimensions, encompassing lifetimes and hugeness with each intricate knot of metaphysical substance, was a web. Its substance was known to me. [...] The plait disappeared into the enormity of possible spaces. Every intention, interaction, motivation, every colour, every body, every action and reaction, every piece of physical reality and the thoughts that it engendered, every connection made, every nuanced moment of history and potentiality, every toothache and flagstone, every emotion and birth and banknote, every possible thing ever is woven into

that limitless, sprawling web. It is without beginning or end. It is complex to a degree that it humbles the mind. It is a work of such beauty that my soul wept. (PSS, 339–40, emphasis in original)

The web is literally all-encompassing: it includes living organisms, dead matter, emotions, thoughts, history, potential futures. Despite its beauty and eternity, there are torn and broken spots in the world weave: as a result of the slake-moths' recent activity, the gossamer of New Crobuzon, for instance, is ruined. As a species, the Weavers have a certain conception of what the web should look like, and by intervening in a world such as Bas-Lag they are able to shape it according to their own particular intellection.[11] In the end, the Weaver encountered in New Crobuzon does not help Isaac and his group because of some moral obligation or bargain, but because the defeat of the slake-moths will fix the torn web. As the giant spider-creature intones in his mystical poetic language: 'LOOK AT THE INTRICATE SKEINS AND THREADLINES WE CORRECT WHERE THE DEADLINGS REAVED WE CAN RESHUFFLE AND SPIN AND FIX IT UP NICE ...' (*PSS*, 655). Since existence never stands still, the web grows and sprawls continuously and hence needs continuous work. In this labour of the Weaver, we can discern a particular lust for the map as an aesthetic object, and also the aesthetic exaggeration enacted in map creation and usage. The world weave is not only the most complete map of everything that was, is, will, and could be, but also, in less grandiose terms, offers the most accurate map available to any of the species in Bas-Lag since it is the most up to date, never ceasing to be a work in progress.[12] The world weave is an eternal impromptu drawing that comes intriguingly close to the conceptualization of the map as a rhizome, in the sense that Gilles Deleuze and Félix Guattari describe: it is 'open and connectable in all of its dimensions; it is detachable, reversible, susceptible to constant modification. It can be torn, reversed, adapted to any kind of mounting' (Deleuze and Guattari, 1987/2009: 13). But even a map as powerful as the Weaver's web in *Perdido Street Station* is not without its flaws: the Weaver continuously moves both around the web, as well as between various locations within New Crobuzon, in order to maintain the web and keep it up to date. In so doing, the Weaver finds itself subjectively located within the map it is continually constructing, and thereby loses the objective sovereignty of an exterior observer. In de Certeau's terms, by moving between the city and the alternative plane of the world weave, the Weaver continuously oscillates between the position of the voyeur and that of the walker, between map producer and map connoisseur, between power and lust. The Weaver is ever alert to the need to adjust the world, and consequently its map, according to its own preferences. This articulation of aesthetic lust is so significant that the map can never be finished.

Lastly, let us turn to mapping strategies that go beyond the production of maps as tangible objects. Yagharek, for example, is mapping the cityscape – but he is doing so without the use of actual, material maps, making use of his bird eyes instead. In general, he seems to get along quite well in the city after a short time of settling in; for example, he surveys New Crobuzon and its landmarks with precision, control and understanding:

> At the top of the Glasshouse, the city seemed to be a gift to him [...]. Everywhere he looked, fingers and hands and fists and spines of architecture *thrust rudely into the sky*. The Ribs like ossified tentacles *reaching always up*; the Spike slammed into the city's heart like a *skewer*; the complex mechanistic vortex of Parliament, glowing darkly; Yagharek mapped them with a cold, strategic eye. (*PSS*, 516, emphasis added)

While other characters need a physical map to traverse New Crobuzon, Yagharek requires only his 'strategic eye' in order to map the cityscape. It becomes clear that his method of mapping – and, thus, the quality of the map he produces – is very different from those of other characters. Looking down on the city, his perception is marked by a strong dynamic of verticality that manifests itself in the narrator's choice of words ('thrust rudely into the sky'; 'reaching always up'; 'like a skewer'). This lexical choice also shows that Yagharek is aware of the brute forces lurking behind this architecture of verticality – almost as if he had read Henri Lefebvre. 'Verticality and great height', as Lefebvre writes, 'have ever been the spatial expression of potentially violent power' (Lefebvre, 1974/1991: 98). Note the discrepancy between this panoramic view,[13] and Yagharek's earlier experience upon arriving in the city, when the wingless bird-man did not possess the ability to enact this way of seeing or, rather, surveying: '*I wonder how this looks from above, no chance for the city to hide then, if you came at it on the wind you would see it from miles away [...]. I could ride the updrafts [...], sail high over the proud towers [...], ride the chaos, alight where I choose*' (*PSS*, 2, emphasis in original). Instead, at the start of the novel Yagharek is '*lost*' (*PSS*, 3, emphasis in original): displaced by his nocturnal entry into New Crobuzon, as well as the unusual mode of transportation, by boat (for him as a flying creature).

While Yagharek's way of mapping relies on visual impressions, the slake-moths seem to peregrinate by means of sound and smell:

> New Crobuzon steamed with the rich taste-scent of prey. [...] Vibrations in a hundred registers and keys beckoned the thing, as forces and emotions and dreams split and were amplified in the brick chambers of the station and blasted outwards into the sky. A massive, invisible flavour trail. (*PSS*, 257)

As with Miéville's extra-textual map of the city, this 'smell map' also proves to be misleading.[14] To paraphrase Ute Schneider, we might argue that although moving through space is a universal feature that constitutes human beings (and other sentient life forms, as we should add when discussing Miéville's fictions), a mobility which presupposes a means of orientation, the ways of perceiving space and relating to it can be very different and are, especially in Yagharek's case, also reflected in the narrator's use of language (Schneider, 2006: 19). The uselessness of printed maps in *Perdido Street Station* could also be read as exploiting Marshall McLuhan's paradigm shift towards visuality (McLuhan, 1962: 125): not so much in its dwarfening of aural/oral culture, but in terms of strengthening different kinds of visuality as ways of accessing the world. Finally, in the interplay of diverse maps, mapping strategies, ways of perception and modes of movement through the city, it transpires that the city space of New Crobuzon is constructed in a productive force field of materiality and discursivity. That is to say, what is out there in the urban space of New Crobuzon is mediated both by the way in which the city's inhabitants interact with it, as well as by the way in which this interaction is narrated by Miéville's use of narrative voice. The body in *Perdido Street Station* thus becomes a projection screen for a dialogic and intersubjective understanding of the construction, and continuous reconstruction, of identity and alterity; a location of conflict between self and other, individual and societal discourses, and their inherent ascriptions of difference (Altnöder, 2009: 302ff.).

Conclusion: Recognition and Misrecognition

As we have seen, maps in *Perdido Street Station* are diverse. In addition to the paratextual map that prefaces Miéville's narrative, designed to aid the reader's understanding of the storyworld through a systematization of its key locations and place names, the novel is also packed with various described maps as well as different modes of map production within the story itself; most of which are obscure, non-scientific and non-institutional. Even the government is unable to establish order through the practices of mapping and therefore unable to execute administrative business in the broadest sense, which is mostly reflected in its lack of control over the city space and over inhabitants' movements through it. My analysis of the way in which maps inform, and misinform, New Crobuzon reveals that this urban topography offers nothing like a functional city ('funktionelle Stadt'), in the sense described by Martina Löw, i.e. a well-planned and well-ordered city featuring a strict separation between housing, work, and recreation as its three main functions (Löw, 2008: 97–102). New Crobuzon's slake-moths cannot be mapped, the weather cannot be regulated, the Weaver is a supernatural force beyond any control, and scientists and adventurers go rogue. Beneath the surface of a dictatorial government, Miéville leaves us in no doubt that there is a whole web of competing structures and movements where mobsters, underground newspapers, rogue scientists, numerous other groups, and 'ruder forms of life struggle and fight and die and are eaten' (*PSS*, 265, emphasis in original), in a city caught between industrial decay and organic sprawl.

The central point is that we are facing two very different levels of observation when it comes to reading the maps in *Perdido Street Station*, both of which are deficient. On the one hand, there is Miéville's reader with his or her abstract paratextual map of New Crobuzon printed in the opening pages of the book which, as I have suggested, does not help the reader as much as one would expect in terms of orientation and imagination. On the other hand, there is the level of the characters within the narrative's storyworld, whose numerous impromptu maps, and different mapping strategies based upon different modes of perception, thwart our general expectation that maps should function as cultural artefacts of preservation and precision. Together, these two levels play a game of recognition and misrecognition with both the reader and the novel's characters in terms of spatial control and topographical verification.[15] Miéville thus forces his readers to mentally map the city at the same time as they encounter, and produce, the city space through their imaginative participation within the storyworld as they read *Perdido Street Station*. While their process of reading imaginatively moves through this complex world and maps the locations that Miéville names, readers are also obliged time and again to interrupt their process of reading, flicking back and forth between the pages of the story and the paratextual map that precedes the narrative. This interrupted process of reading thus enacts what de Certeau describes as the 'authorization' of place names within the travel story through the practice of citation:

> The chain of spatializing operations seems to be marked by references to what it produces (a representation of places) or to what it implies (a local order). We thus have the structure of the travel story: stories of journeys and actions are marked out by the "citation" of the places that result from them or authorize them. (de Certeau, 1980/1984: 120–1)

Miéville, though, is devious enough to allow his readers to attempt to check the place names they encounter in the narrative by offering citations of places without the possibility of verifying them, since only some of the cited place names in the novel are actually referenced in the paratextual map. In fact, the maps of *Perdido Street Station* are deliberately unsuitable in every respect. The printed paratextual map is a non-realistic representation that fails to invoke the characteristics of its quarters in the process of naming them. It is not much help either when we try to track a character's movements through the city, nor would it be helpful to the characters themselves, if they had this very map at their disposal. In addition, the apparent analogy to real-world London is misleading in attempting to understand New Crobuzon as well. The intra-textual maps that Miéville describes within the storyworld are equally misleading and unhelpful: most of them do not exercise power over the territory they refer to – and if they do, they cannot be said to constitute 'artefacts of lust'. In short, the maps encountered both within the narrative as well in its paratextual framework perfectly fit the setting of New Crobuzon as a dark and confusing city where hardly anything is permanent, except change and disorientation. Reading *Perdido Street Station* literally means getting 'perdido' – lost. Such reading is a twisted game that is sometimes lost itself.[16]

Acknowledgements

Attempts were made by the editors to reproduce the paratextual map of New Crobuzon in *Perdido Street Station*, but no clear responses were received.

Notes

1 Objectivity is a contentious issue in cartography. On the one hand, cartographers and geographers seem to be driven by a desire to objectify their maps, i.e. to make them as objective as possible. This desire is grounded in the basic assumption that what one can find out there is objective and real, and that this objectivity or reality can be expressed – in Harley's words, 'that the systematic observation and measurement offer the only route to cartographic truth; and that this truth can be independently verified' (Harley, 1989: 4). On the other hand, true objectivity can never be achieved since map production is always influenced by other factors and rules, e.g. ethnocentrism or culture (see Harley, 1989: 6), and since the map can never refer to the territory in question in a one-to-one representation.

2 The first edition of *Gulliver's Travels*, published by Benjamin Motte, came with four maps of Lilliput, Brobdingnag, and the other fictional places visited by Gulliver. While all these maps are arguably based on Herman Moll's *A New & Correct Map of the Whole World*, their producer remains unknown (see Stockhammer, 2007: 91).

3 To give just a few examples, Eric Bulson (2007: 20) mentions 'the squiggly line over a map of Spain to indicate the direction of Don Quixote's [...] route' and the 'barely legible map of the world to the fourth edition of *Robinson Crusoe*, with a dotted line outlining the course of his protagonist's ill-fated voyage'. Stockhammer examines no less than five novels featuring maps (Jonathan Swift's *Gulliver's Travels*, Johann Gottfried Schnabel's *Insel Felsenburg*, Goethe's *Die Wahlverwandtschaften*, Adalbert Stifter's *Der Nachsommer*, and Herman Melville's *Moby-Dick; or, The Whale*) in great detail (Stockhammer, 2007: 89–210). For a thorough history of literary maps, see Döring (2009).

4 See, for example, Derkhan's train ride in chapter XII (*PSS*, 127–9) and her walk to the communicatrix in chapter XXVII (*PSS*, 313–5).

5 Note also, of course, the central station the novel is named after, which is exemplary for the whole of New Crobuzon: Perdido Street Station (the Portuguese word *perdido* roughly translates as 'veered from the right path' or 'lost').

6 I take Anthony Pavlik's point that a literary map might, due to its artwork and drawing style, add to a novel's overall mood and setting if drawn in a particular way, his example being maps in children's literature. However, I am resistant to label an embellishment of this kind a 'visual dimension [that is being added] to the narrative' (Pavlik, 2010: 29) in the sense that we might be able to literally make the fictional landscape pop up in our minds as we look at the map. Nevertheless, suggestive map designs are a crucial part of the imaginative 'reading game' inherent to virtually all maps (Pavlik, 2010: 40).

7 Although Miéville stated that New Crobuzon is 'analogous to a chaos-fucked London' (Miéville cited in Gordon, 2003: 362), I would say that the similar city layouts make it even more confusing. We might expect a connection, but again: the map is not the territory. Dealing with maps, according to Stockhammer, is related to the lust of dealing with the symbolic (see Stockhammer, 2007: 12) – and in the case of *Perdido Street Station*, maps come to symbolize getting lost.

8   Note, however, that the archetypal vagrant as found in fiction (male, single) is a rather mythological/romanticized construction, as more and more vagrants in our cities are women with children (Löbbermann, 2005: 267).

9   Two features which usually go together since maps are tools of power (Harley, 1989: 12–14; Harley, 2001: 51–81).

10 Montague Vermishank from New Crobuzon University mentions the Fractured Land as a possible origin, but this is not elaborated on further (*PSS*, 373).

11 See the incident right before the travel through the world web: the Weaver cuts off the left ears of Isaac, Derkhan, Lemuel, and twenty militia (*PSS*, 397). Rudgutter's only explanation: 'It made the web prettier! Obviously!' (*PSS*, 406).

12 In so doing, a big problem of ordinary maps is solved: the problem that they are out of date very quickly – sometimes even as soon as they are published.

13 Yagharek's mapping from above should not be confused with the reader's perspective in the sense of De Certeau's voyeur when he looks at the map. One could say that Yagharek comes closer to it than other characters, but besides the fact that he is looking at the city from the Glasshouse, he does not exactly look at it from above. In addition, his mapping is strongly structured by height and vertical extension – which the reader's map is lacking. Furthermore, he still needs the urban experience of the walker in order to be completely absorbed in the city.

14 The moths blindly follow their smell map that Isaac exploits by means of his crisis conductor – and they get killed. Before, their smell map made them superior, they dominated New Crobuzon while any other organism was only prey. With the crisis conductor as a decoy, they only voraciously stare at the map without paying attention to their actual environment of which the map shows a fake and misleading representation.

15 This is a game that Miéville also pursues in other novels. In *The Scar* (2002), he confronts his readers with the nothingness of the ocean where maps are not useful at all, and the constantly changing layout of Armada, a floating city consisting of numerous ships bound together. In *The City & The City* (2009), maps do exist, but in the murder case of Mahalia, it is the traditional flaw of maps that brings down Bowden: Yorjavic, the man who was supposed to make Mahalia's body disappear, was given an out-

dated map by Bowden. Thus, instead of being dropped into the estuary, the body ended up in a more recently built skate park, ready to be found by a group of teenagers. Urban renewal, Beszel's changing topography, is thus what thwarts Bowden's plan.

16 It is not without irony that Bastei Lübbe, publisher of the two-volume German edition of *Perdido Street Station*, not only changed the title(s) to *Die Falter* (which translates as 'The Moths', 2002) and *Der Weber* (which translates as 'The Weaver', 2002), but also omitted the map.

Works Cited

Altnöder, Sonja (2009) 'Die Stadt als Körper: Materialität und Diskursivität in zwei London-Romanen', in Wolfgang Hallet and Birgit Neumann (eds) *Raum und Bewegung in der Literatur: Die Literaturwissen-schaften und der Spatial Turn*, pp. 299–318. Bielefeld: Transcript Verlag.

Barthes, Roland (1970/2000) *Empire of Signs*, trans. 1982 Richard Howard. New York: Hill and Wang.

Bulson, Eric (2007) *Novels, Maps, Modernity: the Spatial Imagination, 1850–2000*. New York: Routledge.

Certeau, Michel de (1984/1980) *The Practice of Everyday Life*, trans. Steven Rendall. Berkeley: University of California Press.

Deleuze, Gilles and Guattari, Félix (1987/2009) *A Thousand Plateaus: Capitalism and Schizophrenia*, trans. Brian Massumi. London: Continuum.

Döring, Jörg (2009) 'Zur Geschichte der Literaturkarte (1907–2008)', in Jörg Döring and Tristan Thielmann (eds) *Mediengeographie: Theorie – Analyse – Diskussion*, pp. 247–89. Bielefeld: Transcript Verlag.

Dünne, Jörg (2013) 'Die Unheimlichkeit des Mapping', in Marion Picker, Véronique Maleval and Florent Gabaude (eds) *Die Zukunft der Kartographie: Neue und Nicht so Neue Epistemologische Krisen*, pp. 221–40. Bielefeld: Transcript Verlag.

Gabaude, Florent and Maleval, Véronique (2013) 'Mapping als Bildrhetorik: Das karto- und abstrakt-graphische Denken der frühneuzeitlichen Publizistik', in Marion Picker, Véronique Maleval and Florent Gabaude (eds) *Die Zukunft der Kartographie: Neue und Nicht so Neue Epistemologische Krisen*, pp. 135–57. Bielefeld: Transcript Verlag.

Genette, Gérard (1997) *Paratexts: Thresholds of Interpretation*. Cambridge: Cambridge University Press.

Gordon, Joan (2003) 'Reveling in Genre: An Interview with China Miéville', *Science Fiction Studies* 30(3): 355–73.

Harley, J. B. (1989) 'Deconstructing the Map', *Cartographica* 26(2): 1–20.

Harley, J. B. (2001) *The New Nature of Maps: Essays in the History of Cartography*. Baltimore, MD: John Hopkins University Press.

Huck, Christian (2010) *Fashioning Society, or, The Mode of Modernity: Observing Fashion in Eighteenth-Century Britain*. Würzburg: Königshausen & Neumann.

Lefebvre, Henri (1974/1991) *The Production of Space*, trans. Donald Nicholson-Smith. Oxford: Blackwell.

Löbbermann, Dorothea (2005) 'Weg(be)schreibungen: *Transients* in New York City', in Robert Stockhammer (ed.) *TopoGraphien der Moderne. Medien zur Repräsentation und Konstruktion von Räumen*, pp. 263–85. München: Fink.

Löw, Martina (2008) *Einführung in die Stadt- und Raumsoziologie*. Opladen: Budrich.

McLuhan, Marshall (1962) *The Gutenberg Galaxy*. Toronto: University of Toronto Press.

Nünning, Ansgar and Vera Nünning (2007) *Grundkurs Anglistisch-amerikanische Literaturwissenschaft*. Stuttgart: Klett.

Pavlik, Anthony (2010) '"A Special Kind of Reading Game": Maps in Children's Literature', *International Research in Children's Literature* 3: 28–43.

Schneider, Ute (2006) *Die Macht der Karten: Eine Geschichte der Kartographie vom Mittelalter bis heute*. Darmstadt: Wissenschaftliche Buchgesellschaft.

Stockhammer, Robert (2005) 'Verortung. Die Macht der Karten und die Literatur', in Robert Stockhammer (ed.) *TopoGraphien der Moderne: Medien zur Repräsentation und Konstruktion von Räumen*, pp. 319–340. Paderborn: Fink.

Stockhammer, Robert (2007) *Kartierung der Erde: Macht und Lust in Karten und Literatur*. München: Fink.

Wood, Michael (2003) 'A Strategic Plan for the International Cartographic Association 2003–2011', Durban: International Cartographic Association (consulted July 2013), http://icaci.org/files/documents/reference_docs/ICA_Strategic_Plan_2003-2011.pdf

4

Failing Better
Iron Council, Benjamin, Revolution

Dougal McNeill

> Utilize the boring eyes of trains as projectors for flashing out schedules of what's happening tomorrow in the arts, like an arrow in swift pursuit.
>
> Velimir Khlebnikov, 'Proposals' (1915)

I. They are always coming

Revolution is, for the socialist, both her primary obsession and desire and her imaginative and representational limit and end-point. Too easily conceived, revolution becomes just another list of ameliorative features all too much like our dreary present; 'gas and water socialism', as the great James Connolly mocked his reformist opponents (cited in Allen, 1990: 106). Too fully represented, though, and scenes of the post-revolutionary 'epoch of rest' will warp and shatter whatever alienated imaginative equipment we have from this era, leaving us with unwillingly comic visions along the lines of Charles Fourier's lemonade seas and multiple moons. Revolution, in the Marxist tradition, thus has a double necessity:

> Both for the production on a mass scale of this communist consciousness, and for the success of the cause itself, the alteration of men on a mass scale is necessary, an alteration which can only take place in a practical movement, a revolution; this revolution is necessary, therefore, not only because the ruling class cannot be overthrown in any other way, but also because the class overthrowing it can only in a revolution succeed in ridding itself of all the muck of ages and become fitted to found society anew. (Marx, 1845: 200)

The 'production on a mass scale of this communist consciousness' is, amongst other things, what *Iron Council* is 'about'. As the third installment of Miéville's 'Bas-Lag' trilogy, its storyworld involves a grisly image of the degrading and damaging impact of capitalism on workers' lives, as the Remade demonstrate. These are criminals with bodies mangled and deformed in ironic pattern, echoing Kafka's Penal Colony; in their redesigned limbs and prosthetic additions, they show the reduction of human nature to corporate use and exploitation. *Iron Council* is both a quest narrative and the imagination of revolution: its quest narrative, in the best traditions of the Western, follows Cutter out into the desert and badlands in search of the mythical Iron Council, a train of revolt escaped from the tyranny of New Crobuzon. The imagination of revolution follows the train back to the city, as intrigue, political organization and open rebellion threaten New Crobuzon's rulers. Hating those who give away good endings, I cannot tell you here how the two stories combine; suffice, for now, to note that their connections give Miéville's political vision its narrative intensity. The revolt of workers, Remade and whole, in the creation of the Iron Council shows us both the ridding of what Marx called 'the muck of ages' (Marx, 1845: 200) which needs to be overthrown, and the novel's tragic *dénouement*. With its 'revolutionary rehearsal' in New Crobuzon 'storming heaven' and facing reaction as it loses, Miéville's *dénouement* links to concerns all too imaginable in the twenty-first century – with its aftermath of revolutionary failure, problems of organization, and resilience.

Miéville's novel is, in other words, a meditation on those moments when 'History felt quicker' (*IC*, 353) and struggle opened up possibilities. He is fascinated with 'alterity, the not-this-ness of this' (Miéville, 2008: 64), and with the 'specific articulations of *alterity*' and the 'unreality function' (Miéville, 2009: 244, emphasis in original) in the world of fantasy and science fiction (SF) – consider the impossibilities and wonder of form-manipulating Vodyanoi, space-bending Tesh and all of Bas-Lag's other richly imagined peoples and dangers. In *Iron Council*, both these fascinations collide productively with a more common and disheartening sense of the 'impossible': namely that carefully cultivated sense that revolutions are themselves a thing of the past and never succeed. Nicholas Birns (2009: 203) calls the revolution we read about in *Iron Council* 'heterodox rather than orthodox'. The details and plot surprises of *Iron Council* are not those we have been trained to expect from the stock accounts of revolutions on our planet. Its clashes are not the stereotyped collisions encountered in some kinds of Marxist writing. The forces of reaction on our planet are unlikely to deploy Handlingers (ghastly parasitic hands able to control the minds of their hosts and victims) against insurgents, to be sure, but there are risks in too quickly closing off points off contact between the world of Bas-Lag and our own. What, after all, is an 'orthodox' revolution? Lenin, who had both practical and theoretical experience with these politics, was convinced that 'whoever expects a "pure" social revolution will never live to see it' (Lenin, 1916: 153). The mess and complexity of the revolutionary situation in New Crobuzon is better understood as a kind of realism-in-Fantasy, a working out of some representational and narrative difficulties common to *all* revolutionary situations, and given new possibility by *Iron Council*'s historical situation within what was the anti-capitalist movement. My argument, in what follows, is that we do not need to choose between a Fantastic aesthetic and the kinds of political and epistemological insights Marxism has traditionally associated with realism. Miéville, in *Iron Council*, shows us how the fantastic contributes to debates around strategy and political theory, and assists in the task of imagining revolution – not elsewhere, but here on Earth.

Iron Council brims with allusions, echoes, asides and all manner of riffs on the revolutionary tradition – a tradition that has been developed both in fantasy literature as well as in history and political philosophy. I want to argue here that these revolutionary echoes can best be read as part of a project to *renew* the fantasy of revolution, the dream of both its desirability, possibility, and of its tragic problems and strategic dilemmas. Tradition may seem an odd term to evoke here, given revolution's associations with ruptures as well as SF's obsession with the new and unimaginable, but it offers a way of thinking about the world *around* the novel loose enough to set associations to work and still precise enough to insist on boundaries. Tradition, in this way of reading, is all manner of objects boxed up together as remnants from a shared project: there is no point in being too precious about where connections begin and end, but one feels still the need to draw limits. *Iron Council* riffs on associations from the leftist world of its production, without ever turning this riffing into a too tightly drawn set of references. 'We Marxists live in traditions' Trotsky insisted in his 1924 work of literary criticism, *Literature and Revolution* (Trotsky, 1924/2005: 115). The revolutionary tradition can be imagined as that body of writing, memory and organization, which reflects on past historical struggle and preserves legacies from the past. Books have a different intellectual and emotional resonance when read this way. Rosa Luxemburg's account of the Russian Revolution, say, may be quarrelled over in materialist historiography, but revolutionary tradition sustains it as a work of *memory* – a text through which one can access revolution – at the same time that it reads Luxemburg's account for theoretical insight. Historical accounts, as well as theoretical abstractions, of revolutionary uprisings within Marxist, socialist and anarchist intellectual traditions thus fuse, and *Iron Council* can best be read *within* this tradition.[1] Miéville draws on many interlocutors and references – from Walter Benjamin most importantly for my purposes here – to reconstitute a tradition, and offers, in his image of revolution, chances for imaginative renewal.

II. The dream of the commons: Another world is possible!

The history of culture, Benjamin (cited in Löwy, 2005: 55) suggests, 'has to be integrated into the history of the class struggle'. *Iron Council* can best be understood if we integrate into our sense of its narrative power a recognition of its moment of production and reception, its part in that period in the class struggle that was known as the *mouvement altermondialiste* (the movement for another globalization) from the turn of the twenty-first century. Miéville has made this connection explicit (he has said in interview that 'the Bas Lag books ... were a response ... very directly to the post-Seattle anti-capitalist movement' [Miéville, 2008: 70]) and although it has not gone unnoticed in criticism so far, much more needs to be made of this contemporary political context.[2] In November 1999, Seattle saw large, vibrant and, in some quarters, unexpected protests against a meeting of the World Trade Organization, and protestors' militancy and energy forced the WTO's apologists into defensive stances. For a heady two years after Seattle – with similar major demonstrations against the World Economic Forum in Melbourne in September 2000, against the World Bank in Prague later that month, and huge World Social Forums across the globe gathering activists and campaigners together – it felt as if, following years of defeat, the left was moving through a cycle of advancing, regrouping, and advancing again. Old ideas regained circulation and new ideas sparked lively debates. *Iron Council* thus needs to be understood as a novel which is explicitly situated within this particular historical moment.

Iron Council's anti-capitalist energies are both imaginative and stylistic. Imaginatively, the novel extends the movement's re-examination and revival of critical Marxist theory; it was written at a time when, in Daniel Bensaïd's words from *Marx for Our Times* (2002), something of a ghostly companion piece to *Iron Council*, theorists were 'disturbing the heavy slumber of orthodoxies' as they produced newly energized radical thought to answer the question: 'whose millennium? Theirs or ours?' (Bensaïd, 2002: 2). In its brash insistence on both revolt ('no pay no lay!' [*IC*, 197]) and revolution as constituent events, *Iron Council* thus restores the centrality of *thinking revolu-*

tion to a left imaginative world which had, through the long years of Thatcherism, various Third Ways and T.I.N.A. (adopted from Thatcher's infamous slogan that 'there is no alternative' to free-market economic liberalism), almost convinced itself that such questions could no longer be asked. This is a *novel*, though, not a political manifesto, and its stylistic pleasures owe something to the anti-capitalist movement too. Miéville's rich, heady wordiness (in such descriptions as 'an integument of pipes and pistons emerging from his flesh' [*IC*, 183]) suggests a certain self-confidence and expansive outlook. *Iron Council* is not afraid of sending its readers to the dictionary; of the stylists on the Anglophone left, only Perry Anderson rivals Miéville for sentences as exacting and vocabulation as expansively lush. The anti-capitalist movement's terminology makes occasional appearance, too:

> "We're a dream," she said. "The dream of the commons. Everything came to this, everything came here. We got to here. This is what we are. History's pushing us."
> *What does that mean?* He thought. *What are you saying?*
> "It's time for us to push through. Whatever happens. We have to come back now, you see? That was all she would say. (*IC*, 430, emphasis in original)[3]

It has been observed that the anti-capitalist movement's self-confidence and energy expressed itself in a stylistic shift, a recasting of old questions and commitments in new languages and codes. In another companion text to *Iron Council* from the movement's headiest years of expansion and intellectual advance, *Fire Alarm*, Michael Löwy (2005: 11) writes of a 'Gothic Marxism': an 'historical materialism sensitive to the magical dimension of the cultures of the past, to the "dark" moments of revolt, to the lightning flash that rends the heavens of revolutionary action'. This is still Marxism, with its commitment to class struggle and belief in the possibility of a socialist future, but it is Gothic Marxism no less: alive to danger, more aware, from the nightmares of the twentieth century, of the unconscious, the 'bad side' to history, the re-appearance of History's repressed.

Fantasy's qualities as a genre made it especially suited as a literary vehicle through which to articulate some of the early twenty-first century anti-capitalist movement's imaginative ambitions, its desire to think alternatives to existing political realities – whether in the form of the manifesto, the programme, or literature itself.[4] One of the tasks of anti-capitalism was 'the revival of social critique' (Callinicos, 2003: 7): *dreaming* other – and, sometimes, impossible – worlds took on particular importance as a part of this renewed critique. The long-maligned late nineteenth-century utopian socialist tradition, articulated by writers such as Charles Fourier, Henri de Saint-Simon, Robert Owen and Edward Carpenter, took on new life as activists and intellectuals, in response to the cynicism of postmodernity, asked pertinent – and radically, estrangingly naive – questions of what other worlds might be possible. Orthodox socialist theory, for much of the twentieth century, had scorned utopian thinking as outdated after the arrival of 'scientific' socialism. Engels's question in *Socialism: Utopian and Scientific* (1880), after all, was socialism utopian *or* scientific (Engels, 1880/1970). The twenty-first-century revival of Utopian thought came in part from anti-capitalism's desire for imaginable futures: it was the future, for many, that neoliberalism had robbed from the present, the sense that in the words of the ubiquitous post-Seattle slogan, borrowed from May 1968 protest graffiti in Paris stating that *Un autre monde est possible*, 'another world is possible'. Early twenty-first-century activism thus picked up, and estranged, what its nineteenth-century Utopian ancestors had left waiting to be rediscovered.

I shall have more to say on how these qualities of fantasy – and with it the potentials for left mythology – draw Miéville and the anti-capitalist movement into confrontation with some of the orthodoxies of left Science Fiction theory below. For now, I want to register a suspicion that, no matter how well Miéville has been served by his leftist critics, some sense of his work's power and reach has been lost in the shift from the political force-field of 1968, that informs most left SF criticism, into the post-Seattle era. Carl Freedman (2008: 270), one of Miéville's most astute leftist critics, sees the use of magic in *Iron Council* as 'best grasped as a set of utopian signs, or figures, or placeholders, for social forces whose precise nature cannot yet be identified but which must be in some way posited if the ultimate ideal of revolutionary social justice is to be maintained'; Freedman (2008:

270) asserts that the 'basic project' of the book is to 'keep hope alive'. Darko Suvin's critique of Fantasy bases itself now on his sense that the post-1989 world order is one marked by defeats and straightened horizons for the Left.[5] The sense of defensiveness and defeat in which Freedman and Suvin couch their comments on hope and sustenance feel quite alien when approached from within the context of anti-capitalism's orientation and energy.

III. Golemetry is an interruption

Evoking the Marxist philosopher Walter Benjamin at this stage in my argument carries dangers all of its own. Benjamin is so regularly cited and discussed by scholars today his work is in danger of losing its revolutionary and disrespectable character. It is worth remembering, therefore, his extra- (and, indeed, anti-) academic location and leftist affiliations. Benjamin was a great enthusiast of the maligned genres of the Western and pulp literature, and some of Miéville's raffish Fantasy might help us to revive Benjamin's pulp predelictions, and help wrest his tradition away from, as he himself wrote, 'a conformism that is about to overpower it' (Benjamin, 1940: 257). Benjamin, after all, scorned the 'pretentious, universal gesture of the book' in favour of nurturing 'inconspicuous forms' and learning from a kind of cultural salvage operation, picking up and studying children's books, street signs, newspapers, and movies alongside classical and canonical literature. His work is both evaluative, discriminating and non-hierarchical. It is a good companion in the world of pulp, Fantasy and Westerns (Benjamin, 1928/1997: 45).

Through the twenty-first century anti-capitalist movement's new interest in time and the actuality of revolution, Benjamin thus re-emerges into communist consciousness, and it is around these themes that his ideas can be discerned in *Iron Council*. Magic and thaumaturgy (a magical process shaping and animating, giving life to matter when 'the universe seemed to flex and stretch at two points' [*IC*, 262]) as well as political organization and action involve choices *in* time, decisions *about* time and its possibilities. Miéville explores the contrasts between what Benjamin (Benjamin, 1940: 263) calls the 'homogenous, empty time' of the concept of historical progress and capitalist normal life, and those revolutionary upheavals charged with qualities of what Benjamin referred to as *Jetztzeit*: that feeling of *newness* when everything seems possible and when the sense of our own lives and of time itself transforms as we change the world. *Iron Council*'s protagonist, Cutter, the friend, lover and follower of the world-shaping Judah Low, leads a group out in search of Judah to bring him and his powers back to the City of New Crobuzon, and back into political activity. At times Cutter's journey in search of Judah is through such 'homogenous, empty time':

> It was not the only moment of the journey when time clotted, and Cutter was stuck fast. A day was only an instant, drawn out. Motion itself – the putter of insects, the appearance-disappearance of a tiny rodent – was an endless repetition of the same. (*IC*, 40–1)

This journey will lead Cutter to Iron Council: a Soviet- or Paris-Commune-like permanent meeting and rebellion travelling to New Corbuzon in a train, carrying with it the promise of political revolution and a Utopian vision of what an alternative socio-political order might look like. This sense of time stands in contrast to the moment when the Iron Council and New Crobuzon almost collide (via Judah's intervention), as the twin historical possibilities of victorious revolution and terrible reaction are caught in the figure of the perpetual train by the 'time golem'. Judah can animate form, he can create golems and, at the novel's climax, his creation of a time golem – time itself gathered together and *used* – becomes both a symbol and a crucial matter for plot and story. 'The same leap in the open air of history', Benjamin argues, 'is the dialectical one, which is how Marx understood revolution' (Benjamin, 1940: 263). Judah has witnessed a closing of the 'open air of history' as other cultures and social formations are crushed by the advance of the railroad; 'the moment has passed him' (*IC*, 140) he realizes as the Stiltspear land (home to an insect-like people with mystical powers and connections) is destroyed. His 'salvation' of Iron Council through its seizure by the golem into a present in tension – in which, as Benjamin analogously writes of the revolutionary arrest, 'time stands still and has come to a stop' (Benjamin, 1940: 264) – is thus an attempt to render the time golem's promise both fulfilled and destroyed in one stroke:

> The time golem stood and was, ignored the linearity around it, only was. It was a violence, a terrible intrusion in the succession of moments, a clot in diachrony, and with the dumb arrogance of its existence it paid the outrage of ontology no mind. (*IC*, 454)

Judah's action here presents the great moral dilemma and tragedy of the book: he 'saves' Iron Council from its imminent destruction by the forces of the state in New Crobuzon only by himself destroying it as an active, democratic revolutionary force. He robs the Councillors of their own decisions, and, in recognizing a Benjaminian 'image of the past as it flashes up in the moment of danger' (Benjamin, 1940: 257), he refuses the Council its chance to act *in* that moment of danger. If golemetry is 'an *interruption*' and 'a subordinating of the static *IS* to the active *AM*' (*IC*, 172, emphasis in original) Judah risks reversing its order and commitment. Who teaches the teachers? Who decides when an historical moment demands revolutionary intervention? Judah freezes time, 'saving' the Council for future generations once he realizes it will lose in the present. But, in doing so, he takes the Councillors – and *their* ability to act in that present – out of the world of political decision and chance taking. The novel's climax, at the level of plot, thus acts out an ethical dilemma of revolutionary politics.

IV. Perpetual Train

Other critics have heard these echoes of Benjamin in *Iron Council*; but connecting them to Miéville's contribution to the anti-capitalist movement helps expand our sense of the imaginative work they carry out.[6] In its theoretical work and its practical interventions disrupting the summits and triumphant processions of globalized capital, the post-Seattle left worked at reviving a politics at once committed and innovative, attuned to liberal complacency over progress and Stalinist delusions of inevitability, to listen for history's moments, its opportunities. There was no homogeneity to what was called anti-capitalism or anti-globalization (the contest between those terms itself indicating areas of disagreement and debate); rather, what unified the movement was a set of shared *questions*. Revolutionary change seemed, at the hinge between the centuries, once again, a realistic and essential desire and strategy, raising the question: which ideas remained productive within inherited political traditions and which have become obsolete? How can revolution as a goal be revived after the defeats and set-backs of the twentieth century? If, as Francis Fukuyama suggested, the time after the Cold War marked the 'end of History', did time then become empty and society unchangeable after the collapse of the Berlin Wall in November 1989? In this new, Fukuyaman, post-historical era, how might the revolutionary tradition of Marxist philosophy restore a sense of hope and the possibility of progressive social change? Daniel Bensaïd (2002: 21) calls this contemporary dilemma 'the decisive notion of the contratemps or non-contemporaneity'. Utopia appears:

> not as some arbitrary invention of the future, but as a project that forces itself on to the horizon of the future. Henceforth, what we are confronted with is not some future City or better world, but a logic of emancipation rooted in conflict. (Bensaïd, 2002: 21)

For all that the anti-capitalist movement is itself now in the past and recent history, its actors and theorists – Miéville not least among them – continue to ask its questions in different venues and as part of different projects. Utopia is not somewhere else, and it is decisively not nowhere, but is located instead *within* the contradictions and experiences of life in the twenty-first century, pressing down as a demand – where is this better world? – on any protest against existing conditions. 'Realising a possibility', as Daniel Bensaïd puts it, 'revolution is in essence untimely and, to some extent, always "premature," a creative imprudence' (Bensaïd, 2002: 54).[7] Bensaïd's timely intervention draws our attention to all those instances when *Iron Council* forces us to confront the *unruly*, unpredictable stuff of history, the moments when revolutionary success or failure rely on choices, conscious action, and timing. Revolution is the product of conscious human activity and organization, and Utopia does not arrive according to some pre-ordained timetable. Political action, insurrection, involves chance, risk, and interventions that seek to change the balance of forces. With its fantastical image of golemetry as interruption, *Iron Council* dramatizes this sense of revolutionary time, in which time is made into a factor both in conflict as well as in a sense of historical possibility. What Miéville describes as the 'revolt of the Iron Council, the renegacy of the perpetual train' (*IC*, 391) thus inspires further revolt within the novel, but attempts by characters to force this revolt into some comforting connection with an 'inevitable' History are rebuffed by the narrative. 'Sometimes there are no choices', Judah says as the train returns to New Crobuzon, 'sometimes it's history decides. Just have to hope history doesn't get it wrong' (*IC*, 352). But history, of course, *does nothing*: the rest of the novel is given over to exploring the choices Judah and the other Councillors make as they face the challenge of building their own history.[8] The novel's tragic dimension makes us aware, as an earlier twentieth-century 'classical Marxism' (developed closely in line with Marx and Engels's orginal writings) could not have been, that a successful resolution of humanity's problems is by no means a certainty:

> We know that the working class has the innate structural *capacity* to achieve the socialist revolution, but whether it can be realised is another issue altogether, which involves questions of consciousness, leadership, strategy, and the extent to which our enemies possess the same qualities. There is also the question of time: the working class may simply continue to be defeated, as it has been until now, until it is too late to prevent the planet becoming uninhabitable. (Davidson, 2009: 166, emphasis in original)

This question of time, of the untimely revolution, perpetual revolt, and disconnected moments the reader encounters in *Iron Council* – crystallized in the image of the train arriving at a destination (revolution) which is no longer there – is developed and extended in the novel into an anti-capitalist analysis of revolutionary time(s). In his 'Proposals' (1915), the Futurist Velimir Khlebnikov (from whom Miéville takes

Iron Council's epigraph) called for a revolt to 'usher in everywhere, instead of the concept of space, the concept of time. For instance, wars on Planet Earth between generations, wars in the trenches of time' (Khlebnikov, 1915/1987: 358). There is not one past, but different historical pasts, different moments coming back into consciousness as the present re-works them in struggles for historical legacies. The Iron Council's frozen train – a moment from a lost revolution visible in a present while still being in the past – is a wonderfully resonant image of this kind of possibility.

V. Leaps! Breaks in gradualness. Leaps! Leaps!

This development of revolutionary time – that time in which revolution becomes possible and a revolutionary sense of time, or awareness of the radical possibility contained within each moment of the present, reveals itself – is impossible without its expression in the genre of *fantasy* literature. What Verity Burgmann (2006: 101) called in 2006 the 'cognitive mapping of a new and global type evident in anti-capitalism' was characterized by an insistence on *dreaming*, on new worlds, on slogans gesturing at their own difficult encounters with alterity, the impossible and the not-yet-thinkable. As one 2001 protest banner proclaimed: 'overthrow global capitalism and replace it with something nicer!'[9] Reviewing a series of interviews with participants in the 1999 Seattle protests, John Charlton (2000: 16) records 'the almost breathless accounts, of people experiencing a birth of the new'. Chris Carlsson similarly called Seattle 'this polyphonous cacophony' as activists woke from a 'long somnambulistic slumber' (cited in Burgmann, 2006: 113). The vocabulary of fantasy – and the work of the utopians whose fantasies, Benjamin argued in 1940 (1940: 261), 'which have so often been ridiculed, prove to be surprisingly sound' – reconnected with political radicalism in the ferment of anti-capitalism. Another world is possible, the slogan went; this stance, in opposition to the older idea that There Is No Alternative, contained an implicit injunction to *dream*, to *fantasize*, to think another world. The anti-utopian models of the twentieth century – most notably Stalinism and reformism – were broken; the left needed to start anew. This reading of the genre of fantasy as enabling political radicalism is not, to be sure, how the majority of Marxist literary critics have viewed fantasy literature. In Darko Suvin's influential analysis, SF is considered to involve cognition whilst Fantasy, based in myth, is criticized for training its readers in seeing the unchanging in what ought to be considered historical and thus open to human transformation. Fantasy, for Suvin and his followers, is a literature of the eternal – its dreams are just ways of making the present order seem unchanging, outside the time of history. For Suvin, the conflation of fantasy (a form that the materialist critic 'may to a large extent rightly dislike') with SF should therefore be considered 'unhealthy' (Suvin, 2000: 210). Suvin links his objections to the fantastic and the 'sense of wonder' to its connection with myth:

> SF's analogical historicity...cannot be mythopoetic in any sense except that most trivial one of possessing a "vast sweep" or "a sense of wonder": another superannuated slogan of much SF criticism due for a deserved retirement into the same limbo as extrapolation. For myth is re-enactment, eternal return, and the opposite of creative human freedom. (Suvin, 2010: 89)

How do we escape from myth and re-enactment, though? Part of the disorientation effected during these long years of neoliberalism has been that what were once accepted truths (concerning class, revolutionary history, and traditions of resistance) have become denigrated as mythical whilst other class myths (such as the so-called wisdom of the economic metaphor of the invisible hand which self-regulates the market) have entered the workers' movement as truth.[10] Anti-capitalism dreamed of new beginnings, and worked with old material – the imagery of 1968, the legacy of past revolutions from Russia in 1917 to China in 1949, and so on – to try and construct a new political rhetoric. As a fictional text which responds both to the anti-capitalist movement as well as to this Marxist tradition, *Iron Council* offers phrases that are recognizable from our own history and our sense of the world scattered throughout its pages, situating Bas-Lag's fantastical elements (as the product of Miéville's world-building) in an uneasy relationship with this real historical past that informs its fantasy setting and contextualizes our reading of the novel. It is a past we may well recognize, and yet in a Fantasy setting it offers unsettling associations with what is familiar to Miéville's readers. The thugs in Quillers, for example, whose violent racism is targeted against the non-human inhabitants of New Crobuzon such as the humanoid scarab beetle race known as the khepri, 'take up the human dust' (*IC*, 302), echoing Trotsky's (1944/2002: 31) description of Nazism as 'human dust'; while the 'Night of the Kinken Shards' (*IC*, 368), in which a khepri ghetto was stormed by the fascist New Quill Party and many khepris murdered, offers another parallel with last century's fascist brutality.

In the early twenty-first century, the anti-capitalist movement struggled between a desire for a new start and a sense that the problems it inherited from a longer tradition of radical leftist and revolutionary praxis anticipated its new forms. Socialists within the movement thus worked to find new rhetorical vehicles in which to couch their political demand for post-capitalist change. That struggle, between maintaining a sense of political and intellectual continuity with a longer radical tradition that still has much to offer in the twenty-first century, and discarding those aspects of its rhetoric that are no longer productive in a contemporary context, can be discerned in the events that take place in *Iron Council*. The image of New Crobuzon's revolt in the novel shows how that very mode of fantasy literature that Darko Suvin suspects of being regressive, conservative and rotten, with its escapist swords and sorcerers, can in fact offer ways out of the deadlock of an eternally recurrent myth of the impossibility of radical political change. New Crobuzon is weird, other to our own contemporary world, and so not reducible to allegorical treatment. At the same time, however, the novel's political message functions through what we might call a sort of metaphorical *jamming* or metaphorical overload: a piling up in Miéville's prose of suggestiveness and connotative baroque luxury that overwhelms any allegorical reduction and keeps an imaginative pact with Benjamin's (1940: 256) insistence that 'nothing that has ever happened should be regarded as lost for history'. *Iron Council*'s revolutionary insurrection thus draws on – and revives an historical sense of – a previous 'tradition of the oppressed' in our own world. In its Brechtian 'FLEXIBLE PUPPET THEATRE' (*IC*, 52) and its fascist Quillers, Miéville's New Crobuzon evokes Weimar Berlin; its urban revolt and threat of war within the city-state draw on the Paris Commune; the train journey and the Caucus factions of merchants opposed to the government suggest Russia in 1905 and 1917; and, finally, the harassed groups of socialist paper sellers meeting in pubs remind us of our own political activism today, from Newcastle to New Zealand. New Crobuzon cannot, of course, be reduced to any one of these historical referents. They are not 'clues' to be read, in allegorical fashion, as 'really' reflecting our world, and Mieville's narrative dexterity (which is ably demonstrated in the racy fight scene early in the novel [*IC*, 56]) insists that we read this material on its own terms. It must be imagined, impossibly, as *all of these moments at once*, a fantasy of reconstituted tradition, a dream of a renewed and viable revolutionary project and shared, common language for new leftist politics. Through this metaphorical, associative jamming, *Iron Council* forces its reader into a recognition of the real historical legacy of political revolt in the twentieth and twenty-first centuries, as well as confounding that recognition through its otherworldly, weird and fantastical landscape. These are images that may stir memories and associations in readers; in Miéville's borrowed phrases from the archive of texts committed to revolution, they figure as parts of a tradition that many on the left had discarded, prior to the resurgence of anti-capitalist activism witnessed at Seattle in 2000. However, such images contain political and rhetorical problems that remain to be worked through. As Marx writes in his 'Preface' to the first edition of *Capital, Vol. 1*:

> Alongside the modern evils, we are oppressed by a whole series of inherited evils, arising from the passive survival of archaic and outdated modes of production, with their accompanying train of anachronistic social and political relations. We suffer not only from the living, but from the dead. (Marx, 1867/1990: 91)

The time is out of joint. Or, as Marx will go on to write, 'we draw the magic cap down over our own eyes and ears so as to deny that there are any monsters' (Marx, 1867/1990: 91). The monster, in this context, is capitalism itself: a monstrous imaginary world studded with details from our own history which may help resuscitate critical, historical thinking. If there is no alternative and this is the End of History, as some in the 1990s claimed, that eternal present may be monstrous; *Iron Council*'s fabulous beasts and fantastic situations give the reader a chance to approach this reality aslant.

VI. Taking metaphors seriously

Miéville has described this process of employing metaphor against allegory as one of Fantasy's great strengths. Allegories must be read reductively, as one uses the captions in a newspaper cartoon to decode the stock figures and translate them into 'real' politicians and so on. Metaphors, however, complicate this one-to-one correspondence. Donkeys in US cartoons are the Democrats, elephants the Republicans; no ambiguity can slip in between. A metaphor *is* whatever it claims to be in the narrative and, at the same time and through this, suggests an abundance of other possible associations. For Miéville (2008: 65, emphasis in original), both SF and Gothic '*literalize their metaphors*'. As he explains: 'to literalize your metaphor does not mean that it stops being a metaphor, but it invigorates the metaphor because it embeds its referent within the totality of the text, with its own integrity and realism' (Miéville, 2008: 65). Against the 'tedious symbolism which mars so much "magic realism" ... in which the fantastic does not trust itself, and which the author is keen to stress is "really about" insert-theme-here', Miéville's aesthetic offers us what he describes as an 'impossible world which *believes in itself*' (Miéville, 2008: 65, emphasis in original). 'Dispensing with allegory cannot mean dispensing with metaphor: fantasy that believes in itself is about itself and *also* about other things' (Miéville, 2012: 49, emphasis in original). The pleasures of story for itself – the pleasure of imagining a richly strange and other world – is not on a lesser plane to the 'real' work of metaphor in this scheme. It is, instead, a companion pleasure, a way of having one's dream and thinking with it.

The detailed vividness of this fantasy that believes in itself is what draws us into the world of Bas-Lag. The horror of Miéville's Remade, for instance, stick in the imagination long after particular plot details of *Iron Council* have been forgotten – and it is this richness that allows fantasy's imperative to be '*also* about other things' (Miéville, 2012: 49, emphasis in original). The Remade may set in train metaphorical associations concerning crime and punishment, capitalism and the reduction of the body to the extraction of surplus value, but they are also monstrously *imaginable*, horrendous:

> a man whose front pullulates with scrawny arms, each from a corpse or an amputation. Chained to him a taller man, his face stoic, a fox stitched embedded in his chest from where it snarls and bites at him in permanent terror. (*IC*, 141)

The junk-yard obsessiveness of this '*also*' is what I am calling 'metaphorical jamming'. These associations pile up into what Walter Benjamin refers to as 'the tradition of the oppressed' (Benjamin, 1940: 257). In *Iron Council*, for instance, the train that 'laid its tracks through history' (*IC*, 359) reminds us of the Russian Revolution, at the same time as the strike that leads to the formation of the Iron Council itself introduces a new generation of readers and activists to the great struggle for unionization on the Dakar-Niger line in 1947–8, as well as the 'march of the women' that the Senegalese writer Ousmane Sembène celebrates in his novel about the railroad strike against colonial Senegal in 1940, *God's Bits of Wood* (1960). Indeed, set on the railroads and including a prostitutes' strike, *Iron Council*'s class struggle borrows very loosely from Sembène. Miéville's tribute to his work in the novel's 'Acknowledgements' can send readers off after links, connections, traditions, and unjustly forgotten texts. However, metaphor and association also function in the novel as unstable and open-ended intertextual references. What role, for instance, does Miéville's Drogon the Whispersmith play in the novel's world, given his intertextual connections to Frank H. Spearman's titular railroad detective in his 1906 Western novel, *Whispering Smith*?

The greatest, most evocative metaphor we're compelled to believe in is the Iron Council itself: a ceaselessly moving train whose rebellious inhabitants must journey to avoid being caught by the New Crobuzon militia. This 'perpetual train' (*IC*, 354) is redolent of Lenin's train journey in April 1917 to St. Petersburg's Finland Station ahead of the October Revolution; or Trotsky's armoured carriage crossing Russia through the Civil War; it also evokes the nineteenth-century locomotives that, as Benjamin (1928/1997: 352) reminds us, were considered to represent unstoppable progress and offered a figure of 'the saint of the future'; or recalls the catastrophic, world-rending railway that we find in Dickens's 1848 novel *Dombey and Son*; *Iron Council* similarly echoes the arrested trains of the 1926 General Strike such as the *Flying Scotsman*, which was derailed by striking train workers; as well as the symbolic train of progress that the Hungarian philosopher Ágnes Heller argued had not delivered Western modernity to the final destination of Utopia (understood as *elsewhere*) but had, in fact, deposited its travellers in the gigantic station of The-End-of-History; modernity had already reached its final destination of life 'after progress' (Löwy, 2005: 113). Miéville's train carrying the Iron Councillors reminds us of all of these historical trains and, probably, many more still. In addition to these carefully interwoven historical references which together demonstrate what I am calling Miéville's metaphorical jamming, the Iron Council is also a train with a carriage that becomes 'a vast membranous cell, three nuclei still vaguely shaped like men and women afloat in cytoplasm' (*IC*, 355). Here, Miéville's dense layering of metaphors must work inside the novel's storyworld to contribute to our sense of Fantasy: any political association we might place upon the text is only possible *after* such metaphors have done their fictional work in convincing us of this fully realized world of Bas-Lag. In addition to this richly delineated world of the train (with all of its associative metaphorical jamming), the readerly pleasures of *Iron Council* are also to be found in its political challenges. The novel reminds Miéville's reader that thinking the unthinkable means stretching ourselves beyond our current mental equipment and expectations. The Council thus represents a wholly new way of managing society that is radically democratic, egalitarian, and communal, and the difficulty of thinking the possibility of a world like this is acknowledged in the text: in the face of such difference, Cutter 'could not map the alterity he felt' (*IC*, 288). Imagination, rather than cognition, may be the keyword with which we are concerned in our politicized reading of *Iron Council* at this juncture: another world, as the text shows us, is possible.

VII. The Distinction of Fiction

Although existing critical commentary acknowledges the quality of Miéville's prose, I am struck by the way in which critics dealing with Miéville and the question of politics confine their appreciation of his political achievement in *Iron Council* to the level of *story* (content), neglecting the important role of *narrative discourse* (and historical intertextuality) in the text. Political discussion and strategic debate within the storyworld of *Iron Council* are essential to the progress of the plot and have therefore attracted critical attention. For example, the jaded outlook of one of Miéville's protagonists, the revolutionary Ori, offers readers a genuine political debate and tension. Ori's disillusionment with the propagandist outlook of New Crobuzon's underground protest publication the *Runagate Rampant*, and his attraction to the militant Toro's anarchist adventures articulate a common problem encountered by radical thinkers and activists in confronting the issue of violence within a revolutionary situation. Although this dilemma works at the level of plot in *Iron Council*, it should also be read at the level of narrative discourse, since it offers a fictionalized account of a real, historical contradiction.[11] But what of *Iron Council's* formal qualities, its organization of this material *in narrative*?

In the novel, Miéville's twin narratives – of the Iron Council's creation and journey back to New Crobuzon, and of organization and insurrection inside the city – combine as a climax when Cutter returns to the city to announce the train's return, which is followed by his subsequent horrified mission to try and save the train from destruction. The rebellion, the Collective, the 'New Crobuzon Commune' has been crushed; 'nightmares of reaction' (*IC*, 368) are triumphant and 'Cutter felt emptied out' (*IC*, 373), as he sees around him evidence that Iron Council's intervention into this revolutionary moment will be too late. If it arrives in New Crobuzon the train will be destroyed: the readerly pleasures and anxieties in the last hundred pages or so of the novel combine as we worry at how, and whether, Cutter will deliver his warning to the train. Because, of course, *as readers*, we know he is right. The moment *has* passed, the train's return would not make a difference, reaction is victorious. In the world of the story, though, the Iron Councillors cannot possibly know any of this, and their reasons for ignoring Cutter's warning and insisting that they still offer 'a hope' (*IC*, 432) to the city are, *within the logic of the story*, perfectly correct and (politically, ethically) essential.

The tragedy that Miéville has established for his readers in this climax involves the manipulation that is a distinctive quality of *all* fiction, shared by both genre fiction (including SF and Fantasy) as well as 'non-genre' fiction such as literary realism, or 'LitFic'. That is, the ordering of time. Narrative discourse can make time warp and bend, can re-order, stretch and linger over order and duration in a variety of different ways. The representation of Miéville's *story* through a splitting of time that is conveyed in the two parallel stories of *Iron Council* forces the reader to experience the catastrophe *as it approaches*, with a knowledge of that catastrophe unavailable to its participants. This experience gives Miéville's readers an insight into what is to come, as well as a pained awareness of the importance of the Councillors' revolutionary stance in what – *for them* – constitutes an historical intervention into the unknown. Revolutionary politics involve a wager, a gamble on timing and the balance of forces in a given moment, and the suspense and tension of *Iron Council* are to do with the ways the reader feels this wager both as a possibility – for characters – and an impossibility, in a story organized so we know its outcome in advance. The qualities of this revolutionary wager (in which one narrative strand lets us know the results of the wager even as we read on to discover them detailed in the other narrative strand) evokes again one of Benjamin's greatest passages:

> The notion of the class war can be misleading. It does not refer to a trial of strength to decide the question, "who shall win, who shall be defeated?" or to a struggle the outcome of which is good for the victor

and bad for the vanquished. To think in this way is to romanticise and to obscure the facts ...The only question is whether the [bourgeoisie's] downfall will come through itself or through the proletariat. The continuance or end of three thousand years of cultural development will be decided by the answer. History knows nothing of the evil infinity contained in the image of the two wrestlers locked in eternal combat. The true politician reckons only in dates. And if the abolition of the bourgeoisie is not completed by an almost calculable moment in economic and technical development (a moment signalled by inflation and poison-gas warfare) all is lost. Before the spark reaches the dynamite, the lighted fuse must be cut. The interventions, dangers, and tempi of politicians are technical – not chivalrous. (Benjamin, 1928/1997: 80)

They are always coming. Benjamin's image is suggestive of his and Brecht's beloved genre of Westerns and, given its frontier atmosphere, is analogous to our reading of *Iron Council*. Like the lit fuse of a burning stick of dynamite, disaster reminds us of both the desperation of Judah's mission and his unforgivable betrayal. Like his namesake Rabbi Judah Loew, the Maharal of Prague, Judah uses golemetry to save the city and its future. His salvation is signified in his successful attempt to ensure that 'Iron Council remains' (*IC*, 462), by suspending the train and its passenger-revolutionaries in a kind of time-outside-of-History through the use of a time golem (discussed above). The very nature of this fixed preservation of the Iron Councillors, however, robs the Iron Council of any chance of intervention, of 'bringing history' (*IC*, 435), or of taking part in the city's revolutionary gamble. Daniel Bensaïd's (2002: 87) reading of Benjamin is instructive here, in his suggestion that revolution consists of 'a suspended present, which is not a transition but a fork and bifurcation; a strategic present for those who stand still on the threshold of time'. It is this bifurcation that Judah destroys, turning the leap of revolutionary possibility in the charged moment of a 'broken political temporality' into a frozen image of tradition; the Iron Council thus becomes held in time as a symbol of revolutionary legacies for the future. That Judah is right to do so changes nothing: as readers we only know that his action is proved right through the temporal manipulations of Miéville's narrative ordering in *Iron Coun-*

cil. At the time of reading this particular narrative strand, however, we are forced to confront the genuine, strategic dilemma facing all of the partisans of the Council. Miéville thus plays here on the availability of proleptic knowledge which is available to a writer within narrative discourse (and, of course, to a reader on a second or subsequent reading of the text), but which is not available to political revolutionaries in the real world. From this perspective, the dissent and objections of the Councillors must be seen as legitimate and worth taking seriously, both as political problems and as imaginative questions for the narrative.

These imaginative questions in narrative link real-world political dilemmas with the resources of Fantasy literature. Literalist readings – the cliché of the SF or Fantasy geek searching for continuity errors or minute details – are an accepted, and, indeed, encouraged, part of serious SF reading in ways that mainstream of 'LitFic' traditions discourage. The proposed solution of the time golem must, therefore, prompt further questioning. How long does a time golem last? How, if Judah is dead, can it be revoked when a new revolutionary situation has need of Iron Council? What happens outside of time in the time golem's reach? Taking Miéville's metaphors seriously adds further complexities to this dilemma. Henry Farrell (2005) identifies in this image a politico-aesthetic problem for Miéville's Benjaminian project:

> If Low is a materialist historian in Benjamin's sense of the word, then Benjamin's enterprise of historic redemption is flawed by design. If it is to do what it is supposed to do (to preserve the myth of Iron Council as an inspiration for struggle), it has to betray the real people who made the Iron Council live and breathe, and turn them into an abstraction. The ability of the historian to act as a messiah, to "redeem" those who fought in the past is at least partly illusory; she can't save them on their own terms. (Farrell, 2005)

It is not the historian who redeems, though, but the revolution itself, and the 'leap in the open air of history', as Benjamin asserts, is a dialectical one: no redemption without the revolution, no revolution without the work of redemption. Miéville's Benjaminian project in *Iron Council* need not be read at the level of story (with Low as a storyworld stand-in for the clarity of insight that Benjamin brings to the revolutionary situation in Germany in the 1930s), but at the level of narrative discourse. That is to say, what is Benjaminian about the novel is Miéville's style of writing, his mode of narration, and the temporal ordering of events in the narrative. Read in this way, we might understand the novel *as a whole* – both in its story and its discourse – to be exploring this question of revolutionary possibility.

VIII. Order prevails?

The image of a revolutionary train frozen in time and ready for insurrectionary revival brings another, final, Benjaminian parallel to mind. As he outlines in *One-Way Street* (1928):

> Threads may have been lost for centuries, that the present course of history erratically, inconspicuously picks up again. The subject matter of history, once released from pure facticity, needs no *appreciation*. For it offers not vague analogies to the present, but constitutes the precise dialectical problem that the present is called upon to resolve. (Benjamin, 1928/1997: 362, emphasis in original)

Inside the storyworld, we can discern such forgotten threads as being encapsulated in the image of the frozen Iron Council itself, stuck in time after Judah's time golem has arrested its progress. The frozen train thus constitutes a thread that may be 'lost for centuries' but which stands ready to resolve a future-present's problem, in the same way as the tactical dilemmas of twentieth-century revolutions will yield political strategies to our grandchildren. Outside the storyworld, this is *Iron Council* the text: a novel that brings to the twenty-first-century anti-capitalist movement echoes and traces of those older revolutionary traditions we had been trained into thinking outdated and dead. The most painful of these echoes, for me, appears just two pages before the novel ends:

RUNAGATE RAMPANT. *Lunuary 1806*

> "Order reigns in New Crobuzon!" You stupid lackeys. Your order is built on sand. Tomorrow the Iron Council will move on again, and to your horror it will proclaim with its whistle blaring: We say, *"We were, we are, we will be."* (IC, 469, emphasis in original)

In its immediate context at the level of story, this short announcement in the *Runagate Rampant* is a message of hope and defiance. Cutter has returned to revolutionary activity and the defeat of the Collective does not imply the end of resistance: *the struggle continues*. However, if we consider the above quotation in terms of its narrative discourse we would note that Miéville quotes almost verbatim in this passage from Rosa Luxemburg's (1971: 415) 'Order Reigns in Berlin', published in the newspaper Luxemburg edited with Karl Liebknecht, *Die Rote Fahne* (The Red Flag), on 14th January 1919:

> "Order reigns in Berlin!" You stupid lackeys! Your "order" is built on sand. The revolution will "raise itself up again clashing," and to your horror it will proclaim to the sound of trumpets:
>
> *I was, I am, I shall be.* (Luxemburg, 1971: 415, emphasis in original)

Luxemburg's short message in *The Red Flag* was also one of defiance and resilience; a promise, after the Social Democrats had colluded in the suppression of communist revolt through the German Revolution of 1918–1919, that progress was to come. As she continues: 'revolutions have brought us nothing but defeats till now, but these unavoidable defeats are only heaping guarantee upon guarantee of the coming final triumph' (Luxemburg, 1971: 41). However, these were the last words that Luxemburg published before her own murder. Since fascism subsequently benefited from the defeat of the German Revolution, the 'final triumph' alluded to here in 1919 is yet to come. In ending with *this* message of resilience, *Iron Council* forces us to confront our historic failures and to realize the uncertainty, risk and 'moment of danger' contained in any revolutionary uprising.

Our final, difficult question should therefore be: does *Iron Council* succeed as a representation of revolution? Of course not, and how could it? After the high point of the WTO protests in Seattle in 2000, and confronted by the subsequent War on Terror, the anti-capitalist movement transformed and lost its exuberance and confident sense of running with the grain of History. Capitalism and war remain. Any representation of a revolution before we have 'plucked the living flower' (Marx, 1843/1977: 132) and been through the process for ourselves is bound to run up against the old aesthico-political barriers blocking all previous attempts. These include the impossibility of imagining any radically different world, and the paralysing sense of difficulty and powerlessness that any truly convincing representation of current suffering and oppression is bound to evoke. The project, as Miéville (2009: 248) has described it, is 'a Benjaminian/Beckettian attempt to fail better and better at thinking an unthinkable'. What we need then, are better failures, and ways to learn at failing better. *Iron Council* helps us along that path.

They are always coming. (IC, 471)

Notes

1 On the idea of revolutionary tradition see Blackledge (2006) and Molyneux (2003).

2 Farrell (2005) and Freedman (2008) remark on Miéville's connections to anti-capitalism but both, being politically and generationally distant from the movement, seem impatient to move on to other points for reflection.

3 The anti-capitalist slogan above all others should be 'defend, extend, and deepen the commons...' (Wall, 2005: 183). See also Naomi Klein: 'The spirit [the movement shares] is a radical reclaiming of the commons' (Klein, 2001: 81).

4 *Iron Council* could be read alongside Michael Albert's *Parecon: Life After Catpitalism* (2002), then, as an example of the anti-capitalist Utopia, a form, as Fredric Jameson (2005: xii) notes, revived by the anti-capitalist movement.

5 Science Fiction, for Suvin, is progressive, and distinguished from Fantasy, in its ability to produce cognitively estranging knowledge and insight. Fantasy, by contrast, was, in his early writings at least, mere wish-fulfilment, myth, and conservatism. Suvin's writings on Fantasy have shifted in his writings of the last decades, so by 2010 he felt the need to consider Fantasy's rise more seriously. His basic stance, however, aligning Fantasy with politically reactionary myth (which 'conceives human relations as

fixed and supernaturally determined' [Suvin, 2005: 26]) and the 'pap' that satisfies 'juvenile taste' (Suvin, 2005: 67), remains unchanged.

6 Henry Farrell (2005) discusses Benjamin in some detail in his contribution to the *Crooked Timber* symposium.

7 'Revolutions never occur on the stroke of time. They persistently miss their deadline. They seem condemned to the infernal dialectic of the "already no longer" and the "still not"' (Bensaïd, 2002: 29–30).

8 As Marx and Engels assert: '*History* does *nothing*, it "possesses *no* immense wealth", it "wages *no* battles". It is *man*, real, living man who does all that, who possesses and fights; "history" is not, as it were, a person apart, using man as a means to achieve *its own* aims; history is *nothing but* the activity of man pursuing his aims' (Marx and Engels cited in Blackledge, 2006: 21, emphasis in original).

9 I saw this not-quite-ironically framed slogan on banners at anti-capitalist demonstrations in Melbourne in May 2001.

10 Surveying shifts in Left thinking since 1990, Perry Anderson identified 'accomodation' as the dominant response to neoliberalism: 'The underlying attitude is: capitalism has come to stay, we must make our peace with it' (Anderson, 2000: 13).

11 Freedman (2008: 263) sees Toro's as 'quasi-Narodnik terrorism', but the immediate resonance is surely with the controversies around anarchism and socialism within the anti-capitalist movement, most especially after Genoa. See Bircham and Charlton (2001).

Works Cited

Albert, Michael (2002/2004) *Parecon: Life After Capitalism*. London: Verso.

Allen, Kieran (1990) *The Politics of James Connolly*. London: Bookmarks.

Anderson, Perry (2000) 'Renewals', *New Left Review* 1: 1–20.

Benjamin, Walter (1928/1997) *One Way Street*, trans. Edmund Jephcott and Kingsley Shorter. London: Verso.

Benjamin, Walter (1940) 'Theses on the Philosophy of History', *Illuminations*, trans. Harry Zohn, pp. 255–66. London: Jonathan Cape.

Bensaïd, Daniel (2002) *Marx for Our Times: Adventures and Misadventures of a Critique*, trans. Gregory Elliott. London: Verso.

Bircham, Emma and Charlton, John (eds) (2001) *Anti-Capitalism: A Guide to the Movement*. London: Bookmarks.

Birns, Nicholas (2009) 'From Cacotopia to Railroad: Rebellion and the Shaping of the Normal in the Bas-Lag Universe', *Extrapolation* 50(2): 200–11.
Blackledge, Paul (2006) *Reflections on the Marxist Theory of History*. Manchester: Manchester University Press.
Burgmann, Verity (2006) 'Archaeologies of Anti-Capitalist Utopianism', *Arena* 25–26: 99–122.
Callinicos, Alex (2003) *An Anti-Capitalist Manifesto*. Oxford: Polity.
Charlton, John (2000) 'Talking Seattle', *International Socialism* 86: 3–18.
Davidson, Neil (2009) 'Walter Benjamin and Classical Marxism', *International Socialism* 121: 157–72.
Engels, Frederick (1880/1970) *Socialism: Utopian and Scientific*, trans. Edward Aveling. Moscow: Progress Publishers. Available at the *Marxist Internet Archive*, URL (consulted 1 October 2014), https://www.marxists.org/archive/marx/works/1880/soc-utop/
Farrell, Henry (2005) 'An Argument in Time', *Discussing Iron Council*, URL (consulted 1 October 2012), http://www.utsc.utoronto.ca/~farrell/ironcouncil.pdf
Freedman, Carl (2008) 'To the Perdido Street Station: the Representation of Revolution in China Miéville's *Iron Council*', in Donald M. Hassler and Clyde Wilcox (eds) *New Boundaries in Political Science Fiction*, pp. 259–71. Columbia: University of South Carolina Press.
Jameson, Fredric (2005) *Archaeologies of the Future: the Desire Called Utopia and Other Science Fictions*. London: Verso.
Khlebnikov, Velimir (1915/1987) 'Proposals', in Charlotte Douglas (ed.) *Collected Works of Velimir Khlebnikov*, Vol. 1, trans. Paul Schmidt. Cambridge: Harvard University Press.
Klein, Naomi (2001) 'Reclaiming the Commons', *New Left Review* 2(9): 81–9.
Lenin, Vladimir (1916) 'The Discussion on Self Determination Summed Up', *Collected Works*, Vol. 22. Moscow: Progress.
Löwy, Michael (2005) *Fire Alarm: Reading Walter Benjamin's 'On the Concept of History'*, trans. Chris Turner. London: Verso.
Luxemburg, Rosa (1971) *Selected Political Writings*, ed. Dick Howard, trans. Peggy Fallen Wright. New York: Monthly Review.
Marx, Karl (1867/1990) 'Preface to the First Edition', *Capital*, Vol. 1, trans. Ben Fowkes. Harmondsworth: Penguin.
Marx, Karl (1843/1977) *Critique of Hegel's Philosophy of Right*, ed. Joseph O'Malley. Cambridge: Cambridge University Press.

Marx, Karl (1845) *The German Ideology*, in Karl Marx and Frederick Engels, *Collected Works*, Vol. 5. London: Lawrence and Wishart.

Miéville, China (2009) 'Cognition as Ideology: a Dialectic of SF Theory', in Mark Bould and China Miéville (eds) *Red Planets: Marxism and Science Fiction*, pp. 231–248. London: Pluto.

Miéville, China (2008) 'Gothic Politics: a Discussion with China Miéville', *Gothic Studies* 10 (1): 61–70.

Miéville, China (2012) 'With One Bound We Are Free: Pulp, Fantasy, and Revolution', *Discussing Iron Council*, URL (consulted 1 October 2012), http://www.utsc.utoronto.ca/~farrell/ironcouncil.pdf

Molyneux, John (2003) *What is the Real Marxist Tradition?* Chicago: Haymarket.

Suvin, Darko (2000) 'Considering the Sense of "Fantasy" or "Fantastic Fiction": an Effusion', *Extrapolation* 41(3): 209–47.

Suvin, Darko (2005) 'Estrangement and Cognition', in James Gunn and Matthew Candelaria (eds), *Speculations on Speculation*. Lanham, MD: Scarecrow.

Suvin, Darko (2010) *Defined by a Hollow: Essays on Utopia, Science Fiction and Political Epistemology*. Oxford: Peter Lang.

Trotsky, Leon (1944/2002) *Fascism: What it is and How to Fight it*. New York: Pathfinder.

Trotsky, Leon (1924/2005) *Literature and Revolution*, ed. William Keach. Chicago: Haymarket.

Wall, Derek (2005) *Babylon and Beyond*. London: Pluto.

5

'BLATANTLY COMING BACK'
THE ARBITRARY LINE BETWEEN HERE AND THERE, CHILD AND ADULT, FANTASY AND REAL, LONDON AND UNLONDON

Joe Sutliff Sanders

Reviews of China Miéville's first book for young readers, *Un Lun Dun* (2007), routinely list its main successes as a result of how it complicates old standbys of children's fantasy. *School Library Journal*, for example, praises *Un Lun Dun* for revealing that 'sometimes the chosen one doesn't get to save the city, and [...] sometimes steps in a preordained quest don't come out as planned' (Kunz, 2007: 143). Similarly, *SFReviews.net* delights that the novel 'grabs onto the most recycled YA fantasy there is' and 'then proceeds to suborn it at every turn' (Wagner, 2006), and the *Observer* raves that the novel 'breathes fresh air into a familiar formula' (Fox, 2007).

But for all the attention given to how *Un Lun Dun* upends the clichés of prophecy and formula, most readings have missed an important argument the novel makes with a bizarrely tenacious trend in classic children's fantasy. Perhaps this argument has been missed because it comes very near the end of the novel, indeed after the climax, and takes up only about two pages. Nonetheless, careful attention to this scene can spotlight a problematic ideology that has underwritten the endings of even progressive classics of children's fantasy. In many significant masterpieces of the field, the child protagonist who has used magic to leave her homeland is forced to leave the world of her adventure, often with much hand-wringing and disappointment over the loss of the discovered world. *Un Lun Dun*, however, rejects this pattern. By laughingly dismissing the tradition of forcing the child protagonist to foreswear the magical world in favour of the mundane world of her origin, Miéville's book hints at a way out of a tendency of children's fantasy that has consequences for both genre and ideology.

Un Lun Dun tells the story of an 'abcity' known as Unlondon into which two London girls stumble. Although the novel is Miéville's first for young readers, it boasts an inventiveness that melds Miéville's own weird tastes with those of previous masterpieces of children's fantasy, including Norton Juster's *The Phantom Tollbooth* (1961) and Lewis Carroll's *Alice's Adventures in Wonderland* (1865). The girls first travel to the abcity by using a common tool of modern society (in this case, a rusty spigot rather than a tollbooth), and while there they negotiate Unlondon with the help of Rosa and Jones, a displaced bus driver and conductor. They come to the attention of a talking book and the 'propheseers' who study it, and they subsequently team up with odd characters whose numbers include a hybrid ghost-boy, a cuddly – if rancid – discarded milk carton, and a school of fish who cooperate to animate a diving suit. The propheseers have long foretold the coming of the girls, and the entire population is abuzz with anticipation that Zanna, the blonde, popular, athletic girl, will fulfill prophecy and defeat the sentient smog that threatens to engulf Unlondon. Zanna, however, is unceremoniously thunked on the head in her first battle with the smog, and Deeba – the short, witty sidekick – carries her back to London. But as Zanna recovers, forgetting Unlondon in the process, Deeba realizes that the friends she has left behind are being duped by an agent of the smog. Careful analysis of the one token she has kept from the abcity leads her to believe that she can re-enter

Unlondon by climbing library bookshelves, and soon Deeba is embroiled in a battle not just with the smog, but with the weapons and even the police officers it has imported from London with the help of an underhanded civil servant named Murgatroyd.

The novel is full of challenges to classics of children's fantasy, from its jettisoning of the prophesied heroine to its grotesque setting, but the end of the novel provides what is perhaps its most pointed argument with other works in the genre. *Un Lun Dun* draws to its conclusion by at first apparently rehearsing the conventional edict that, having had their fun in the exotic lands of the fantasy novel, children must go home. As one of the propheseers gently puts it, 'You're talking as if you'll be back again, Deeba... [b]ut it isn't easy to cross between the worlds. Every time you breach the Odd, the membrane between two whole *universes* is strained' (*ULD*, 509, emphasis in original). Mortar goes on to explain that although Deeba would be welcome as a permanent resident of Unlondon, her companions and allies all understand that they cannot ask her to give up her home in London. 'We'll miss you if you go,' he tells Deeba, '[b]ut you have to choose' (*ULD*, 509). Deeba thinks over her options and finally replies that she cannot remain in Unlondon, that she must return to the mundane world, and, in an echo of classic children's fantasy, she speaks of the deep place in her heart that her adventures in the magical world will always keep. This is, as my next section will demonstrate, a familiar move in children's fantasy texts: the tragic final sacrifice of the child hero who has gained power in the magical world and now willingly returns to the pale world of school, homework, and curfews. And in the same way that *Un Lun Dun* opens with an apparent willingness to conform to the clichés of children's fantasy, here it appears to be content to send Deeba on her way.

But just as the novel opened by invoking the clichés of the field only to reject them, here it closes by doing the same. Deeba, suddenly laughing the tragic spirit away, continues by saying: 'Part of the reason I won't forget you... is 'cause I'll be back all the time' (*ULD*, 509). With a smile, she adds:

What you even *talking* about, Mortar? It's *easy* to get from London to here. I got here by *turning a tap*, then by *climbing shelves*. Jones is here, Rosa got here, all the conductors got here. The police came in a digging machine. For God's sake, Unstible and Murgatroyd put an elevator in. People are *always* going between, and you don't see either universe collapsing, do you? (*ULD*, 510, emphasis in original)

Deeba concludes her little speech with a line that might be directed as much at other children's fantasy texts as it is at the characters surrounding her. 'You just think it's hard to go between the two 'cause you've always thought it must be,' she says. 'You're just saying that 'cause you sort of think you should' (*ULD*, 510). When Mortar replies that the trans-universal methods Deeba lists 'aren't reliable,' that '[t]hey may not always work; the rules aren't always clear,' Deeba interrupts him to answer, 'Well then, I'll try others. Till one of them does' (*ULD*, 510). Deeba's responses to Mortar highlight the arbitrariness of the fantasy narrative logic that explains the required separation of the newly knowledgeable child protagonist from the wondrous place of adventure.

The traditional separation of magical and mundane at the end of children's fantasy is an absurdity. It is of course contrary to the laws of reality as we understand them to skip from one universe to another, but since children's fantasy is content to break that rule to allow an adventure to begin, why is it that the boundary between universes becomes sacrosanct as soon as the adventure is over? Fantasy takes for granted that there are exceptions to the laws of consensus reality; suddenly to declare that the very laws whose violation gave rise to the plot are now inviolable is, frankly, silly. When natural law in a fantasy novel is inflexible, there is only one reason for this: because the author has decided it needs to be.

Further evidence of the arbitrariness of this pattern in children's fantasy is the fact that not all children's fantasy follows this rule. Enid Blyton's *Faraway Tree* (1939–51) stories, for example, utilize a magic that requires the children to get back home from the magical world before a window closes, but after each adventure, they can use the same magical technology to enter a new magical world. E. Nesbit's

Psammead series, beginning with *Five Children and It* (1902), gives its children fairly extensive powers to leave home, return, and then leave again, and the extended *Oz* series (1900–20) by L. Frank Baum – though not, interestingly, the first book, which ends with Dorothy and her companions weeping at their 'sorrowful parting' (Baum, 1900/1986: 249) – allows repeated passage between the magical and mundane worlds. But in a great deal of children's fantasy, indeed in a great deal of pivotal children's fantasy published over many decades and from a variety of aesthetic and political positions, the argument is made again and again that children must leave the world of magic after the crisis of that world has been solved. I will give three key examples in the next section, but for now, it is worth noting that the pattern is so familiar that it provides the underlying irony for a strip from Randall Munroe's web comic, *xkcd* (Figure 1).

Figure 1. (Image credit: Randall Munroe under a CC BY-NC license, http://xkcd.com/693/)

The strip highlights several of the conventions of this pattern: the protagonist's growth, the potency he achieves in the strange (two-mooned, in this case) magical world, and the infinitely precious token of remembrance. The final panel then pokes fun at the empty mundanity of the protagonist's life upon his return home. The joke only works, though, if the first panels are familiar and the last panel touches on a truth inherent in the convention. At the heart of the joke is a contrast between the joy of the magical world and the emptiness of the 'real' world in which the 'young hero' must live out his life.

Given that this pattern is not structurally necessary, indeed that it is not even always followed, the important question becomes this: what is at stake when children's fantasy *does* follow the pattern? To answer this question, I will take a closer look at three important works of children's fantasy that insist on the ultimate separation of child hero from the newly discovered land. These three books – and, as Sarah Gilead's essay on children's fantasy (1991) demonstrates, there are many, many more examples – are all major works of children's fantasy, classics by virtually any standard, and they span a history that both precedes and follows the publication of *Un Lun Dun*.

'It's All Arranged': Three Arbitrary Boundaries

The first work to consider is C. S. Lewis's *Narnia Chronicles* (1950–6). Travel between the world of the story and the magical world of Narnia is a frequent concern of the books, as are the limitations placed upon that travel. The series' most extensive analysis of the logic behind the transfer between universes comes in *Prince Caspian* (1951), which bears the relevant subtitle *The Return to Narnia*. In the novel's denouement, the novel's main figure of authority, the lion Aslan, is in the process of expelling from Narnia a group of humans who have tried their best to frustrate the forces of good. Then, in a moment of evident incongruity, Peter and Susan, the oldest of the four Pevensie children, tell the younger two that it is time for the children to change their clothes. Edmund and Lucy, the younger children, reply with confusion: 'But our other things are at Caspian's castle,' protests Edmund, to which Peter replies, 'No, they're not.... They're all here. They were brought down in bundles this morning. It's all arranged' (Lewis, 1951/1994: 221). That last phrase – 'It's all arranged' – is an excellent summary of the logic that governs the transfer between worlds. What Peter means in this moment is that Aslan has already taken the older children aside and explained that all four children must have their clothes on hand and be ready to return to Earth on this day. But Peter's phrase is applicable to much more than this one moment in the text. The movement of the children between the mundane and magical worlds is 'all arranged,' completely out of their hands and at the arbitrary whim of powers the children themselves can hardly hope to understand. The hour of their departure is appointed by Aslan, and he has seen to the arrangement of all the conditions allowing for that departure.

That logic has been implicit since the children's first visit to Narnia, becoming clearest in the closing pages of *The Lion, The Witch and the Wardrobe* (1950). There, Professor Digory Kirke debriefs the children, who have just returned from Narnia. Although Kirke is certain that the children will one day return to Narnia, he warns them: 'But don't go trying to use the same route twice. Indeed, don't try to get there at all. It'll happen when you're not looking for it' (Lewis, 1950/1970: 186). When the children do return at the beginning of *Prince Caspian*, their passage into Narnia is clearly not of their own design, and indeed it has the air of something one would very much like to avoid. Lucy, the youngest, 'gave a sharp little cry, like someone who has been stung by a wasp' (Lewis, 1950/1970: 2). Similarly, Edmund remarks on a 'most frightful pulling', Peter complains that he feels as though someone were 'dragging' him, and Susan cries, 'Oh—oh—oh—stop it!' (Lewis, 1951/1994: 4–5). The children's entrance into the magical world in this novel is very similar to their departure: it is all arranged. When the children arrive in Narnia, they do so because they have been summoned to intervene in the history of Narnia at a specific moment, and when they depart, it is because Aslan has finished with them.[1]

It is easy, though, (and, frankly, cliché) to criticize Lewis, whose heavy moralism and wink-wink, nudge-nudge allegory sit uneasily with contemporary trends in fantasy for children *or* adults. Indeed, one of the most voluble critics of Lewis is Philip Pullman, author of the brilliant and thoughtful *His Dark Materials* (1995–2000) trilogy. One of Pullman's favourite refrains is his disdain for Lewis – he told one interviewer that 'I hate the Narnia books, and I hate them with deep and bitter passion' (Vulliamy, 2001: 18). The real challenge, in fact, may be to find an interview in which he does *not* wax eloquent about his disdain for Lewis. And yet Pullman's trilogy, too, ends by locking his child heroes, Lyra and Will, in the mundane worlds of their origin, and the logic explaining this necessity is just as arbitrary as is Lewis's. Will's father has discovered by painful experience that one cannot live in another's universe for years without debilitating illness, and an angel explains to the children that every window between worlds must be closed and the tool for their creation destroyed because, as Lyra's dæmon puts it, 'otherwise everything good will fade away and die' (Pullman, 2000: 483), which, one must admit, would be disappointing. As the angel learns from Will how to close the windows, the novel similarly closes down every possible way for the children to visit one another's worlds. One solitary window may be left open, for example, but someone else has a better claim on it than do the children, so the novel closes down that possibility (Pullman, 2000: 492). And although angels still know how to move between worlds, this process is really more akin to seeing the other world than what Lyra calls *real* traveling' (Pullman, 2000: 494–5, emphasis in original), so the novel flags that solution as unsatisfactory. The rules explained at the end of the trilogy that prevent the children from traveling between worlds are airtight.

These narrative rules are also arbitrary. To understand just how arbitrary they are, even within the context of the book's own logic, consider for example the sources of the information confirming that the worlds must be kept separate: Will's father and an emissary of Heaven. The novel gives no sign that either should be doubted, but throughout the rest of the trilogy, parents and angels are never presented as perfect models of reliable authority – indeed, they are routinely the enemies against which Lyra and Will must struggle.[2] And yet when it comes to safeguarding the boundaries between magical and mundane, for some reason their word is reliable. Elizabeth Rose Gruner (2011) has reluctantly hinted at similar frustrations with the story, as she explains how 'narrative causality seems in some ways to undermine Pullman's emancipatory impulses. While Lyra is free of the fundamentalism of the Church that has controlled her world, she is still in thrall to a story that she did not invent' (Gruner, 2011: 282). 'Lyra can do many things', Gruner concludes, 'but ultimately she is subject to the same mysteries that animate the alethiometer, mysteries that Pullman as author refuses to dispel' (Gruner, 2011: 284). Pullman's trilogy is an extraordinary unraveling of many of the didactic and moralistic impulses evident in, to take just the obvious example, Lewis's series. However, *His Dark Materials* seems to retain the arbitrary prohibition against children remaining in the worlds they have discovered because, to paraphrase Deeba, it sort of thinks it should.

Two more patterns in the arbitrary logic of children's fantasy connect Lewis's *Narnia* and Pullman's *His Dark Materials*, and those patterns also become visible in a third crucial work of children's fantasy, this one published the year after *Un Lun Dun*: Neil Gaiman's *The Graveyard Book* (2008).[3] Gaiman's book, too, ends with the human boy, named Bod, forced out of the magical graveyard into which he stumbled as a small child. Bod has grown up in the graveyard, protected by its temporarily resident vampire, tutored by a werewolf, and adopted by good, solid – if in fact dead and ethereal – English ghosts. But in the final chapter, Bod is expelled from the graveyard. The reason for his expulsion is, the book implies, tied to his maturation, especially his physical maturation. In the closing scenes of the book, one of the ghosts realizes with surprise that he has become 'a young man,' and Bod guesses that he is now 'about fifteen' (Gaiman, 2008: 298). When he goes to visit Silas the vampire, Bod is now unable to see inside the chapel, and Silas's response – 'Already?' – seems to indicate a regrettable fall from mystery through the inevitable path of maturation (Gaiman, 2008: 301). Similarly, Bod's looming sexual maturation seems to mark his increasing unsuitedness to the magical place, which becomes clear when Liza 'the witch-girl' whispers in Bod's ear, touches his hand, and kisses 'the corner of his lips' (Gaiman, 2008: 300). Bod, evidently dimly aware of the dance of sexual play, is 'too perplexed, too utterly wrong-footed, to know what to do', and Liza says her farewell (Gaiman, 2008: 300). If he were completely innocent of sexual impulse, Liza's actions might seem odd, but they are unlikely to have left him 'utterly wrong-footed', as though Bod were a boy at his first school dance. Gaiman's novel thus directly links Bod's arrival at the cusp of physical and sexual maturity to the moment at which he must leave the graveyard. The implication is that the former is in fact the reason for the latter.

This sense that a child must leave the magical world because of his or her ageing body is also familiar from major classics of children's fantasy. Pullman has complained, for example, of *Narnia*'s 'view of childhood as a golden age from which sexuality and adulthood are a falling away' (cited in Vulliamy, 2001: 18). In another interview, Pullman bemoans Susan's absence from the Narnian heaven in the last book of Lewis's series, in which Peter intones that Susan 'is no longer a friend of Narnia' and other friends complain that Susan has relegated the stuff of Narnia to mere child's play in favour of a reported exclusive interest in 'nylons and lipstick and invitations' (Lewis, 1956/1994: 154). Pullman interprets this interest as a natural 'awareness of her own sexuality' and complains that Narnia cannot tolerate such a thing in its child heroes (cited in Wavell, 2001: 3).

Pullman's argument certainly seems accurate, but it is an argument that, if we are looking at how these books end, seems awfully relevant to *His Dark Materials* as well. After all, one of the ultimate ironies of *His Dark Materials* is that the entrance into carnal knowledge that reverses the damage done to the multiverse also sets up the restoration of the worlds to, as the children's trusted angel puts it, 'their proper relations with one another' (Pullman, 2000: 503). For those relations to remain proper, the two children who got to have sex – once – must now be locked away from each other. In Narnia, the prohibition is imposed because sex cannot even be named directly. In Gaiman's graveyard, it is because becoming sexual is part of being alive, and in Pullman's Oxford it is because sexual contact lays the groundwork for delicious tragedy. In all cases, however, the ultimate end is the same: children who come into contact with sexual knowledge can look forward to a future in the world of their parents, eyes misty with the recollection of the other world they used to know.

Gaiman's novel also points to a final pattern in children's fantasy, and here we find a further connection with tragedy. As Bod leaves the graveyard, his sorrow is perhaps mitigated by his reflection that at the end of his life, 'he would, finally, return to the graveyard' (Gaiman, 2008: 307). The same is true for the children who visited Narnia, children who have now turned into adults and who, in the last book, return not quite to Narnia itself, but to a heaven that is '[m]ore like the real thing,' as one of them puts it (Lewis, 1956/1994: 193). Aslan reveals that the reason they are here is that they have all died, and now they get to live out eternity not in Narnia, but in a sort of Super-

Narnia with brighter colours (Lewis, 1956/1994: 210). Despite Pullman's disdain for Lewis, the same is true for the children of *His Dark Materials*. As Lyra and Will savour their despair over being separated from each other, Will promises eternal love: 'and after I die, and when I find my way out of the land of the dead, I'll drift about forever, all my atoms, till I find you again...', and Lyra promises the same (Pullman, 2000: 497). Thus, in all three books, the children forced back to their original worlds *can* hope to escape their prison ... but only when they are dead.

The Consequences of Arbitrary Boundaries: Genre

Normally, I would not write about literature with this level of sarcasm, especially about books I rather like. And I certainly do like these books: I relish Gaiman's edgy, trademark blend of pathos and horror; applaud Pullman's erudite rewriting of *Paradise Lost* in a tone that takes for granted the intelligence of his readers; and I admire even Lewis's fantasy, which, for all its allegorical didacticism, uses a terrific pace to reveal a world that Lewis himself loves without a hint of self-conscious irony. Indeed, my guess is that one reason I am so bilious about these books is that they *are* so good ... and their brilliance is routinely undercut by their adherence to a pattern of separating child heroes from magical settings for reasons that are, at best, poor. But there is more to my frustration with these otherwise excellent books. In addition to being poor aesthetic choices, these ridiculous endings have ramifications that extend beyond the threat they pose to the artistry of otherwise good books.

One of the consequences I find so dissatisfying about this pattern is that there is a sense in which this ending requires that children's fantasy foreswear itself, that, as the protagonist moves from magical to mundane, a proper, grown-up reader will also eventually choose mimesis over fantasy. In Sarah Gilead's essay on what she calls the 're-turn-to-reality' pattern in children's fantasy (Gilead, 1991: 277), she toys with the idea that such a pattern portrays 'the fantasy narrative as a necessary lapse from structured reality, a lapse that paradoxically supports reality' (Gilead, 1991: 278). For Gilead, this is important for its psychological reasons: reality and fantasy are concepts that figure prominently in identity formation, and fantasy novels, Gilead suggests, help children negotiate reality and fantasy better. My complaint is not about any individual case of maturation, but about how the lapse into *and return from* fantasy supports the idea of *mimesis* as a literature inherently more valuable. When a work of children's fantasy requires that maturation coincide with the abandonment of magic, it argues that genres that can talk about magic without smirking must also be abandoned by mature readers.

In the USA, the champions of children's literature have been frequent propagators of the idea that fantasy is best understood as something to grow out of. The American Library Association (ALA), the influential organization that awards the Caldecott medal (to outstanding American picture books) and the Newbery medal (to outstanding American book-length works for children), for example, is a tireless advocate of excellent literature for children and perhaps the staunchest opponent to censorship in the nation's history. But, as Leonard S. Marcus's history of children's publishing in the USA explains, the ALA's history is also marked by an aversion to fantasy. Take Madeleine L'Engle's *A Wrinkle in Time* (1962) as an example. Although the novel is now universally regarded as a masterpiece, the ALA's selection of the novel for a Newbery medal was at the time startling. The book may even have been lucky to see publication at all: 'Twenty-six publishers had in fact been baffled or surprised enough by *A Wrinkle in Time*', Marcus writes, 'to have rejected it before Farrar, Straus and Giroux finally took a chance on the experiment' (Marcus, 2008: 226). Again, the notion that publishing one of the greatest children's fantasy novels of the century would be an 'experiment' now seems bizarre, but for much of the history of children's publishing in the USA, the genre of fantasy was presumed to be a genre of intellectual laziness, unable to provide the kind of moral and mental rigour that good children's literature was supposed to foster. 'Most American children's book editors and librarians still looked askance at fantasy fiction as a form of fringy, escapist reading, little better than the comics', Marcus recalls of the time in which L'Engle's now-classic novel was published (Marcus,

2008: 226). The choice for *Wrinkle in Time*, then, was a choice made *in spite* of its genre. Marcus himself wonders at '[j]ust what had impelled the Newbery-Caldecott Committee to select' L'Engle's novel, concluding that 'clearly the committee had been in a maverick mood' (Marcus, 2008: 226–7).[4]

Times have changed, and in the twenty-first century the idea that fantasy is inherently bad is no longer the default opinion of children's librarians, editors, or publishers, especially not those who want to keep their jobs. Yet the endings of books such as Gaiman's *The Graveyard Book* (another Newbery medalist) recall a time when fantasy for children occupied a second-class status. Such endings seem to imply that fantasy is simply not that important in comparison with mimesis, a position that Gaiman certainly does not hold. If there is any value whatsoever to fantasy, and I am going to take as an article of faith that there is, an ending that aligns growing up with turning one's back on magic is an ending that betrays the value of the preceding narrative, indeed of the genre in which it resides.

The Consequences of Arbitrary Boundaries: 'Childhood'

But as much as children's fantasy's abdication of its own value bothers me, more significant than that complaint about genre is a complaint concerning the participation of children's fantasy in an ideology that is problematic well beyond the purview of genre. When children's fantasy insists that children must leave the magic behind, what it is saying is that childhood and adulthood must be understood as separate, indeed, that they must be *maintained* as separate. This is most obvious in the physical and sexual maturation that marks the children's lack of access to the magical world of their youth: no matter what the author's feelings about sexuality in the lives of young people might be, each of the three classic works of children's fantasy I have examined manages to lock children away from the worlds they have discovered once they begin to mature sexually and physically. As I have already shown, the adults responsible for the production, distribution, and awarding of children's literature played a key role in developing the opinion that fantasy was bad for children. Furthermore, those adults also participated in the development of a literature for children that imagines childhood to be an empirical category separate from literature for adults. Nathalie op de Beeck has written of this process in her history of picture books. She paints a picture of 'business and education communities' who happily colluded to make 'child- and age-specific books' a centerpiece of the picture book market. 'Publishers', she argues, 'not only promoted a dominant discourse and targeted avid shoppers, they also constructed a definition of childhood that remains prevalent today. Ultimately, children were redefined as market groups distinct from adult readers, with books scientifically calibrated to their age-related needs' (Op de Beeck, 2010: 18). Therefore, children's fantasy that insists on a firm line between child and adult, a line described by maturation, is no accident, but a function of its participation in a marketplace that benefits from discrete, factitious consumer categories.

The Consequences of Arbitrary Boundaries: Fetishization

Still, the fact that children's literature has long participated in constructing a division between adult and child does not at all lessen the consequences that follow from children's fantasy insisting on a line between adulthood and childhood, a line reflected in the division between magical world and mundane. Current theory proposes that all the cultural effort invested in insisting that children and adults are different from one another has an effect that should be very familiar from other historical periods in which various cultures have worked very hard at enforcing arbitrary boundaries. By repeatedly, arbitrarily, and, one might say, romantically insisting on a distinction between the species-known-as-child and the species-known-as-adult, children's fantasy fetishizes the boundary between the two. James R. Kincaid (1992) has written the most extensively on this theory, and although his work focuses on Victorian English culture and contemporary American media, his explanation provides excellent critical tools for thinking about children's fantasy. In the Romantic vision of childhood Kincaid locates, '[t]he child was figured as *free of* adult corruptions; *not yet burdened with* the weight of responsibility, mortality, and sexuality; *liberated from* "the light of common day"' (Kincaid, 1992: 15, emphasis in original). 'The irony', he writes, 'is not hard to miss: defining something entirely as a negation brings irresistibly before us that which we're trying to banish' (Kincaid, 1992: 55). It is useful here to extend Kincaid's point about Romantic thought to those works of children's fantasy that kick children out of the new world when they achieve a level of maturity. Such books' fervent policing of the line between magical, which links with child, and mundane, which links with knowing/sexual/growing adult, can be read as part of a broader cultural tradition of fetishizing the arbitrary line between childhood and adulthood. That fetishization is *implicit* in the work of Lewis and Gaiman, but it is actually *explicit* in Pullman's trilogy. Consider, for example, the angel's explanation of the 'proper relation' between the lovers' worlds when the windows between them have closed: 'Lyra's Oxford and Will's would lie over each other again, like transparent images on two sheets of film being moved closer and closer until they merged—although they would never truly touch' (Pullman, 2000: 503). Or consider Lyra's plan that, although doomed to separate Oxfords, she and Will could each find parallel benches in parallel Oxford parks and be *almost* together. She explains:

> What I thought was that if you—maybe just once a year—if we could come here at the same time, just for an hour or something, then we could pretend we were close again—because we *would* be close, if you sat *here* and I sat just *here* in my world—'
> 'Yes,' he said, 'as long as I live, I'll come back. Wherever I am in the world, I'll come back here—'
> 'On Midsummer Day,' she said. 'At midday. As long as I live. As long as I live...' (Pullman, 2000: 507–8, emphasis in original)

All of this tantalizing closeness—the *almost touching* of the two children, sitting on benches that are *almost* the same, this 'proper relation' of places that '*would* be close'—comes together to energize longing, the same sort of fetishization that Kincaid has decried in other venues of literary and popular culture.

This pattern in much important children's fantasy, a pattern *Un Lun Dun* rejects,[5] functions as a form of fetishization, and, if Kincaid is right, this fetishization claims to privilege children in the same way that chivalry claimed to privilege women, which is to say, it does not help any actual children and routinely does them harm. Its only product is a longing for what has been lost: a longing for a magical, better time whose loss eroticizes the arbitrary boundary between here and there, magical and mundane, child and adult.

Conclusion: Applications for Miéville's Adult Fiction

My academic home is in children's literature, so the real goal of this essay has been to demonstrate the context in which I think one ought to read Miéville's refusal to limit his protagonist to one world. My argument has been that the ending of *Un Lun Dun* addresses artistic, generic, and ideological failures inherent in many other masterpieces of children's fantasy by rejecting the arbitrary division between the discovered world and the world of Deeba's origin. The consequences of that arbitrary division in other works are significant: first, fantasy appears as something out of which one must grow; and, second, the culturally policed boundary between adult and child becomes more deeply fetishized. Thus, neither the genre nor the actual children reading it are well served. These are fundamentally observations about children's literature and culture, theorized through texts useful to those fields.

Un Lun Dun does, however, hint at implications for the study of Miéville's body of work beyond his novels for children, especially if the novel's end is read as an antidote to a deeply problematic fetishization. Nowhere is this more obvious than in *The City & The City* (2009), a novel set in a geographical space that is characterized by its duality and in a political space defined by its aggressive lack of attention to that duality. Consider for example this line, taken from a description of a place where students researching the archaeology of the two cities can pass between the worlds, in spite of and yet in constant knowledge of their society's prohibition against exactly such passage. The narrator observes, 'It was here in the crosshatch that the students might stand, scandalously, touching distance from a foreign power, a pornography of separation' (*CC*, 336). This brief quotation touches twice – 'scandalously,' 'pornography' – on the erotic energy generated by the egregiously ignored overlap between cities. It is not a fetishization that has anything directly to do with the division between adulthood and childhood, but it is exactly a fetishization preserved by authorities that sound otherwise similar to the authorities of children's fantasy with whom Deeba argues: well-intentioned and arbitrary. Indeed, although *The City & The City* is obviously in dialogue with noir and pulp traditions, it might be that the more important comparison is not with other texts in those traditions, but with *Un Lun Dun*, a novel published only two years earlier, populated by misguided authority figures, and set in a place that is pointedly itself and not itself. In this way, my arguments about the ending of *Un Lun Dun* have implications for Miéville's fiction for taller readers.

The insights afforded by Deeba's rejection of the line between London and Unlondon also carry further, even into Miéville's ideas about genre. In his Afterword to *Red Planets: Marxism and Science Fiction* (2009), Miéville concludes that, despite the subtitle, a theory of science fiction must not exclude fantasy: '*Red Planets* we have. We should not neglect the red dragons' (Miéville, 2009: 245, emphasis in original). The Afterword is reflective and at times even self-critical, so it is not perfectly accurate to say that in its pages, Miéville rejects any boundary between science fiction and fantasy, but it *is* fair to say that the Afterword can be understood as a place in which Miéville is struggling with the validity of such a boundary. At times, he presents that boundary as doomed (Miéville, 2009: 244), and at others, as the origin point of unfortunate consequences for the fantastic. 'Indeed,' he argues at one point, 'I believe that the embedded condescension and even despite towards fantasy that this paradigm has bequeathed stands as perhaps the major obstruction to theoretical progress in the field' (Miéville, 2009: 232). Elsewhere, he tempers that claim by writing that 'both the boundaries and their breaching might continue both to enable and constrain creativity and innovation in fantastic fiction' (Miéville, 2009: 244). In *Un Lun Dun*, the boundaries are mocked, and such is not quite the case in Miéville's genre theory, but still, there is a sense that boundaries should not be taken for granted. Further, there is a sense that the boundaries – whatever their artistic and even erotic potential – are the problematic, arbitrary product of authorities who are invested in the maintenance of those boundaries for reasons about which they are rarely forthcoming.

What *Un Lun Dun* urges us to recognize in the body of Miéville's work is an impulse to interrogate the prohibitions – and their consequences – of popular constructions of space and identity. That impulse is best understood through the theories offered by the study of children's literature, but the implications of that impulse extend well beyond.

Notes

1 This is also true of the arrival and departure of the earthly *adults* who would lead to the line of Telmarine adults who depart Narnia at the end of *Prince Caspian*. Although Aslan says that those original adults 'fell, or rose, or blundered, or dropped right through' 'one of the chinks or chasms between that world and this,' there is a sense that the reason they came to Narnia was so that a child of earthly heritage – a 'Son of Adam', as Aslan puts it – could take over as the rightful king of Narnia (Lewis, 1951/1994: 217). With Caspian now poised for legitimate rule, the descendants of Earth are sent back to Earth. As Peter's phrase 'It's all arranged' indicates, when people – children or adults – come to or leave Narnia, they do so because of Aslan's fiat, not because of any solid narrative logic or character motivation.

2 Amelia A. Rutledge (2008: 119) has made excellent points about the trilogy's surprisingly 'conservative view of adult authority'.

3 If Pullman's story is in part a response to the *Chronicles of Narnia*, Gaiman's is in part a rewriting of Rudyard Kipling's *The Jungle Book* (1894) and Peter S. Beagle's *A Fine and Private Place* (1960). Thus, it is not unreasonable to see Gaiman, like Pullman, as revising earlier fantasy, even if he is not quite so preachy about it.

4 Marcus points out that it is this same committee that selected *The Snowy Day*, a picture book with a black protagonist for the Caldecott Medal – this in America in 1963. To call either choice a conservative or even safe choice would be to ignore some fraught headlines of the day.

5 Notice, too, that in the closing pages of *Un Lun Dun*, Deeba explains that her single-minded drive to get back to her mundane world was driven in part by the fact that she was forbidden to go there. 'Now that I *can*', she explains, 'I'll go back and forth all the time. You seriously think I'm not coming to see you again? Not coming to see this place?' (*ULD*, 510).

Works Cited

Baum, L. Frank (1900/1986) *The Wonderful Wizard of Oz*. Berkeley: University of California Press.

Blyton, Enid (1939/2007) *The Enchanted Wood*. Copenhagen: Egmont Books.

Blyton, Enid (1943/2011) *The Magic Faraway Tree*. Copenhagen: Egmont Books.

Blyton, Enid (1946/2012) *The Folk of the Faraway Tree*. Copenhagen: Egmont Books.

Blyton, Enid (1951/2005) *Up the Faraway Tree*. Copenhagen: Egmont Books.

Carroll, Lewis (1865/2011) *Alice's Adventures in Wonderland*. Buffalo, NY: Broadview Press.

Fox, Killian (2007) 'Review of *Un Lun Dun*', *The Observer*. 7 April 2007 (consulted 14 August 2012), http://www.theguardian.com/books/2007/apr/08/booksforchildrenandteenagers.features2

Gaiman, Neil (2008) *The Graveyard Book*. New York: HarperCollins.

Gilead, Sarah (1991) 'Closure in Children's Fantasy Fiction', *PMLA* 106(2): 277–93.

Gruner, Elisabeth Rose (2011) 'Wrestling with Religion: Pullman, Pratchett, and the Uses of Story', *Children's Literature Association Quarterly* 36(3): 276–95.

Juster, Norton (1961) *The Phantom Tollbooth*. New York: Random House.

Kincaid, James R. (1992) *Child-Loving: The Erotic Child and Victorian Culture*. New York: Routledge.

Kunz, Nancy (2007) 'Review of *Un Lun Dun* by China Miéville', *School Library Journal* 53(4): 142–3.

Lewis, C. S. (1950/1970) *The Lion, the Witch and the Wardrobe*, illus. Pauline Baynes. New York: Collier Books.

Lewis, C. S. (1951/1994) *Prince Caspian: The Return to Narnia*, illus. Pauline Baynes. New York: HarperTrophy.

Lewis, C.S. (1956/1994) *The Last Battle*, illus. Pauline Baynes. New York: HarperTrophy.

Marcus, Leonard S. (2008) *Minders of Make-Believe: Idealists, Entrepreneurs, and the Shaping of American Children's Literature*. Boston, MA: Houghton Mifflin.

Miéville, China (2009) 'Afterword: Cognition as Ideology: A Dialectic of SF Theory', in Mark Bould and China Miéville (eds) *Red Planets: Marxism and Science Fiction*, pp. 231–48. Middletown, CT: Wesleyan University Press.

Munroe, Randall (n.d.) 'Children's Fantasy', *xkcd: A Web Comic of Romance, Sarcasm, Myth, and Language* (consulted 15 July 2013), http://xkcd.com/693/

Nesbit, Edith (1902/1905) *Five Children and It*. New York: Dodd and Mead.

Op de Beeck, Nathalie (2010) *Suspended Animation: Children's Picture Books and the Fairy Tale of Modernity*. Minneapolis: University of Minnesota Press.

Pullman, Philip (2000) *The Amber Spyglass*. New York: Alfred A. Knopf.

Rutledge, Amelia A. (2008) 'Reconfiguring Nurture in Philip Pullman's *His Dark Materials*', *Children's Literature Association Quarterly* 33(2): 119–34.

Vulliamy, Edward (2001) 'Author Angers the Bible Belt', *The Observer*, 26 August 2001 (consulted 14 August 2012), http://www.theguardian.com/books/2001/aug/26/bookerprize2001.bookerprize

Wagner, Thomas M. (2006) 'Review of *Un Lun Dun*', *SFReviews.net* (consulted 14 August 2012), shttp://www.sfreviews.net/unlundun.html

Wavell, Stuart (2001) 'The Lost Children: An Interview with Philip Pullman', *The Sunday Times* 11 November 2001 (consulted 14 August 2012), *Expanded Academic ASAP*. Web. 28 October 2014. Gale Document Number, GALE|A80240626 (p. 3).

6

SIGNATURES OF THE INVISIBLE
READING BETWEEN *THE CITY & THE CITY* AND
CHRISTOPHER PRIEST'S *THE GLAMOUR*

Paul March-Russell

Upon its publication in 2009, *The City & The City* was praised for its originality. Michael Moorcock, for example, wrote that 'Miéville again proves himself as intelligent as he is original' (Moorcock, 2009). Miéville's intelligence is undisputed but the thornier issue of originality raises questions as to how Miéville's fiction should be read. To some extent, Miéville already addresses this concern: on the acknowledgements page (as is his custom) Miéville includes some of the authors whose work has informed the writing of *The City & The City*. This list features the American crime novelist, Raymond Chandler, the *Mittel* European modernists, Franz Kafka, Alfred Kubin and Bruno Schulz, and the travel writer and historian, Jan Morris. At the same time, Miéville also implies the presence of other writers: the novel's central conceit – the co-existence of two cities, Besźel and Ul

Qoma, within the same geometrical space – clearly invokes the improbable stories of Jorge Luis Borges.

The social consequence of this co-habitation is that their respective citizens have been socialized, from childhood, into 'unseeing' their neighbours. The perpetual anxiety of not doing so is that they will breach the intersections at which their cities meet and be punished by the mysterious agency that polices the borderlines. The process of unseeing echoes the means by which invisibility operates in *The Glamour* (1984), Christopher Priest's tale of doomed love between the 'partially' invisible Sue, the 'deeply invisible' Niall and the 'incipient, halfway' Richard Grey (Priest, 2005a: 107, 109). Wounded in a terrorist explosion, and suffering from amnesia, Richard has to piece together the evidence about his relationship to Sue, the alleged presence of Niall, and the possibility of his own social invisibility.

Miéville's lack of acknowledgement of Priest's earlier novel is not necessarily intentional for, as Priest himself has observed, invisibility is one of the most widely-used tropes within science fiction, fantastical literature, children's fiction, cinema and popular entertainment (Priest, 2005b: xvii –xxiii). Instead, in pairing *The Glamour* with *The City & The City*, this chapter will examine the mutual dynamic between Miéville and Priest: their distinct although complementary uses of invisibility and its function within the wider intertextual associations afforded by the trope. Although their differences describe contrasting aesthetic and political ambitions, a common exploration of the secretive interactions between writer, reader and text can also be discerned in each novel. Both authors exhibit a sceptical regard for the role of invisibility made manifest in the suspension of a rational call to judgement. Taking this scepticism as integral to modernist and science fictional discourses, the chapter will conclude that both novels reveal an underlying absence, silence or indeed invisibility at the heart of not only sf but also modernist fiction.

Another way of considering this question of originality in Miéville's work would be to re-think the publication of *The City & The City* as an occasion. Occasional writing is often taken to mean the commemoration in verse or prose of a moment in time – more often a private, rather than a public, event – presented to its reader(s) as a gift. The work of the American poet, Frank O'Hara, would be the supreme post-war example of this type of occasional writing. Yet, as David Herd has argued of O'Hara's fellow New York Poet, John Ashbery, occasional writing can mean something more than this: it can also commemorate the occasion of the writing; the circumstances of its creation (Herd, 2000: 10). As Boris Pasternak writes in his autobiography:

> The clearest, most memorable and important feature of art is how it arises, and in their telling of the most varied things, the finest works in the world in fact all tell us of their own birth. (Pasternak, 1959: 213)

Pasternak also suggested in 1922 that art is less 'like a fountain' than 'a sponge'; its purpose is not 'to flow forth' but to 'absorb and become saturated' (cited in Davie, 1969: 23). In other words, the artwork is less about self-expression and more a record of those social, aesthetic and political circumstances which acted upon the artist. This re-conception of the way in which art is produced, and for what purpose, does not diminish the need for discernment and artistic selection; rather, the artist becomes more acutely aware of the phenomena acting upon him/her, as in Miéville's sense of indebtedness and his need to make acknowledgement. The self finds itself *within* the co-mingling of others: 'You in others are yourself, your soul. This is what you are' (Pasternak, 1996: 70). For Miéville, the political implications of such communal activity are crucial.

The aim here is not to propose Pasternak as one of Miéville's unspoken intertexts but to think through the function of Miéville's intertextuality via Pasternak's sentiments. Miéville's novels are known to be dense – in their very size, geographical and topographical scale, historical awareness, political scope, and wordplay – but part of their saturation (to paraphrase Pasternak) is their absorption of other sources. Although working with generic material, Miéville's use of acknowledgement amounts to a form of gifting often associated with more avant-garde forms of literature; consider O'Hara's casual remark that concludes his poem, 'A Step Away from Them' (1956): 'My heart is in my / pocket, it is Poems by Pierre Reverdy' (O'Hara, 2008: 110). The casualness disguises the importance that these poems have for

O'Hara – they are his 'heart' – and the pleasure that they might have for his readers, in exchange for the time they have given to reading his poem. Equally, Miéville's uses of intertextuality and acknowledgement function as an exchange with his readers. In the context of *The City & The City*, where each community has its own existence but neither is independent of the other, this shadowy exchange takes on immediate political resonances.

By contrast, Priest's novel seems less willing to acknowledge its predecessors although, as his 2005 introduction to H. G. Wells's *The Invisible Man* (1897) makes clear, Priest is steeped in the literature of invisibility and its range of meanings: from the allegorical to the political to the psychological, the supernatural and the scientific. Both Miéville and Priest can be seen as extending the rational-sceptical approach of Wells – who literalizes Plato's allegory of Gyges and the ring of invisibility from Book 2 of *The Republic* (which affords its wearer the power of invisibility through an act of will) – by concentrating upon the material constraints that would befall such power (see Holt, 1992: 236–47). Like Wells, Priest ventures a scientific explanation for the phenomenon of invisibility – Dr Hurdis's suggestion that 'it might have been a form of negative hallucination' (Priest 2005a: 209) – but the novel's ambiguous closure questions whether that truly explains the glamour. Unlike Plato's ring of Gyges then, or other magical tokens which enable invisibility in legends, folktales and fantasies (such as those by J. K. Rowling or J. R. R. Tolkien), the invisibility in both Priest's and Miéville's novels has no external agency.

In this respect, however, Priest's term for the condition of invisibility is his novel's clearest intertextual reference. Mrs Quayle, the psychic who befriends Sue, explains to her the etymology of the glamour:

> It was an old Scottish word, brought into general English before its meaning became corrupted. In the original sense a 'glammer' was a spell, an enchantment. A young man in love would approach the wisest old woman of his village and pay her for a charm of invisibility to be placed on his beloved, so that she should no longer be coveted by the other young men. Once she had been glammered, or made glamorous, she was safe from prying eyes. (Priest, 2005a: 118)

Besides forming an analogy to the hold that Niall seeks to maintain over Sue, this description complements the etymology of the word as offered by the *Oxford English Dictionary*. The *OED* further indicates that it was Sir Walter Scott who, in 1830, facilitated the transmission of the word into English via his recounting of traditional Scottish folklore: 'This species of Witchcraft is well known in Scotland as the glamour, or *deceptio visus*, and was supposed to be a special attribute of the race of Gipsies.' Yet, the *OED* also indicates that the word was itself a corruption from the Old French, *gramarye*, meaning a form of occult learning, the sense of which was also revived by Scott in 1805. Furthermore, this word was related to a derivation from the Anglo-Norman *glomerie* which was applied to a college position at the University of Cambridge: for several centuries the Master of Glomery taught Latin to the undergraduates. Consequently, both *gramarye* and *glomerie* are etymologically tied to the more familiar 'grammar', a connection that links the teaching of the fundamentals of language to occult practices such as spell-binding. As Priest indicates then, by his choice of title, to submit to the grammar of his novel is to be made glamorous: to become spellbound. The intertextual associations of the word, 'glamour', presage the novel's metafictional concerns upon the relationship between the author (as enchanter) and reader (as enchanted).

Although *The Glamour* has been described as a work of magical realism (Mendlesohn and James, 2009: 132–3), *The City & The City* more clearly demonstrates the stylistic and thematic qualities associated with this genre. In particular, its stylistic inheritance of the European tradition of not only Kafka and Schulz but also its debt to Italo Calvino's novel of imaginary dialogues about fantastical cities between Marco Polo and the emperor Kublai Khan, *Invisible Cities* (1972). Yet, this tradition also extends to nineteenth-century tales of the fantastic, for example Nikolai Gogol's 'The Overcoat' (1844), and the narrative resources of the older European folktale, such as 'The Twelve Dancing Princesses' (1812) by the Brothers Grimm. As Priest asks: 'Who as a child did not sometimes dream of the possibilities of invisibility?' (Priest, 2005b: xvii). Strengthening this connection between the trope of invisibility and children's literature, Miéville has argued that adults are effectively socialized out of a juvenile love of fantasy (Miéville, 2011).[1] Appropriately, then, both novels evoke the childlike wonder of children's fantasy fiction. The shared existence of Besźel and Ul Qoma, for instance, is prefigured in one of English literature's earliest urban fantasies – E. Nesbit's *Five Children and It* (1902):

> You know, we wished the servants shouldn't notice any difference when we got wishes. And nothing happens to the Lamb unless we specially wish it to. So of course they don't notice the castle or anything. But then the castle is on the same place where our house was – is, I mean – and the servants have to go on being in the house, or else they would notice. But you can't have a castle mixed up with our house – and so we can't see the house, because we see the castle; and they can't see the castle, because they go on seeing the house. (Nesbit, 2008: 141)

The children's invisibility from their servants is the result, however, of an external agent – 'It', the wish-fulfilling Psammead. The lack of an external cause in both *The City & The City* and *The Glamour* might be said to resemble another children's fantasy instead: T. H. White's retelling of medieval Arthurian legend, *The Sword in the Stone* (1938). In their confrontation with the giant Galapas, the invisibility of Merlyn and the Wart is sustained by 'an exercise of will-power' (White, 1971: 243) rather than an actual spell, an episode of mind control that compares with the Wart's earlier reflection upon Athene's invisibility:

> Athene was invisible, or at least the Wart never remembered having seen her afterwards. At the time he did not notice that she was invisible [...] because he was aware of her without seeing her [...] the suffering which had brought her there had left her with a kind of supernatural *good manners*. (White, 1971: 232, emphasis in original)

Similarly, in *The Glamour*, Sue describes invisibility as 'a natural condition', stating that: 'Many ordinary people have talents, both positive and negative [...]. Some people, a few, one or two like me, are inherently unnoticeable, evanescent, invisible' (Priest, 2005a: 119).

Borrowing the terminology of her dead friend, Mrs Quayle, Sue refers to a 'cloud' in order to describe her invisible state: 'I was not invisible in the sense that I was transparent, or that the science of optics was somehow being breached, but that the cloud made it difficult for me to be *noticed*' (Priest, 2005a: 120, emphasis in original). At the same time, Sue distances herself from mysticism: 'I felt no rapport with psychic sensitives like clairaudients or spirit mediums' (Priest, 2005a: 119). To some extent, Sue can choose to be either visible or hidden, but since her choice is affected by the presence of those around her – the irredeemably glamorous Niall or the unaware Richard – it also causes her profound misery. Like Merlyn, Sue's invisibility is an act of will-power but her sovereignty as an invisible woman is corrupted by her close social and sexual relations, no more so than when she conceals from Richard her rape by Niall in a shocking display of polite conduct: 'When I was sure I would not disturb you I slipped out of the bed and went to the bathroom. I showered as quietly as I could, scrubbing myself clean' (Priest, 2005a: 160–1).

In Miéville's novel, good manners – the ability to 'unsee' the inhabitants of the spatially co-existent cities of Besźel and Ul Qoma – are something learnt from childhood:

> The early years of a Besz (and presumably an Ul Qoman) child are intense learnings of cues. We pick up styles of clothing, ways of walking and holding oneself, very fast. Before we were eight or so most of us could be trusted not to breach embarrassingly and illegally, though licence of course is granted children every moment they are in the street. (CC, 80)

The thematic tension of *The City & The City* hinges upon the possibility of two cities, two peoples and two distinct cultures existing within the same location but being entirely unseen by one another. In clarifying this spatial-ontological premise, Miéville introduces a consideration of the issue of language, which might be read as prefiguring his later novel, *Embassytown* (2011):

> Anyway whether in its original or later written form, Illitan bears no resemblance to Besz. Nor does it sound similar. But these distinctions

are not as deep as they appear. Despite careful cultural differentiation [...] the languages are closely related – they share a common ancestor, after all. It feels almost seditious to say so. Still. (*CC*, 51)

In other words, the obscure history of what Miéville's protagonist, the investigating detective Borlú, refers to as 'the Cleavage' (*CC*, 51) is inscribed in the differences between Besz and Illitan that shape the consciousness of the citizens to regard themselves as separate. But, also inscribed here is the dim, distant suggestion that these two cities were once unified, lending succour to the claims of Unificationists on both sides of the divide. By reading Miéville's text alongside Priest's *The Glamour*, it is possible to argue that, although both writers demystify invisibility in order to present it as either a natural or a learnt condition to which the individual has to be socialized, Priest emphasizes the subjective experience of his characters whereas Miéville foregrounds their objective social reality – albeit one that is irrevocably split.

In establishing the condition of invisibility within their texts, both writers use familiar reference-points to ease the reader's suspension of disbelief: Miéville cites historically split cities, such as Berlin and Jerusalem, whilst Priest depicts Sue as attempting to persuade Richard of her invisibility by citing common social occasions where someone will pass unnoticed (Priest, 2005a: 161–3). As Sue recognizes, reality is all a matter of perception: 'I had never been invisible to myself in mirrors, because I looked in them purposely to see myself, as everyone does, and in expecting to see I noticed and *saw*' (Priest, 2005a: 120, emphasis in original). Equally, when Borlú accidentally sees a woman from Ul Qoma, 'With a hard start, I realized that she was not on GunterStrász at all, and that I should not have seen her' (*CC*, 14), the reader's initial perception is that Borlú has seen a ghost; an absence made present whose irruption into the sentence is registered by Miéville's repeated use of the negative.

Although both Priest and Miéville question the function of invisibility, their texts nevertheless invoke folkloric and popular cultural beliefs in spectres and vampires; in anonymous things that cast neither shadow nor reflection. In *The City & The City*, this playing upon irrational fears forms part of the novel's overturning of conspiracy theory: Breach, the mysterious power that patrols the borders between Besźel and Ul Qoma, is revealed to be no more than a competent police force whose concealment relies upon its superior knowledge of the interstices between the cities and its ability to navigate them undetected. Whilst Miéville denies any supernatural abilities of invisibility, then, in *The Glamour*, Priest reveals the visceral horror of poltergeists as underpinning the final confrontation between Richard and Niall:

> Grey swung about, groping with one hand at the air around him, prodding and punching with the rolled-up pages in his other fist. He moved awkwardly to the door, snatched it open to peer outside, then slammed it closed. He reached blindly for me as the air swirled about us both. (Priest, 2005a: 231)

The insertion of 'me' into the final sentence announces the shift from third- to first-person narration and Niall's revelation that Richard and Sue are in his 'control' (Priest, 2005a: 232). In other words, whereas Miéville's novel is concerned with the exposure of power as an institutional force, Priest's text is preoccupied with the seductive glamour (magic, charm) of power: the invisible hold that Niall has over Sue, its destructive effect upon Sue's relationship with Richard, and the sexual tensions – desires, wants, fears – that such control possesses.

It is at these points that *The Glamour*, perhaps surprisingly, recalls one of the key radical texts of Gothic fiction: William Godwin's denunciation of political authority, *Caleb Williams* (1794). Consider, for example, the passage in which Caleb realizes that during his flight he has never once been free from his master's gaze:

> I had my eye upon you in all your wanderings. You have taken no material step through their whole course with which I have not been acquainted. [...] Do you think you are out of the reach of my power, because a court of justice has acquitted you? (Godwin, 1988: 291–2)

Falkland's power over Caleb is such that he 'haunts' him 'like a demon'. As Caleb says: 'I cannot wake but I think of him. I cannot sleep but I see him. He poisons all my pleasures' (Godwin, 1988: 33). The sexual subtext to Caleb's possession chimes with Priest's description of Niall's hold over Sue in *The Glamour*. But elsewhere in Godwin's novel, Caleb also observes: 'I was ignorant of the power which the institutions of society give to one man over others' (Godwin, 1988: 264). Falkland's panoptical hold over Caleb clearly relates the narrative to what Martin Jay has termed 'scopic regimes of modernity' (Jay, 1988: 3–23), but it can also be compared with the networking of intertextual references present in both Miéville and Priest. To some extent, their readers share Caleb's subject position insofar as total comprehension is impossible. However, Miéville and Priest do not acquiesce to a God-like dominion over the reader. For one thing, they too are subject to the potential play of unseen allusions; for another, they both seek to demystify the author's function as originator (*auctor*).

The political aspect of Godwin's Gothic novel – the revelation that Falkland is not 'like a demon' at all but the embodiment of capital and misrule – prefigures Miéville's treatment of invisibility as an instrument of state power. Although in one sense the liminal existence of Besźel-Ul Qoma means that these cities could be located anywhere on the map, in another sense the East European nature of this setting is profoundly significant. The internalized skill of unseeing one's neighbours literalizes the culture of disavowal that existed within the Soviet Union: a culture that operated on the level of everyday discourse, since disavowing what might be one's true thoughts was a necessary survival mechanism when the person one knows as a friend, a work colleague, a relation, a neighbour might at the same time be a police informer or state agent. Disavowal marks the literature of the Soviet period, for example, in Arkady and Boris Strugatsky's *The Second Invasion from Mars* (1968), in which the major events happen off-stage and are only felt indirectly – even invisibly – by an isolated Russian community. In Abram Tertz's (Andrei Sinyavsky) short story, 'Pkhentz' (1966), the narrator is a hunchback whose social and sexual unease seems, initially, to arise from his disability and an unspecified psychological trauma. In the course of the story, he becomes obsessed with a fellow hunchback whom he spies upon at the local laundrette.

Finally, he engages his counterpart in conversation but finds him sadly ignorant:

> 'Cut it out,' I said quietly. 'I recognized you at first sight. You and I come from the same place. We're relatives, so to speak. PKHENTZ! PKHENTZ!' I whispered, to remind him of a name sacred to us both. (Tertz, 1987: 230)

In despair, the narrator explains away the hunchback's lack of awareness by claiming that he has 'entered too fully into his part, gone native, become human', only to realize that 'he was a normal human, the most normal of humans' (Tertz, 1987: 231–2). For the narrator believes himself to be an extraterrestial who has only taken the form of a hunchback as 'fancy dress', 'a bit better-looking than the rest of them here, though they are monsters too' (Tertz, 1987: 225). The self-division of the narrator's identity, of being (perhaps) two in one, is further compounded by the superficial mirroring with his physical other: a literal manifestation of the invisible effects of totalitarianism upon the psyche in terms of psychological disavowal and social alienation.

So, to return to *The City & The City*, it is 'still' an 'almost seditious' act within the two worlds of the novel to even consider that Besźel and Ul Qoma could have had a common linguistic ancestor. The spectral presence of Breach signifies that such thinking is not paranoiac – as in the Soviet Union, there *literally* were state powers capable of expunging the individual. Instead, the object of *The City & The City* is to demystify such forces in a way that the literature of the Soviet era could not do except by allegorical suggestion (cf. Etkind, 2009: 182–200). In both *The Second Invasion from Mars* (1968) and the Strugatskys's later novel, *Roadside Picnic* (1972), the aliens – who may or may not be read as substitutes for the Soviet authorities – are knowable only by their collateral effects. In *Roadside Picnic*, these consist of the mysterious artefacts abandoned within the so-called Zone that defy human comprehension, and to which have been ascribed names such as 'witches' jelly': appellations that describe the depths of an Eastern European folkloric imaginary. By contrast, in *The City & The City* such an imaginary is subjected to scrutiny. In particular, the conspiracy that surrounds the hypothetical third city, Orciny, is revealed to be symptomatic of the state-induced paranoia that binds Besźel and Ul Qoma together, whilst distracting their populations from the reality of political and commercial corruption.

It might be tempting to read *The City & The City* as a play upon the historical 'cleavage' of the collapse of the Soviet Union in and around 1989, with Besźel identified as representing one of the authoritarian satellite states of the USSR and Ul Qoma as its more Western-orientated, free-market but, in truth, no less authoritarian counterpart. However, Miéville's use of unseeing also has a less allegorical function. It could be read more generally as Miéville's commentary on the way in which national communities imagine themselves, as in Benedict Anderson's influential description: 'the members of even the smallest nation will never know most of their fellow-members, meet them, or even hear of them, yet in the minds of each lives the image of their communion' (Anderson, 1991: 6). In reformulating Anderson's terms, it is possible to argue that to remain part of a 'limited' and 'sovereign' state, the citizens of Besźel and Ul Qoma must therefore unsee one another. Yet, just as Sue's sovereign status as an independent woman is compromised in *The Glamour*, so the sovereignty of Besźel and Ul Qoma is also shown to be flawed: the cities are nevertheless reliant upon one another, although each disavows the existence of the other. Unlike Sue's storyline, however, the exposure of each city's lack of sovereignty in Miéville's text is potentially emancipatory. At the novel's ending, Borlú's self-professed 'liberal' position suggests that living in 'the city and the city' means also living 'in the interstice', and vice versa (*CC*, 373). By contrast, although the political uprising of Unificationists determined to remove the borders between the two cities fails, one possibility if it had succeeded might have been the imposition of a sovereign, and therefore false, national identity that would have subsumed both Besźel and Ul Qoma. Borlú's invisibility – his disappearance from both cities and into Breach – amounts to his acceptance of the contradictions that define lived experience, in contrast to the abstract ideals that underwrite the imagined national community.

This abstraction may be best understood in terms of Michel de Certeau's distinction between 'the urban *fact*' and 'the *concept* of a city' (de Certeau, 1984: 94, emphasis in original). The Concept-city is not only rationally organized, transparent and centrally administered, it also disregards the momentary behaviour of the citizens who move within its environs; 'a way of being in the world' that is 'forgotten' within the Concept-city's panoptical gaze: the inscription of 'a totalizing and reversible line on the map' that 'has the effect of making invisible the operation that made it possible' (de Certeau, 1984: 97). Thus, the rationalizing tendencies of the Concept-city not only disappear the particularities of lived experience, which Borlú seeks to accept, but also habituate the citizens to unsee both one another and the global relations of power, economics and trade that permit their urban existence. By contrast, the novel's final chase sequence, circumnavigating the intersections between the two cities in avoidance of Breach, can be read as a re-inscription of the physical movement of humans in defiance of the Concept-city.

The open ending to *The City & The City* is thus indicative of what Miéville calls his 'anguished optimism' (Miéville, 2012). By contrast, the ambiguous ending of Priest's *The Glamour*, in which it becomes radically indeterminate as to who is writing whose narrative, Richard or Niall, may be indicative of Priest's pessimism: the reader is encouraged to conclude that there is no escape from the illusions that his characters have invented for themselves. In the novel's final confrontation, Priest's object becomes clear as long as the reader believes the putative author, Niall, who has not only raped Sue, has also violated Richard's memories:

> We are all fictions: you are one, Susan is another, I am also one to a lesser extent. I have used you to speak for me. I have made you, Grey. You disbelieve in me, but not nearly so much as I disbelieve in you.
> Why resist the idea? We all make fictions. Not one of us is what we seem [...]. The urge to rewrite ourselves as real-seeming fictions is present in us all. In the glamour of our wishes we hope that our real selves will not be visible. (Priest, 2005a: 234)

By contrast, Miéville only lightly touches upon the metafictional possibilities of his text when Borlú comments:

> I watched and with occasional over-the-shoulder suggestions helped Dhatt construct a letter saying polite and regretful nothing to Mr and Mrs Geary [...]. It was not a good feeling of power, to be present a ghost in that holding message, knowing them, seeing them from inside the words which would be like one-way glass, so that they could not look back in and see me, one of the writers. (CC, 271)

The single, subjective point of view from which *The City & The City* is narrated, in contrast with *The Glamour*'s constant shifting between multiple narrators and perspectives, means that Miéville's text has less opportunity for metafictional devices than Priest's. Although, in *The Glamour*, Niall's self-aggrandizement as the text's nominal author-figure cannot be trusted – in addition to the shifts in perspective, the final paragraph suggests that Niall might be a character within Richard's narrative – invisibility nevertheless acts as a metaphor for the occult relationship between the author, the reader and the text in Priest's fiction.

Writing in the academic journal, *Foundation*, Priest observed that: 'All fiction [...] succeeds or fails on the plausibility, oddness, originality, accuracy, etc. of its metaphors' (Priest, 1978: 48). The crystalline narrative structure of *The Glamour* invites the reader to read the text metaphorically, and not as a metonym for the world beyond the text. Although divided cities such as Berlin and Jerusalem are invoked in *The City & The City* as a means of comparison with Besźel-Ul Qoma, the characters insist that they cannot be compared (CC, 90–1). Miéville anticipates the reader's desire to read the text allegorically, in other words as metaphor, and instead encourages him/her to read the environment of *The City & The City* as a metonym: as a compressed substitute for the reality beyond the text. The theme of invisibility, then, should be understood here as relating also to the issue of mimesis – the illusion or appearance of reality – within science fiction. As Roger Luckhurst has neatly summarized, the discursive strategies associated with metaphor and metonymy underwrite, respectively, the approaches of Darko Suvin and Samuel R. Delany to the reading of science fiction:

> So, for Suvin, "it should be made clear that the sf universe of discourse [...] presents possible worlds [...] as totalising and thematic metaphors", whilst for Delany the focus is on "the most basic level of sentence meaning [where] we read words differently when we read them as science fiction". Suvin, in other words, isolates the specificity of science fiction in the rigour of its cognitive leap between levels (metaphor), whereas Delany insists that the conjunctions and disjunctions of science fiction be located as "a specific way of reading", an abuse of "particular syntactical rules" in the science fictional sentence (metonymy). (Luckhurst, 2000: 70)

In his subsequent analysis of primarily New Wave sf, Luckhurst identifies this distinction between metaphor and metonymy as the twin linguistic poles advanced by the Russian literary theorist and structuralist critic, Roman Jakobson, a theoretical model based upon a study of aphasia, in which the sufferer loses either one or other of their capacities for speech. For Luckhurst, sf 'bears the anxieties of its perceived "low" cultural status internally, and at the point where the voice begins to speak' (Luckhurst, 2000: 71): dysfunctional loss of either the metaphoric or metonymic capacities is symptomatic of a disabling, internalized sense of cultural insecurity. Following Luckhurst, then, we might want to read the invisibility of *The Glamour* as opening-up a space in which narrative coherence is overwhelmed by competing voices, whereas the invisibility of *The City & The City* encourages a lack of voice; since the coherence of Besźel-Ul Qoma is held together at the end only by the now illusory power of Breach as a higher authority. In both instances, the comprehensibility of the sf text teeters upon an abyss, in that in the former, there is an excess of possible meanings and narrative discourses whilst, in the latter, there is a deficit of meaning since the transcendental claims of Breach as an enforcer not only of legal and spatial definitions but also linguistic ones have been discredited.

Luckhurst's critique, though, is tied to the logic of the New Wave and its persistent demands to erase the generic boundaries surrounding sf and to disappear into a nebulous mainstream fiction (see Luckhurst, 2005: 168). Despite his injunction to read science fiction in terms of its own discourse, it is notable how often Delany, for example, reads the genre through decadent, modernist and avant-garde literature (see Delany, 2009, 2012). The aesthetic tendencies of the New Wave further inspired *Science Fiction Studies*, co-founded in 1973 by Suvin. Priest, who was closely associated with *New Worlds* in the 1960s and other similar titles, might be regarded as continuing this tendency; he is often described as abandoning sf by the late 1970s. Yet, as Priest remarked of his relationship to sf in 1983: 'I haven't renounced it – it has renounced me!' (cited in Ruddick, 1989: 89); whilst more recently, he has described himself as a 'writer of the fantastic'.[2] Unencumbered by the legacy of the New Wave, Miéville has repeatedly insisted upon the viability of working within, or between, genres as opposed to what he regards as a sterile form of literary realism: 'Narrow "realism" is as partial and ideological as "reality" itself. [...] "Realistic" books may pretend to be about "the real world" but that does not mean they reverberate within it with more integrity and insight' (Miéville, 2002: 42). And, although Priest has sought to qualify Miéville's position (Priest, 2011), he has nevertheless been a constant critic of writers such as Julian Barnes and Ian McEwan, who typify contemporary British mainstream fiction for those readers who adopt the Man Booker Prize as their barometer of literary taste. In other words, the variance between excess and loss that Luckhurst detects within the science fictional register may be symptomatic of a particular moment within the history of the genre rather than of the genre itself.

Or, to put the same point another way, these 'vicissitudes' (to use Luckhurst's word) may be symptomatic of what New Wave sf was hoping to disappear into – broadly speaking, modernism. As David Lodge has shown in *The Modes of Modern Writing* (1977), Jakobson's model can be usefully applied to modernist literature in which the modernist text frequently verges upon loss, silence or invisibility. Examples include: 'the faint ring of incomprehensible words cried from afar' (Conrad, 1973: 119) during Marlow's interview with Kurtz's Intended in *Heart of Darkness* (1899); the 'wedge-shaped core of darkness' (Woolf, 1977: 60) into which Mrs Ramsay dissolves in *To The Lighthouse* (1927); or, the voices heard 'as though they were speaking out of the air' (Faulkner, 1963: 19) that narrate William Faulkner's *As I Lay Dying* (1930). Both Priest's championing of the slipstream and Miéville's redefinition of the Weird are rooted in a modernist aesthetic with, coincidentally, Borges and Schulz as common reference-points (Gordon, 2003: 363–4; Priest 2003). In her essay, 'The Aesthetics of Silence' (1967), Susan Sontag observes that '[a] person who becomes silent becomes opaque for the other; somebody's silence opens up an array of possibilities for interpreting that silence, for imputing speech to it' (Sontag, 1994: 16). It is possible to rephrase Sontag's observation in terms of Pasternak's image of the sponge: art absorbs the intertexts of speech to become dense and saturated. Within their joint occlusion, both Miéville and Priest invite their readers to experience a plenitude of meaning. In that sense, then, both texts recapture the sense of childlike wonder – without losing the hard sceptical edge of control and manipulation – that underscores the speculative tradition of tales concerned with invisibility.

Notes

1 For a more extensive reading of Miéville's engagement with the genre of young adult fantasy, see Joe Sutliff Sanders's previous chapter 'Blatantly Coming Back.'
2 In conversation with the author, Paul Kincaid and Maureen Speller at the Folkestone Book Festival (November 2012).

Works Cited

Anderson, Benedict (1991) *Imagined Communities: Reflections on the Origin and Spread of Nationalism*, 2nd edition. London: Verso.
Conrad, Joseph (1973) *Heart of Darkness*. London: Penguin.
Davie, Donald (1969) 'Introduction', in Donald Davie and Angela Livingstone (eds) *Pasternak: Modern Judgements*, pp. 11–34. London: Macmillan.
De Certeau, Michel (1984) *The Practice of Everyday Life*, trans. Steven Rendall. Berkeley, CA: University of California Press.
Delany, Samuel R. (2009) *The Jewel-Hinged Jaw: Notes on the Language of Science Fiction*. Middletown, CT: Wesleyan University Press.

Delany, Samuel R. (2012) *Starboard Wine: More Notes on the Language of Science Fiction*. Middletown, CT: Wesleyan University Press.

Etkind, Alexander (2009) 'Post-Soviet Hauntology: Cultural Memory of the Soviet Terror', *Constellations* 16(1): 182–200.

Faulkner, William (1963) *As I Lay Dying*. London: Penguin.

Godwin, William (1988) *Caleb Williams*, ed. Maurice Hindle. London: Penguin.

Gordon, Joan (2003) 'Revelling in Genre: An Interview with China Miéville', *Science Fiction Studies* 30(3): 355–73.

Herd, David (2000) *John Ashbery and American Poetry*. Manchester: Manchester University Press.

Holt, Philip (1992) 'H. G. Wells and the Ring of Gyges', *Science Fiction Studies* 19(2): 236–47.

Jay, Martin (1988) 'Scopic Regimes of Modernity', in Hal Foster (ed.) *Vision and Visuality*, pp. 3–23. Seattle: Bay Press.

Lodge, David (1977) *The Modes of Modern Writing: Metaphor, Metonymy, and the Typology of Modern Literature*. London: Edward Arnold.

Luckhurst, Roger (2000) 'Vicissitudes of the Voice, Speaking Science Fiction', in Andy Sawyer and David Seed (eds) *Speaking Science Fiction*, pp. 69–81. Liverpool: Liverpool University Press.

Luckhurst, Roger (2005) *Science Fiction*. Cambridge: Polity.

Mendlesohn, Farah and Edward James (2009) *A Short History of Fantasy*. London: Middlesex University Press.

Miéville, China (2002) Editorial introduction to 'Symposium: Marxism and Fantasy', *Historical Materialism* 10(4): 39–49.

Miéville, China (2011) 'A Life in Writing', *Guardian*, URL (consulted January 2013), http://www.guardian.co.uk/books/2011/may/14/china-mieville-life-writing-genre

Miéville, China (2012) 'The Future of the Novel', *Guardian*, URL (consulted September 2012), http://www.guardian.co.uk/books/2012/aug/21/china-mieville-the-future-of-the-novel

Moorcock, Michael (2009) 'The Spaces In Between', *Guardian*, URL (consulted January 2013), http://www.guardian.co.uk/books/2009/may/30/china-mieville-fiction

Nesbit, E. (2008) *Five Children and It*, 2nd edition [1902]. London: Puffin Classics.

O'Hara, Frank (2008) 'A Step Away from Them', in *Selected Poems*, ed. Mark Ford, pp. 109–10. New York: Knopf.

Oxford English Dictionary. URL (consulted January 2013), http://www.oed.com

Pasternak, Boris (1959) *Safe Conduct: An Early Autobiography and Other Works*, trans. Alec Brown. London: Elek Books.

Pasternak, Boris (1996) *Doctor Zhivago*, trans. Max Hayward and Manya Harari. London: Harvill.

Priest, Christopher (1978) 'Letter to Malcolm Edwards', *Foundation* 14: 48–9.

Priest, Christopher (2003) 'Top 10 Slipstream Books', *Guardian*, URL (consulted September 2012), http://www.guardian.co.uk/books/2003/may/28/top10s.slipstream

Priest, Christopher (2005a) *The Glamour*. London: Gollancz.

Priest, Christopher (2005b) Introduction to H. G. Wells, *The Invisible Man*, edited by Patrick Parrinder, pp. xiii–xxv. London: Penguin.

Priest, Christopher (2011) 'Another Damned Label', URL (consulted January 2013), http://www.christopher-priest.co.uk/journal/410/14-may-2011/

Ruddick, Nicholas (1989) *Christopher Priest*. Mercer Island, WA: Starmont House.

Sontag, Susan (1994) 'The Aesthetics of Silence' in *Styles of Radical Will*, pp. 3–34. London: Vintage.

Strugatsky, Arkady and Boris (1981) *Far Rainbow/The Second Invasion from Mars*, trans. Antonina W. Bouis. London: Collier.

Strugatsky, Arkady and Boris (2007) *Roadside Picnic*, trans. Antonina W. Bouis. London: Gollancz.

Tertz, Abram (1987) 'Pkhentz', in *Fantastic Stories*, trans. Manya Harari, pp. 215–45. Evanston, IL: Northwestern University Press.

White, T. H. (1971) *The Sword in the Stone*. London: Lions.

Woolf, Virginia (1977) *To the Lighthouse*. London: Grafton.

7

'YOU SHOULD BE TEACHING'
CREATIVE WRITING AND EXTRAMURAL ACADEMICS IN
PERDIDO STREET STATION AND EMBASSYTOWN

Ben de Bruyn

Weird Campus Novels

Although the literature on China Miéville, British author of genre-bending 'weird fiction', continues to grow, and deals with topics as diverse as genre, Marxism and the representation of cities, it has so far ignored another important aspect of his books: to a greater or lesser extent, they are all campus novels.[1] Even to those who are familiar with Miéville's work, this characterization may seem wilfully obscure. By definition, campus novels evoke academic settings, whereas Miéville's books take their readers to lavishly imagined alternative worlds, as their titles often inform us. The reader of these novels visits the 'weird' settings of *Perdido Street Station* (2000), *Un Lun Dun*

(2007), *The City & The City* (2009), *Embassytown* (2011) and *Railsea* (2012), not the campuses of Harvard, Cambridge or the University of Warwick. If anything, these books take us *away from*, rather than *to*, the more or less familiar habitats of students and scholars that feature in campus novels. In *Un Lun Dun*, for instance, an intelligent cloud of smog threatens to take over the alternative, 'weird' version of London – the 'abcity' called UnLondon – with the help of such unlikely allies as smog-junkies and smog-zombies. Even though she is not the prophesied chosen one, a London girl comes to the rescue of UnLondon, battling or befriending such odd creatures as carnivorous giraffes, spider-windows, living words, animate 'unbrellas' and a tribe of roof-dwellers. In *Railsea*, likewise, the reader follows a young boy across the endless tracks that have replaced the world's oceans, evading pirates, mutated wildlife and a hostile 'ferronavy' in order to recover ancient salvage, to hunt an elusive monster-mole (in an extended nod to Herman Melville's *Moby-Dick* [1851]), and to discover the place where, impossibly, the rails end. Academics may dream of living words and elusive objects, but still, these books sharply differ from such immediately recognizable campus novels as Jeffrey Eugenides's *The Marriage Plot* (2011), in which readers encounter university students, are shown a highly competitive research lab and follow characters on a typical post-collegiate trip abroad. So why do I insist, seemingly perversely, that Miéville's books are campus novels?

To present the descriptive predicament more clearly, let me return to the novels I mentioned. If the young characters of *Un Lun Dun* appear to escape from the tedious playground of the novel's opening, first of all, various elements of the story nevertheless remain related to education. The guardians of UnLondon are the Propheseers or 'Prophs' (*ULD*, 49), 'magicians and scholars [...] with reputations built on generations of study' (*ULD*, 394). Furthermore, a 'Proph' who was researching London smog is transformed by the evil monster into a Faust-like parody of the modern researcher. On the first page, he is bravely reading several books at the same time, and when we hear his delirious ravings at the end, his goal is still to 'learn everything' (*ULD*, 480) he can. In the real world, 'Professor Lipster' (*ULD*, 169) unwittingly helps to decipher the enemy's plan and the protagonist is able to return to UnLondon by climbing the stacks of her 'school library' (*ULD*, 178). What we might call the 'academic unconscious' of *Railsea* is even clearer. Choosing as protagonist a young boy who recalls 'Hunt Studies' (*R*, 5) and 'geography lessons' (*R*, 57) seems like a mere strategy to introduce readers to the workings of this fictional world, but the language of the school also emerges elsewhere; we hear of the 'Diffuse College' (*R*, 97) of foraging technology-salvors, of the 'scholarocracy of Rockvane' (*R*, 56), of 'railseaologists' (*R*, 286) and the crucial discipline of 'ferrovia-oceanology' (*R*, 192), which is the study of the railsea's iron lines and extends across all fields, including metallurgy, biology and theology. And what should we think of Captain Naphi, the Ahab-like figure who is interested in journals like '*Captain-Philosopher's Quarterly*' (*R*, 123) and in books on subjects like 'Floating Signifiers' (*R*, 122)? Most captains discuss their beloved preys in 'lectures' (*R*, 91), we hear, their nemesis turning into 'principle[s] of [...] obsession, modernity, nostalgia' and Naphi's Mocker-Jack is no exception; his meaning is obscure, she teaches, as the beast evades her harpoon and 'resist[s] close reading' (*R*, 92). Whatever their ironies, in reading such passages, we do not appear to be in UnLondon or on the railsea at all, but at Harvard or Cambridge, where Miéville studied, or at Warwick, where Miéville has taught creative writing.[2] These academic elements are typical of his novels, as I will demonstrate, despite their frequent critique of university life.

The Institution is the Message

From a certain perspective, the presence of academic terms in Miéville's work is neither surprising nor significant. It could be argued that the language of the university is simply one of the jargons making up the social fabric of his novels, and he is obviously not the first science fiction or young adult writer to represent scientists and schools. Yet the presence of the academy in his work merits further scrutiny, if only because it has not received much attention, despite Miéville's connection with various universities. That such connections are important is amply demonstrated in Mark McGurl's *The*

Program Era (2009), a study that identifies the intimate ties between twentieth-century American literature and the institutions of higher education, the creative writing programme especially. McGurl's book not only invites us to re-examine the connections between individual authors and academic institutions, but also traces the history of the writing programme and simultaneously provides a productive template for institutional readings of modern novels including, as I will show, those by Miéville. Let me first summarize McGurl's book in some detail, not only because his approach is novel but also because I will draw on several aspects of his work in my subsequent analysis of the 'academic unconscious' in Miéville's fiction, particularly *Embassytown*.[3]

In general terms, McGurl's thesis is simple: we should study the impact of creative writing programmes in more detail, as they amount to 'a genuine literary historical novelty' (McGurl, 2009: 21) in their rise to prominence and their counterintuitive conjunction of individual creativity and institutional constraints. Beginning that work, McGurl's book offers a sweeping history of the programme (in the US) that simultaneously counters snobbish dismissals of creative writing. The historical narrative reads as follows. In the course of the twentieth century, the agency of the school ensured that the three (partly conflicting) creeds of the writing programme – self-expression ('write what you know'), craft ('show, don't tell') and creativity ('find your voice') – gradually became embedded in the work of every important postwar writer. If the progressive education movement introduced the pleasurable character-building of 'creative self-expression' (McGurl, 2009: 86) in American schools, the concomitant outpouring of emotions was reined in by the 'imposition of [...] institutional constraints upon unfettered creativity' (McGurl, 2009: 131) via notions like craft. These notions were in turn modified by the institutional embrace of countercultural creativity in the 1960s, a large-scale '*institutionalization of anti-institutionality*' (McGurl, 2009: 221, emphasis in original). This paradox implies that the desire to escape from institutions expressed by alternative writers like Ken Kesey in fact revealed that their work was *not opposed to, but continuous with*, the logic underpinning creative writing instruction. Together with writers like

Younghill Kang and Sandra Cisneros, who introduced the related value of 'cultural pluralism' (McGurl, 2009: 84), these socio-historical developments culminated in the creative writing programme as we know it now, with its celebration of personal expression, literary craft and nonconformist creativity.

The result has been criticized by many commentators, who argue that it is a cynical plan propounded by academic administrators to cash in on the literary ambitions of aspiring writers and a misguided attempt to institutionalize the creativity of individual genius. Drawing on his historical knowledge, McGurl argues that these critiques are unjustified. For one thing, creative writing and the broader 'culture of the school' (McGurl, 2009: 30) have shaped the work of most twentieth-century writers, even those whose unorthodox, counter-academic position – what McGurl calls their '"extramural" consciousness' (McGurl, 2009: 24) – most resists the association with the university. Without modern colleges in the United States, there would have been no Vladimir Nabokov, no Philip Roth, no Octavia Butler and no Cormac McCarthy. It is true that literature is instrumentalized by universities, which eagerly imagine creative writing 'as a way of keeping the student-writer, and through him the institution itself, open to "the outside" which is the source of the unpredictable and new' (McGurl, 2009: 386). Yet it is also true that literature has benefited from this arrangement. For starters, 'serious readers' are nowadays mostly created by the school, 'where millions of students [a]re first introduced to the refined pleasures of the literary' (McGurl, 2009: 64).[4] Additionally, creative writing professorships and other forms of writer-in-residency imply that the university has become 'the most important patron of artistically ambitious literary practice in the United States' (McGurl, 2009: 22). Without academic funding and training, there might not be much literary fiction left.

McGurl's study also introduces a specific reading method that can be employed to uncover the academic unconscious in China Miéville's fiction. Apart from unearthing the close biographical ties between specific authors and certain institutions, McGurl analyses many widely anthologized texts to show that the modern educational environment manifests itself on different levels in the literary text, 'as a kind of watermark' (McGurl, 2009: 4). First of all, 'the era of the writer-teacher' (McGurl, 2009: 388) coincides with a proliferation of academic characters and settings. Wherever you look in modern novels, you find students and professors who are 'in close proximity to universities' (McGurl, 2009: 383). Despite its educational theme, McGurl refrains from calling Toni Morrison's *Beloved* (1987) a 'campus novel' (McGurl, 2009: 348), but his argument nonetheless raises the question of whether all postwar American novels should not be considered 'campus novels of a sort' (McGurl, 2009: 47). Refuting the Romantic characterization of authors as disconnected from their broader literary-institutional and educational surroundings, and the associated claim that metafictional techniques are the sole reserve of withdrawn experimentalists, McGurl's account thus reveals the remarkable extent to which modern novels process the educational experiences of their authors. To McGurl's mind, every novel is nowadays, on one level, a Joycean 'portrait of the artist as a student' (McGurl, 2009: 338). A substantial part of the job of authorship in the programme era is 'job description itself' (McGurl, 2009: 48), a fictional form of self-monitoring that explains why he is able to find 'metafiction' (McGurl, 2009: 136, 305) in unlikely places. McGurl further contends that many postwar novels explicitly or implicitly consider education, often navigating between models of cold or 'bad institutionality' – represented as akin to a form of slavery – and good or 'warm institutionality' – as in the ideal family (McGurl, 2009: 158). What is more, these texts frequently concentrate on groups approximately the size of a creative writing seminar – work gangs, group therapy sessions – leading to an 'inventory of potentially analogical small groups' that help us to understand 'the workshop as a social form' (McGurl, 2009: 385). In their novels, these teacher-writers thus offer allegories of this quintessential educational experience. The impact of creative writing also manifests itself on a formal level; in writers' preference for economic forms like the 'short story' (McGurl, 2009: 144) or for the minimalist aesthetic that is the programme's 'house style' (McGurl, 2009: 294). The emphasis on craft and pluralism also encourages an exploration of 'point of view' (McGurl, 2009: 49), in which teacher-writers reveal their indebtedness to techniques outlined in creative writing textbooks and writing manuals. A story by Robert Olen Butler can thus be identified as sharing its formal properties with a 'suggested exercis[e]' (McGurl, 2009: 390) in a colleague's writing manual, for instance. On each of these levels, the *institution* is the message of modern fiction.

McGurl also reflects on the programme's geographic and generic limits. He concedes that creative writing originally emerged in North-American universities. Yet he also mentions the spiritually related work of the French Oulipo group and points out that writing programmes have started proliferating in countries like Canada, Mexico and the United Kingdom (McGurl, 2009: 364). Despite its roots in the US, in other words, these insights probably have a wider applicability. As far as genre is concerned, McGurl disapprovingly notes the programme's snobbish attitude towards genre fiction; there is a systematic 'aversion to genre fiction' (McGurl, 2009: 329) in most university-based programmes, he feels, which explains why academic programmes pay little or no attention to commercial genres like science fiction. This dismissive attitude is partly due to the programme's uncomfortable contiguity with such lowly genres; like formula fiction, after all, creative writing is heavily invested in notions like craft. This situation explains why aspiring genre fiction writers need to enrol in unofficial, extramural programmes: internet courses like The Gotham Writers' Workshop or the famous Clarion Workshops (McGurl, 2009: 306, 396).

McGurl's ground-breaking study raises a number of important points pertinent to the study of contemporary literature. Most notably, that we should study the institutional impact of creative writing programmes in the US and the UK in more detail in order to broaden our conceptions not just of the generic campus novel but, more significantly, of metafiction and experimental writing in general. This requires replacing the Romantic view of discrete, isolated authorship with an understanding of the way in which contemporary authors work, teach and produce literature within the university, this weird institution which instructs its students to combine personal expression, unorthodox creativity and self-conscious craft in the service of a pluralist project. In short, we should include another topic in our interpretive toolkit for modern fiction, namely 'education' (McGurl, 2009: 347). These are productive insights for interrogating the institutional parameters underpinning writing in the twenty-first century. Moreover, if we consider Miéville's work through the lens of McGurl's argument, we can begin to uncover an alternative pedagogy of creativity which is characteristic of creative writing's extramural consciousness.

Extramural Academics

At first sight, the links between Miéville, the university and creative writing appear tenuous, despite his postings at various universities. In interviews, for instance, Miéville's earlier research in international law and politics is often stressed whereas his work in creative writing is downplayed. These publications mention that he is an assistant professor but there are no questions put to Miéville concerning his teaching practice, which receives very little attention compared to his theorization of genre or his political engagement. Nor is Miéville himself eager to correct the assumption that creative writing is not an academic pursuit worthy of discussion. In one interview, he actually begins by saying that he 'was going to be an academic' and that he 'still enjoys research' (thinking of his work in law), brushing aside his current academic status as a creative writing professor (Pearl, 2011). Elsewhere he says that he wanted to finish his PhD in international law when his writing took off 'because you never know how long you will be able to write professionally, and it's good to have other possibilities' (Naimon, 2011: 55). Apparently, you are not an academic when you teach creative writing, and writing and research are other pursuits.[5]

Miéville not only distances himself from the university, but also from creative writing. He objects to the fact that 'parsimony has become the norm for skilful literary writing' (Derbyshire, 2012: 47) and rather promotes a maximalist, pulp fiction agenda that ignores the programme's minimalist creeds. 'The whole kind of "kill your darlings" cliché of writing is a very good injunction', he says, 'but at the same time, sometimes I think [...] let that darling live' (Chatfield, 2012). In another publication, he approvingly notes that J. G. Ballard '[b]lithely ignor[ed] the injunction beloved of creative writing teachers everywhere to "show, not tell" [by occasionally using] the SF technique known as the "infodump", in which undigestible nuggets of necessary facticity are simply thrown in' (Miéville, 2010b). What surprises the students of his weird fiction course at Warwick, he observes elsewhere, is that 'a certain kind of lush purple prose isn't necessarily a failure' (VanderMeer, 2012). Even though his presence in the writing department is salutary for all concerned, he therefore remains an outsider: '[a] lot of my students write what I think of as mainstream "literary" fiction, and I think it's very, very helpful for me to see what people from that tradition are working on, and very helpful for them to get feedback from someone with a rather different eye from their main readers' (Miéville, 2010a: 88). Like many of the authors discussed by McGurl, Miéville might be *a part of* the programme, but he is also *apart from* the programme.

This impression of an extramural consciousness is reinforced by his fiction. For Miéville's books not only consider university life but also criticize it systematically. The different aspects of that critique are present in a passage from the opening pages of his breakthrough novel *Perdido Street Station*, where the protagonist, Isaac, reflects on his academic status and unorthodox relationship with a non-human or 'xenian' beetle-woman, Lin:

> [Isaac] was [...] the scientist-outcast, the disreputable thinker who walked out of a lucrative teaching post to engage in experiments too outrageous [...] for the tiny minds who ran the university. What did he care for convention? He would sleep with whomever [...] he liked, surely! [...] That was his story, and it was at least half true. He had walked out of the university [but] only because he realized [...] that he was a terrible teacher. He had looked out at the quizzical faces, listened to the frantic scrawling of the panicking students, and realized that [...] he could not impart the understanding he so loved. [...] In another twist to the myth, his Head of Department [...] was [...] an exceptional bio-thaumaturge, who had nixed Isaac's research less because it was unorthodox than because it was going nowhere.

> Isaac could be brilliant, but he was undisciplined. Vermishank had [made] him beg for work as a freelance researcher on terrible pay, but with limited access to the university laboratories. And it was this [...] which kept Isaac circumspect about his lover. [And] the academy did not just play at being old-fashioned. Xenian students had only been admitted as degree candidates in New Crobuzon for twenty years. (*PSS*, 12–13)

This extended passage not only punctures Isaac's own self-mythologizing account of his extramural status, but also contains many features of Miéville's critical representation of the university. In his novels, the official representative of the university often proves treacherous: whether it is Isaac's supervisor Vermishank, the failed academic Dr David Bowden in *The City & The City*, or Professor Patrick Vardy in *Kraken*. In these novels, it is not the butler but the *professor* who did it. Additionally, they frequently evoke a tension between extra- and intramural forms of research whereby fringe sciences turn out to be more interesting than orthodox approaches, even if they are dangerous or frowned upon. Although the above passage praises Vermishank's work, the reader ultimately learns that Isaac's extramural research in 'unified field theory' leads to far more important results (and a similar endorsement of innovative research conducted outside of traditional institutions can be seen in the treatment of other renegade academics like Bowden in *The City & The City* or Cole in *Kraken*). The above passage of *Perdido Street Station* also draws attention to teaching gone wrong, a motif that recurs throughout the book; we hear of 'didactic barks' (*PSS*, 611) emanating from a school, of a speech by Vermishank which sounds 'as if he was giving a seminar' (*PSS*, 374), and of an evil mayor, who shakes his head 'like a teacher correcting a normally reliable student' (*PSS*, 271). Some educational experiences are depicted in positive terms – when Isaac explains his research in 'non-technical' (*PSS*, 222) terms, for instance, Yagharek finally understands the relevant scientific principles and is described as 'a model pupil' (*PSS*, 170) – but these moments always take place, as in *Railsea* or *The City & The City, outside* the official education system. Finally, the passage outlining Isaac's extramural status implies that in the Bas-Lag world universities are conservative bureaucracies, which even exclude certain species groups from entering their grounds, in an unmistakable reference to past race (and gender) relations. Given these observations, we might conclude that the implied author of these urban fictions, like the protagonist of *Kraken*, breathes a sigh of relief when he is able to run 'out of the university grounds, back into the city proper and away' (*K*, 348).

The advantage of adapting McGurl's account of the extensive influence of creative writing programmes upon both the form and content of contemporary fictions to a reading of Miéville's fiction is twofold here. Not only does it demonstrate the importance of these scattered references to the university throughout Miéville's oeuvre, but it also allows us to see how such attempts at distancing oneself from orthodox forms of education are part of an equally systematic, alternative pedagogy of creativity, which is a crucial part of Miéville's aesthetic sensibility. To stay with the example of *Perdido Street Station*, its indictment of repressive race relations may be a critique of this fictional university but the book's implicit embrace of cultural pluralism simultaneously fits into the agenda of real-world universities. Like modern college administrators, Miéville believes these institutions should be open to everyone. This pluralist agenda can further be seen in Isaac's romantic relationship with the *non-human* xenian artist Lin, as well as in the remarkable passage where he unwittingly taps into the dreams of all the inhabitants of New Crobuzon; an experience which reveals that dream logic is 'shared by all the sentient races of Bas-Lag' (*PSS*, 185). Here, Miéville's narration obliges the reader to inhabit the different points of view of a variety of characters, including Isaac, his lover Lin, his bird- and frog-people helpers, and even his otherworldly antagonists, the slake-moths. This mode of storytelling, with its frequent shifts in point of view, enables Miéville to reconnect the different identities and communities that threaten to clash in the fictional world of Bas-Lag. If the novel can be read as distancing itself from a conservative model of the university as a bastion of cultural elitism, it hence also realigns itself with a progressive, pluralist conception of higher education, using to that purpose literary techniques, like focalization, that are a central part of the creative writing curriculum.

Although I am primarily interested in the textual repercussions of Miéville's exchanges with the academic world, certain biographical elements should be mentioned here as well. The unexpected connection with the university is reinforced, for instance, if we realize that *Perdido Street Station* was actually written while Miéville was finishing his PhD at the London School of Economics. Like that of his fictional character Isaac, Miéville's student life was hence devoted to a semi-illicit research project that led to an important, if partly non-academic, breakthrough. Despite what the negative representation of the university in *Perdido Street Station* might suggest about his feelings towards academic institutions, moreover, Miéville has indicated that academic life actually *enabled* his creativity. Discussing his first novel *King Rat* (1998), he says that he was only able to finish the book because student life left him with time on his hands. He found it hard to write while working in an office, but this changed when he enrolled at the university:

> It was only when I did a Masters degree that I could get a lot of work done on the book. That doesn't mean I wasn't doing any studying, it's just that your time is more flexible, so you can catch up with late nights or whatever. I finished the book in Harvard while I was on this scholarship thing. (Miéville cited in Guran, 1999)

We can trace the positive role of educational institutions even further in Miéville's past. It turns out that school was one of the prime instigators of Miéville's writing career. Asked to submit his first story for an anthology of early work by famous science fiction writers, *Before They Were Giants* (2010), he sent in a text he wrote at the age of thirteen, 'Highway 61 Revisited'; a post-apocalyptic story that functioned, he recalls, as 'the kind of validation that probably made me think I could actually do this a bit' (Miéville, 2010a: 87). The figure behind that story was *a teacher*, who acted like creative writing teachers do, namely by setting an 'assignment', providing the constraint of a fixed 'title' and helping the student enter 'competition[s]' (Miéville, 2010a: 86). It proved an encouraging experience, as the story ended up winning a prize, and hence marked the beginning of Miéville's long history of winning writing awards. Having received so much input from the educational system, Miéville has recently returned the favour, allowing *King Rat* to be used by the British Council as a tool to teach English to foreign students.[6]

The ties between Miéville and his academic environment become even stronger if we consider – in the spirit of McGurl's analysis of the importance of institutional contexts to contemporary writers – related handbooks like *The Cambridge Introduction to Creative Writing* (2007) written by David Morley, one of Miéville's former colleagues in the Warwick writing department. Once again, we find traces of what I have called an extramural consciousness. Morley argues that academia can be 'a very healthy place' for writers and that literary writing is a 'version of research' (Morley, 2007: 30, 44). Yet he also concedes that the programme risks becoming 'a machine' that churns out work which 'sounds like a teacher writing' (Morley, 2007: 54, 250). Morley concludes that writers rightly prefer to be on the 'outside' of groups, adding that creative writing 'needs more rooms of its own outside the arena of formal education' (Morley, 2007: 48, 240). Like weird fiction and Isaac's unified field theory, perhaps creative writing properly belongs *outside* the university, where it is sufficiently liberated to become *the* central embodiment, paradoxically, of the academic virtue of 'creativity' (Morley, 2007: 252).

Miéville's view of authorship might also be considered to echo David Morley's emphasis upon the discipline of writing which, as he sternly observes, negates the 'romanticised view of writing' as spontaneously inspired by a 'divine wind' (Morley, 2007: 82, 109). In a recent polemic, Miéville brought his political beliefs to bear upon the business of writing for a living, arguing that good writers should get a fixed salary, like any other type of 'skilled worker' (Miéville, 2012). Authors are not that special, he writes, criticizing the 'ahistorical Olympian simpering at the specialness of writers' in reaction to the perceived existence of 'novel-writing kits' available to everyone (Miéville, 2012). Writers may be undervalued, but so are 'nurses, teachers, public transport staff, cleaners, social workers' (Miéville, 2012). Miéville also agrees that writers should not write to please their audience (thereby criticizing 'novel-writing kits' himself):

> I heard a writer on the radio the other day and she said that the most important thing she'd learnt from her creative writing MA was to write the books that readers want to read. That made me really sad. I hate that approach. [...] I think our job should be to make readers want to read the books that we write. (Miéville cited in Slatter, 2012)

Again, the advice is to strike out on your own and hope the reader will follow. Both teachers even agree, more or less, about genre. For despite the fact that Morley's handbook, like creative writing more generally, is wary of 'commercial genres' (Morley, 2007: 156) and '[o]verwriting' (Morley, 2007: 94, 110) and suggests that novels mainly portray '*small,* new worlds' (Morley, 2007: 3, emphasis added), it often mentions genre writers, advises aspiring writers to experiment with 'genre[s] that openly challeng[e] you to change your style' (Morley, 2007: 126) and describes literary writing as an exercise in imagining 'land[s] you do not know' (Morley, 2007: 10) and in inhabiting strange points of view, like that of 'a worn-out tablecloth' (Morley, 2007: 17) or a 'snail' (Morley, 2007: 141). In fact, Morley's introduction goes on to describe great literature in a way that should appeal to Miéville, famous writer of 'weird fiction', namely in terms of its '*weirdness*' (Morley, 2007: 20, emphasis in original). It is impossible to 'draw up a curriculum in which we teach *weirdness*' systematically, Morley asserts, yet schools where we can write genre fiction and practise a certain '*wildness*' (Morley, 2007: 20, emphasis in original) are a good thing. It appears that Miéville's extramural consciousness is shared by his academic colleagues.

Portrait of the Alien as a Young Student

Although the educational dimension of Miéville's other novels merits further scrutiny, I will concentrate here on the novel which seems furthest removed from pedagogical debates and creative writing programmes, as it is not even set on earth: the science fiction novel *Embassytown*. Let me summarize the story before teasing out its academic elements. Set in a far future where the human race, as '*Homo diaspora*' (*E*, 57), has colonized other planets, the protagonist Avice is a female human living in the international hub of a larger alien city on Arieka, a planet at the outskirts of the known universe. This planet is prized for its strategic location, its production of strangely organic tools and the remarkable language of its indigenous inhabitants. The 'Language' of the Ariekei or 'Hosts' has two striking features. Given their peculiar anatomy and psychology (if we can call it that), words only make sense to the Hosts if they are spoken by two separate voices working in tandem, forcing the human colonists to train peculiar, twin-like Ambassadors who, via special training, are able to express a unified message in the alien tongue by speaking different parts of utterances simultaneously. What makes the Language of the Ariekei even more unique is that words only make sense to the Hosts if they have real referents, meaning that lies, metaphors and counterfactual statements can neither be spoken nor truly thought unless a real-life equivalent has been found or theatrically staged for that purpose. Crucially, these stagings occasionally involve ordinary (single-voiced) humans, who thus become elements of Language: physical stand-ins for words and concepts. Especially important are the human similes because these figures of speech hint at unprecedented meanings but can still be spoken and thought by the Ariekei; in contrast to literally untrue metaphors ('I am a lion'), the comparisons of similes ('I am *like* a lion') remain explicit and are hence conceivable without real problems. This prelapsarian Language and the peaceful coexistence of Hosts and humans are threatened when a new Ambassador arrives whose slightly off-key speeches provoke a stultifying addiction in the Hosts, resulting in the neglect of their farming and maintenance duties and the slow collapse of life on Arieka. During these cataclysmic events, Avice turns out to be a pivotal figure: not only because she is an important simile, but also because she helps to avert a planetary catastrophe by transforming the god-like Language into a less truthful but more human-like language.

From a cursory glance, readers of *Embassytown* would be forgiven for querying my reading of the novel as engaging with the realm of contemporary academia. As with *Railsea*, however, academic language turns up in unexpected places in this distant world. At an early stage in the narrative, Avice and the other human similes are invited to events where Hosts celebrate their peculiar Language and flirt, largely unsuccessfully, with the ability to tell untruths. These gatherings are described as festivals, ceremonies, athletic competitions and literary performances, but they are also depicted, less obviously, as academic conferences:

> There had for a while been a vogue among the Hosts for what were, more or less, conventions. [...] They would gather as many of us necessary constructed facts as they could in one place [...] and come to look at us, use and theorise us, without consensus. We sat polite through wheezing, stuttering, sung arguments [...] about us. [...] Hosts stamped back and forward, disagreeing in factions. (*E*, 112–3)

These events are not only like concerts, masses or matches but are also described as evoking the atmosphere of 'conferences and conventions' (*E*, 114). And if this choice of words sounds innocuous, consider the fact that the most advanced competitors or 'liars' are described as 'Professors' (*E*, 146). Some Hosts consider the human similes as mere spectacle, but the best liars behave like academics, circling individual similes as 'exhibit[s] in a gallery', uttering 'opaque things' and creatively 'stretch[ing] the logic of analogy' (*E*, 146). To some extent, Miéville is poking fun at academic life here, associating it with the incomprehensible disputes of stuttering non-speakers. Yet this ironic dimension should not blind us to the fact that these 'conventions' and 'professors' also exert a positive influence within the novel, as they are instrumental in transforming the god-like Language into the less literal and more creative alternative that will ultimately save Arieka's inhabitants.

The reader of *Embassytown* meets real academics as well. The protagonist Avice is initially characterized as a non-academic figure; she may have passed the 'arcane exams' (*E*, 30) necessary to travel beyond Arieka, but she was 'never an intellectual' (*E*, 28). As the reader never leaves Avice's perspective throughout the novel, we therefore approach the real academic characters we meet at the beginning of the novel from what might again be characterized as an 'extramural' point of view. Entering a bar on an alien planet, Avice observes that she is familiar with its various types of patrons, with the exception of the 'academics' (*E*, 38) who are participating in a local conference. Through her outsider eyes, we visit this 'Conference of Human Exoterre Linguistics' (*E*, 38) and hear about outlandish languages as well as Avice's impromptu presentation on the most 'weird' (*E*, 39) specimen of all: the Language of Arieka. At this event Avice also meets her future husband Scile, a linguist from a 'parochial university town' (*E*, 42) who had been working on a comparison of languages from different worlds in a fruitless search for linguistic essences. Upon meeting Avice, however, he quickly starts an ambitious new project about Language. Even if the reader never leaves Avice's outsider perspective – she 'never made much effort to understand [Scile's] academic world' (*E*, 55) – we are hence introduced to an explicitly academic figure, who not only tells us about the unique character of Language but also about research and its practical organization. The novel describes Scile's trips to 'libraries' (*E*, 43) and 'archives' (*E*, 55), his 'nightly' (*E*, 84) and 'antisocial' (*E*, 165) research, his reading of (what must be shockingly ancient) books by Lakoff and Ricoeur, his search for 'epigraphs' (*E*, 60) for his projected monograph on Language and his practical arrangements with his 'employers-cum-supervisors' (*E*, 55). Scile's research prompts Avice to reconsider the special character of her home planet, so these scholarly activities are seen to be important. Yet, as so often in Miéville's work, official academic characters prove untrustworthy. In line with his earlier interest in linguistic essences, Scile is convinced that the Ariekei should be protected from 'changing Language' (*E*, 164), arguing that only 'punk[s]' (*E*, 162) would want to lie and alter this uniquely truthful, quasi-divine form of speech. Scile is not a diabolical figure, but his scholarly views nonetheless provoke two cowardly political murders. In the final analysis, this academic tries to stave off change and prevent the alien Hosts from acquiring a real language replete with lies, metaphors and creativity.

The novel not only mentions research, but also teaching. From the very first page, it draws attention to Embassytown's peculiar educational system, with its rotation of 'teachers and shiftparents' (*E*, 1), and the book further mentions the violent 'fight-crèche' (*E*, 95) of the Ariekei, the more familiar situation where children are raised by adults who are related 'by direct genetics' (*E*, 82) and the 'institutional raising' (*E*, 16) of Embassytown Ambassadors. The complex process of training Ambassadors is particularly singled out; despite being made up of two people, Ambassadors have to speak with one mind, which requires the special forms of breeding and training of 'the Ambassador-farm' (*E*, 66). There is something disquieting about this regime of education, where pupils are trained to think alike and small physical differences are daily corrected. The regime is also unsuccessful, for Avice eventually learns that some trainee Ambassadors fail to coalesce and that Embassytown therefore has a secret facility, a disquietingly ambiguous 'infirmary and asylum and jail' (*E*, 247) for these failed adults and 'unfixable children' (*E*, 248). What we have here is the bad institutionality of a failed school, you might say, a 'monstrous' (*E*, 251) place that will only cease operation at the novel's very end, when Avice and her friends open the jail's 'doors' (*E*, 396). This negative image of education returns when the evil ambassador EzRa captures a rebellious Host. Before torturing his captive, EzRa describes the prisoner's physiognomy in 'a lecture hall', 'like [...] an ancient lecturer, in some pre-diaspora centre of learning' (*E*, 329). Not all Embassytown '[s]chools' (*E*, 216) are bad and Avice says that her shiftparents are 'good people' (*E*, 16), but official institutions of learning nevertheless have a dark underside in this fictional world.

It is striking to note, however, that the novel also contains a unilaterally positive image of teachers in the figure of Avice. Despite her initially anti-academic profile, the impending doom of Embassytown forces Avice to consult Scile's 'books' (*E*, 331, 345) and to become a researcher and *teacher* of sorts. Because Avice is a simile, and a simile that can signify change as well as resignation, she is popular among the 'Professors', those Hosts who were nearly able to lie before EzRa's addictive speech turned the Ariekei into mindless zombies. With the help of rogue Ambassadors, she helps these lie-athletes to think new things in order to break the hold of EzRa's speech over the Ariekei, effectively turning herself into a teacher and the 'Professors' into 'students' (*E*, 340) or 'pupils' (*E*, 342), as she puts it. At the end of the novel, in other words, when the very fate of the planet is at stake, the Embassytown resistance's crucial mission is *a pedagogi-*

cal one: '[e]verything [...] depended on whether we could teach the Ariekei what we had to' (*E*, 358). After this small group of Ariekei finally acquires figurative, human language and casts off the unique but inflexible alien, non-conceptual Language, the individual pupils will have to continue this mission on a planetary scale, desperately trying to rescue their addicted compatriots from mindlessness and death. These developments explain why the concluding sections of *Embassytown* keep returning to the importance of education. Desperately trying to prevent a cataclysmic clash between the Embassytown resistance forces and the rebellious Ariekei, Avice 'kept up efforts to teach' (*E*, 350), we are informed. Her 'priority was to teach' (*E*, 359) and, when she relents at a certain point, a friend quickly admonishes her: '[y]ou should be teaching' (*E*, 354).

Avice, then, might productively be read as teaching her alien students to use metaphors and adopt a more creative language. In *Embassytown*, Miéville is thus presenting his reader with a correlated set of circumstances in which teaching – and specifically the teaching of new, creative modes of thinking and writing – is foregrounded. The festivals of lies, for instance, are represented as recognisably *literary* events: 'eisteddfods' (*E*, 96), which take place in an arena with 'theatrical seating' (*E*, 179). Meanwhile, Avice, we are informed, demonstrated *literary* talent at school, doing well in 'rhetoric and some performative elements of literature' (*E*, 30). Given the way in which Miéville consistently draws his reader's attention to such literary and pedagogical details, surely it is not a huge leap to conclude that Avice is in fact a teacher *of literature*, which can be understood metonymically as a practice of metaphor, or a 'lie that truths' (*E*, 395), on a larger scale. Instead of denouncing metaphors as evil, as Scile does, Avice sees them as creative instruments; after the Professors have learnt to use metaphors, there is 'slippage between word and referent, with which they could play' (*E*, 363), enabling 'unprecedented formulations' (*E*, 362). This flexible mindset enables the Ariekei to escape from their addiction to the uncreative speeches of EzRa, who, like a bad creative writing student, cannot stop talking about himself; even when his reign is over, '[h]e wanted to continue telling [Avice] about his life' (*E*, 236). Before Avice teaches them metaphors, the

Hosts crave these 'stories of [...] youth' (*E*, 222), with their obvious 'cliffhanger[s]' (*E*, 215) and stock phrases like '*I always felt different from the others around me*' (*E*, 215, emphasis in original) and '[w]*hen my father died I was sad but there was a freedom in it too*' (*E*, 228, emphasis in original). Here, the Anglo-American creative writing programme's dictum to 'write what you know' has run amok and the stock phrases of writing kits are recycled with fatal effects. The alternative, properly creative language is taught by Avice, in a manner reminiscent of a writing teacher; by asking her pupils to imagine variations on a set theme, in this case herself: '"What am I like? What is like me?" [...] I willed them to strive for poetry. Closed my eyes. They asserted similarities. I didn't let them stop. After quite a time their suggestions grew more interesting' (*E*, 341). This scene offers us an interesting allegory of what McGurl calls 'the workshop as a social form' (McGurl, 2009: 385), since Avice is teaching literary techniques to a group of Ariekei roughly the size of a writing seminar. The direct result of this workshop, additionally, is the proto-poetic description of Embassytown that features in the victory speech of Avice's brightest student: 'the city is a pit and a hill and a standard and an animal that hunts and a vessel on the sea and the sea and how we are fish in it' (*E*, 394). Via her creative teaching, Avice has not only *humanized* these aliens but has also transformed them into creative *writers*. If the latter conclusion seems too strong, consider that Avice's pupils develop a new writing system with startling 'ideograms' (*E*, 80), leading her to imagine a Host writer, 'pen' (*E*, 387) in alien 'hand'. This is not just her imagination, because at the novel's end her best pupil begins to write its account of 'the story of the war' (*E*, 403), much like a version of *Embassytown* from the alien point of view. The creative writing lesson, in other words, has reached its logical conclusion.

What is more, the educational theme continues until the novel's end and, presumably, beyond the end of the narrative's story-time. Having taught the Ariekei the human language of 'Anglo-Ubiq' (*E*, 403), Avice not only goes on to teach them 'French' (*E*, 402) but actually returns to the school herself; becoming 'a student' of the new dialect of 'Anglo-Ariekei' (*E*, 403) as well as learning the new alien script, 'like a young Ariekes' (*E*, 401). If the alien 'Professors' become 'pupils' in Avice's workshop, in other words, this human teacher finally also turns into a 'student'. Miéville's novel thus not only suggests that everyone is engaged in a learning process of some sort, but also that the positions of teacher and student are not always easy to distinguish. Avice further relinquishes her anti-academic stance by 'studying' (*E*, 405) official navigation techniques, no longer relying on her natural abilities but truly applying herself for the first time. Through her work as a teacher, it seems, she has become fully convinced of the value of education. *Embassytown* is therefore an ideal novel for school syllabi, effective, like *One Flew Over the Cuckoo's Nest*, to 'reel [...] unsuspecting "disaffected youth" back into the educational groove' (McGurl, 2009: 202).

Conclusion

As I have demonstrated, Miéville's putatively idiosyncratic novels have all the trappings of what McGurl has called 'programme fiction'. Even when the readers of these fantastic fictions embark on a journey to an alien planet such as Arieka, they are arguably being schooled in the art of creative writing. *Embassytown* is particularly instructive in this regard, as the reader hears the story of a teacher-like woman who teaches student-like aliens to practise creative forms of language so that they can use metaphors and write stories. On one level, these fictions might therefore be read as processing Miéville's extensive experiences as a student, a scholar and a teacher. Whatever their weird character and their critique of the university system, we can consider his fictions to be campus novels or weird campus novels, if you will. It might be fruitful therefore to analyse the academic component of Miéville's other writings in more detail (in texts such as *Kraken* and *The City & The City* particularly), examining the way in which academic institutions, as well as those extramural research environments defined in opposition to institutional norms and hierarchies, are a central preoccupation in Miéville's aesthetic universes. Furthermore, I think we should pay closer attention to the ways in which at a broader institutional and ideological level higher education informs even those contemporary texts whose content does not, at first glance, appear to be informed by creative writing programmes in the USA or UK. But these are subjects for another chapter. Because now, you see, like Avice and Miéville, I should really be teaching.

Notes

1 For a good discussion of space, hybridity and dialectics in Miéville's work, see Gordon (2003a). For Miéville's views on 'weird fiction', see his manifesto (2008). His thoughts on genre are discussed in the interview with Gordon (2003b) and in two essays where he complicates the distinction between science fiction and fantasy literature (Miéville, 2002, 2009). Although it does not discuss education or the academy in detail, Samuel Collins has an interesting essay on the connections between science fiction writers like Ursula Le Guin and anthropologists like Margaret Mead in the postwar period, pointing out facts like the existence of joint conferences and the use of science fiction novels in anthropology courses (Collins, 2003).

2 Miéville was for some years an associate professor in creative writing at the University of Warwick. He has also taught creative writing at other institutions, including Roosevelt University and the Clarion Workshop (Howle, 2002/2003: 1).

3 Although my further analysis will identify certain similarities between US and UK fiction, there are obviously important historical and institutional differences between the literatures and writing programmes of the UK and USA. Bould offers a relevant discussion of the position of British fantasy and science fiction, 'poised somewhere between the USA and Europe while trying to maintain indigenous identities and traditions' (Bould, 2003: 395). As far as the programme is concerned, creative writing was originally taught at polytechnics in England, which implies that it developed a large-scale presence much later than its US counterpart (Dawson, 2007: 82–3). Another difference is that the American system is geared towards the MFA degree, which concentrates on 'the production of original creative output', whereas English students usually acquire a more traditional, 'critical' MA (Harper, 2007: 348).

4 Praising McGurl for the fact that he sees university novels as 'a regular part' of postwar fiction, Jeffrey J. Williams (2012: 578, 579) has nevertheless argued that 'the profusion of the academic novel results less from the advent of MFAs than from an audience for whom higher education

is natural'. Williams correctly highlights what you might call the era of the student-reader, but this is compatible with McGurl's argument, in my view. Williams's distinction between student-centric 'campus novels' and professor-focused 'academic novels' strikes me as less important, furthermore, than the fact that the campus novel has infiltrated other novelistic subgenres, turning the academic experience into a central component of many contemporary novels, including those that do not at first appear to be university novels at all, like those by Miéville.

5 Miéville's response to my characterization of the books as campus novels reinforces this point. He mentioned his amused pleasure on hearing one academic characterize *The City & The City* as 'the best novel ever about writing a PhD'. Yet he continues as follows: 'I am not a trained teacher, certainly not of creative writing, and when I thought I would be an academic it was in International Law' (Miéville, private correspondence).

6 See the 'Teacher Notes', for instance (British Council, 2012).

Works Cited

Bould, Mark (2003) 'What Kind of Monster Are You? Situating the Boom', *Science Fiction Studies* 30(3): 394–416.

British Council (2012) 'King Rat – China Miéville. Teacher Support Worksheet', January 2012, URL (consulted 12 November 2012), http://www.teachingenglish.org.uk/sites/teacheng/files/King%20Rat%20teacher.pdf

Chatfield, Tom (2012) 'An Interview with China Miéville', *Boing Boing*, May 2012, URL (consulted 12 November 2012), http://boingboing.net/2012/05/31/an-interview-with-china-mievil.html

Collins, Samuel Gerald (2003) 'Sail on! Sail on! Anthropology, Science Fiction, and the Enticing Future', *Science Fiction Studies* 30(2) (2003): 180–98.

Dawson, Paul (2007) 'The Future of Creative Writing', in Steven Earnshaw (ed.) *The Handbook of Creative Writing*, pp. 78–89. Edinburgh: Edinburgh University Press.

Derbyshire, Jonathan (2012) 'China Miéville: The Books Interview', *New Statesman*, 4 June 2012, p. 47.

Eugenides, Jeffrey (2011) *The Marriage Plot*. London: Fourth Estate.

Gordon, Joan (2003a) 'Hybridity, Heterotopia, and Mateship in China Miéville's *Perdido Street Station*', *Science Fiction Studies* 30(3): 456–76.

Gordon, Joan (2003b) 'Reveling in Genre. An Interview with China Miéville', *Science Fiction Studies* 30(3): 355–73.

Guran, Paula (1999) 'China Miéville: Making His Name with a Darkly Brilliant Debut' in *DarkEcho/HorrorOnline*, October 1999, URL (consulted 12 November 2012), http://www.darkecho.com/darkecho/horroronline/mieville.html

Harper, Graeme (2007) 'Creative Writing Doctorates' in Steven Earnshaw (ed.) *The Handbook of Creative Writing*, pp. 345-52. Edinburgh: Edinburgh University Press.

Howle, Leslie (2002/2003) 'A Milestone Approaches' in *The Seventh Week: Clarion West Writers Workshop*, Winter Issue: 1-2.

McGurl, Mark (2009) *The Program Era. Postwar Fiction and the Rise of Creative Writing*. Cambridge, MA: Harvard University Press.

Miéville, China (2002) 'Marxism and Fantasy: Editorial Introduction', *Historical Materialism* 10(4): 39-49.

Miéville, China (2008) 'M. R. James and the Quantum Vampire: Weird; Hauntological: Versus and/or and and/or or?' in R. Mackay (ed.) *Collapse IV*, pp. 105-28. Falmouth: Urbanomic.

Miéville, China (2009) 'Afterword. Cognition as Ideology: A Dialectic of SF Theory in Mark Bould and China Miéville (eds) *Red Planets. Marxism and Science Fiction*, pp. 231-48. London: Pluto Press.

Miéville, China (2010a) 'Highway 61 Revisited', in James L. Sutter (ed.) *Before They Were Giants: First Works from Science Fiction Greats*, pp. 77-89. Redmont, WA: Paizo Publishing.

Miéville, China (2010b) 'In Disobedient Rooms', *The Nation*, 15 March 2010, URL (consulted 12 November 2012), http://www.thenation.com/article/disobedient-rooms#

Miéville, China (2012) 'The Future of the Novel', *Guardian*, August 2012, URL (consulted 12 November 2012), http://www.guardian.co.uk/books/2012/aug/21/china-mieville-the-future-of-the-novel

Morley, David (2007) *The Cambridge Introduction to Creative Writing*. Cambridge: Cambridge University Press.

Naimon, David (2011) 'A Conversation with China Miéville', *The Missouri Review* 34(4): 52-66.

Pearl, Nancy (2011) 'Book Lust with Nancy Pearl, featuring China Miéville', 1 July 2011, URL (consulted 12 November 2012), http://seattletimes.com/html/books/2015475443_booklust01.html

Slatter, Angela (2012) 'China Miéville in Da Lair', blog entry, 4 January 2012, URL (consulted 12 November 2012), http://www.angelaslatter.com/china-mieville-in-da-lair/

VanderMeer, Jeff (2012) 'China Miéville and Monsters: Unsatisfy me, frustrate me, I beg you', *Weird Fiction Review*, 20 March 2012, URL (consulted 12 November 2012), http://weirdfictionreview.com/2012/03/china-mieville-and-monsters-unsatisfy-me-frustrate-me-i-beg-you/

Williams, Jeffrey J. (2012) 'The Rise of the Academic Novel', *American Literary History* 24(3): 561–89.

8

Iron Council, Bas-Lag and Generic
Expectations

Matthew Sangster

When we read the first pages of a book, we do so possessed by a number of pre-existing expectations. Some of these expectations arise from paratexts apprehended before the business of reading begins. For any given book, these might include the picture on the cover, the colour of the cover, the font and prominence of the title and author's name, the publisher's imprint, the date of publication, a synopsis on the back and blurbs from writers and publications. This list is by no means exhaustive. Factors external to the book also shape expectations, including the opinions of reviewers and friends; knowledge of the author's biography and other works; and prior acquaintances with the genre or genres in which the book has been marketed or placed. The texts of books may uphold or undercut these conjured expectations, but the subversion of generic expectations carries the greater risk. A reader who buys a book liveried in the distinctive garb of the romance novel but who finds a techno-thriller inside will usually feel cheated. Such subversions can sometimes be employed for a purpose, inspiring unanticipated readerly responses through provocation. Were it to turn out that our hypothetical techno-thriller was critiquing the eroticization of technology, it might succeed in winning round some of its readers by making their initial qualms and confusion seem significant. However, readers are often powerfully invested in their expectations, and when books' realities fail to conform to these, disappointment can forestall both enjoyment and any productive critical questioning of the text.

In this chapter, I will be focusing on the manifestations of a specific set of expectations relating to the quintessential post-Tolkienian fantasy form: the trilogy. In particular, I will be examining the reception of *Iron Council* (2004), China Miéville's third novel set in the world of Bas-Lag, which follows on from his hugely successful *Perdido Street Station* (2000) and its sequel, *The Scar* (2002). While the Bas-Lag books in general – and *Iron Council* in particular – are resistant to many of the conventions of fantasy, including those of trilogies, they are generally acknowledged as existing within the fantasy genre. The first descriptor on Miéville's Wikipedia page is 'English fantasy fiction author'. His books are most commonly shelved in Fantasy and Science Fiction sections in bookshops and they are reviewed most frequently in genre periodicals and in genre-bounded sections in newspapers. His talents have been recognized through his receiving World Fantasy, Locus and Arthur C. Clarke awards, but he has not thus far been nominated for more self-consciously 'literary' prizes such as the Booker. While he has broken through to more diverse audiences than many authors of fantasy and science fiction, his works speak to, are grounded in, and are most highly valued by, genre commentators and communities. These contexts make them subject to patterns of reading which conform to expectations shaped by other fantastical works. As I will demonstrate, many readers have approached *Iron Council* expecting to find within it the culmination of patterns they have identified as being initiated in *Perdido Street Station* and developed in *The Scar*. However, *Iron Council* does not conform to these expectations and as a consequence it has left some admirers of Miéville's previous

Bas-Lag books cold. In a 2008 interview with Steve Haynes, Miéville acknowledged that it appeared to him that *Iron Council* was 'the most controversial, the least loved of those books' (Haynes, 2008). In what follows, I will explore the truth of this statement through considering quantitative and qualitative data on readers' responses to *Iron Council*, which I will contextualize by examining reactions to Miéville's other works and to a framework of comparable texts and series. Through this examination, I will contend that readers' negative reactions to *Iron Council* have often had less to do with its inherent narrative and aesthetic qualities and more to do with how those qualities fail to conform to their expectations of its author and genre. However, I will also argue that *Iron Council's* failure to conform comprises an intrinsic part of a deliberate narrative strategy of generic subversion and that its truculence is the source of some of its greatest strengths as a work of fiction.

Generic Subversion: The Critical Reception of *Iron Council*

In her 2004 review for the *Daily Telegraph*, Ruth Killick takes considerable pains in setting *Iron Council* up for her readers' approval. While admitting in her first line that '[f]antasy is often dismissed as formulaic genre fiction', she contends that 'the act of transporting readers into an alien world can be a powerful way of addressing big themes' (Killick, 2004). Killick presents *Iron Council* as a success according to this criterion, contending that Miéville 'uncovers new dimensions to such themes as justice, power, revolution, idealism, love and betrayal in his fiction'. Miéville is characterized as a universal thinker – 'a presenter on Radio 3's Nightwaves', no less. This positioning is noticeably different from the one employed in Andrew McKie's review (2002) of *The Scar* in the same publication, which opens, 'China Miéville doesn't let the improbable stand in the way of his ambition to reshape the world. This is, after all, a bloke who chose to stand for the Socialist Alliance in Kensington'. McKie's review places Miéville on the margins and describes his work as a 'triumphant reworking of fantasy', dwelling on its beasts and bizarreness. By contrast, Killick makes less genre-specific claims, describing *Iron Council* as asking 'tough questions' and making 'exhilarating demands on the imagination'. *Iron Council's* particular specificities and its status as a work of fantasy are asserted, but are carefully framed with arguments about its literary depth, formal complexity and wider social relevance that serve to commend it to Killick's readers. While Killick praised *Iron Council* as a work that transcended genre categories, other reviewers who similarly identified divergences were less positive about the book's departures from the conventions of its Bas-Lag predecessors. After delighting in detailing some of 'Miéville's signature tangential inventions', Steven Poole writes with a degree of disappointment in his *Guardian* review that 'in comparison with *The Scar*, such ideas are fewer and less indulgently elaborated' (Poole, 2004).

Poole and Killick were not the only readers to register the impact of *Iron Council's* generic deviations from the first two novels in the Bas-Lag trilogy. In a 2005 interview with Lou Anders, Miéville himself observed that:

> *Iron Council* has had the most profoundly contradictory response that any of my books have had [...] you have people saying, "This is Miéville's breakthrough book. He's moved to a different level." And then you've also had it described as "the crushing disappointment of 2004. Completely lost it." To the extent that I can generalize, the critical reception at the pro level has been quite, quite good; the critical reception at fan level has been troubled. (Anders, 2005)

The reactions Miéville describes here register the shared perception among the book's admirers and detractors that it represented a major change when compared with his previous works. In his 2008 interview with Haynes, Miéville responded directly to this perceived change in style and tone:

> I was aware of it being quite different, of it being more overtly political, and I was definitely aware of it being somewhat more demanding of the reader in terms of prose style [...] for *Iron Council* I wanted something more mediating between the reader and the writing, and asking a bit of an effort. (Haynes, 2008)

In this interview, *Iron Council* is characterized by Miéville as providing a consciously different experience than *Perdido Street Station* and *The Scar*, introducing overt and potentially divisive political material, using more complex prose and employing more involved narrative strategies. Perhaps unsurprisingly, these innovative generic divergences drew praise from many critics. The judges who awarded *Iron Council* the Arthur C. Clarke Award in 2005 selected it as 'the best science fiction novel first published in the United Kingdom during the previous year'.[1] The novel has also proved to be of particular interest to scholars; see, for example, Dougal McNeill's chapter in this collection (McNeill, 2015) and the numerous articles published in the speculative fiction journal *Extrapolation* by academics including Nicholas Birns (2009), Carl Freedman (2005), Christopher Palmer (2009) and Sandy Rankin (2009). Such professional readers, we might argue, have a vested interest in identifying and praising fictional works which challenge generic conventions and employ stylistic novelties. After all, their positions as expert arbiters of literary taste depend, to a large extent, on their ability to persuade others that the complexities of the literary works with which they are professionally concerned have value. For those readers without such authority claims in mind, though, generic continuities and repetitions often comprise a great part of the pleasure of reading – especially for readers who favour series, in which patterns are usually reiterated and developed rather than discarded or contradicted. For such readers, as I will show, the impressive nature of Miéville's generic deviations in *Iron Council* were of secondary importance to the fact that the novel had radically departed from the techniques and themes they had enjoyed in its admired predecessors.

Goodreads and Twenty-first-century Reader Responses

To demonstrate the impact of Miéville's critically acclaimed generic subversion in *Iron Council* upon his lay readership, I will draw on the unprecedentedly rich datasets of reader responses currently accumulating online. I will focus particularly on the social cataloguing site

Goodreads, which is, in the words of its own FAQ, 'the largest site for readers and book recommendations in the world', with, as of January 2013, a community of 'more than 13,000,000 members who have added more than 440,000,000 books to their shelves' (Goodreads, 2013).² To give a sense of its scale relative to the resources available to scholars studying literary reception in earlier centuries: the Open University's *Reading Experience Database* (*RED*) has between its launch in 1996 and January 2013 painstakingly assembled 'over 30,000 easily searchable records documenting the history of reading in Britain from 1450 to 1945' (*RED*, 2013). As of January 2013, Goodreads hosts more than two-and-a-half times that number of user reviews for Stephanie Meyer's best-selling young adult novel *Twilight* (2005) alone.

It is worth rehearsing here the ways in which Goodreads collates its vast cache of data. Goodreads allows its users to log their responses to books in three main ways. First, they can add books to their own personalized shelves, indicating that they have read them, that they intend to read them, or that they are interested in reading them in the future. Second, they can give star ratings to books that they have already read (or that they purport to have read – by its very nature, Goodreads is a space of social performance, with readers recording and advertising their tastes and adding to a collective body of opinion). The hover text that appears for the various star ratings suggests that one star should indicate that the reader 'didn't like' the book, two stars that 'it was ok', three stars that they 'liked it', four stars that they 'really liked it' and five stars that 'it was amazing' (Goodreads, 2013). While the extent to which the site's users follow these indications is impossible to gauge, it is important to note that these criteria invite readers to express subjective opinions – they do not ask for a judgement of a book's cultural value, but for an assessment of its affect. Third, users can add written reviews in order to give more considered and critical reactions. These reviews can range from a few disconnected words to long and complex analyses incorporating pictures and diagrams.

Conveniently for those seeking to use the site's quantitative data, Goodreads provides a 'rating details' tab on each book's page. This tab gives figures for the number of users who have added, rated and reviewed the book, provides a bar chart that shows the number of one-, two-, three-, four- and five-star ratings the book has received, and calculates an average star rating for each book (given to two decimal places). Theoretically, this average can be anything from one to five, but, as with most online reviewing communities, in practice a far smaller range is commonly employed – very few books with more than a handful of reviews have ratings lower than three or higher than four point five.[3]

Harvesting data from Goodreads' book pages allows for comparisons which can indicate the relative popularity of books and suggest the enthusiasm with which readers have responded to them. Obviously, this numerical data must be handled with care. Potential problems include the co-existence of diverse reading communities with different assessment criteria within the Goodreads user base and the issue of the site's age – Goodreads was launched in January 2007, so books published after that date could be reviewed by users in the initial flush of their popularity; this is reflected in a noticeably greater number of reviews relative to the numbers of logged ratings and 'adds' (the statistic Goodreads uses for counting the number of users who have added a given book to their own personalized shelves on the website). The site is also being continually modified and updated. To try and minimize the effects of such additions on my comparisons, all the data presented in this chapter was collected within a twenty-minute window on the 15 January 2013.[4]

The handful of fairly arbitrary choices given in Table 1 will serve to demonstrate the sorts of discrepancies that Goodreads' data can reveal. Among many other things, these examples make clear Goodreads' potential for showing the disparities in readerships between mass-market bestsellers, classics and more esoteric fare. Despite being published ten years after David Foster Wallace's *Infinite Jest* (1996), Stephanie Meyer's *Twilight* (2005) has been rated more than sixty-nine times more frequently by Goodreads users. The figures also suggest that readers at large ascribe substantially different values to books than those propagated within institutions of education, where Foster Wallace's works are commonly taught as undergraduate and

Table 1. Some Examples

Book	Adds	Ratings	Reviews	Average Rating
A Game of Thrones (George R.R. Martin)	492057	323204	20882	4.42
Infinite Jest (David Foster Wallace)	67718	20273	3361	4.33
To the Lighthouse (Virginia Woolf)	69010	38445	2031	3.72
Ulysses (James Joyce)	95773	38140	2596	3.72
Twilight (Stephanie Meyer)	1603302	1411022	76980	3.59

postgraduate texts, whilst Meyer's works are rarely lauded. Such differences in readerships' responses have often been posited, but empirical data from Goodreads gives us the means directly to access and evidence many previously elusive perspectives. James Joyce's *Ulysses* (1922) and Virginia Woolf's *To the Lighthouse* (1927) are commonly placed among the greatest novels of the twentieth century, but the table demonstrates that Goodreads' users have generally found George R. R. Martin's *A Game of Thrones* (1996) a great deal more enjoyable. This raises questions about the different criteria by which books are judged: referring to our earlier consideration of a book's production of affect, a researcher might choose to explore this area by seeking to find out if readers would rate the modernist classics higher were they asked how important or innovative they thought such texts were, rather than how much they'd enjoyed reading them. The data also raises questions about the ways in which readers engage, and persevere, with books. Only about 40% of those Goodreads users who have added *Ulysses* as a text that they are interested in reading have ended up rating it. This discrepancy between adds and ratings on the site is even more apparent in the case of Foster Wallace's *Infinite Jest*, which has only been rated by about 29% of the users who have added it. By contrast, Meyer's *Twilight* has been rated by around 88% of those who have it displayed on their virtual bookshelves. This significant discrepancy might be attributed to a number of different causes, including: the power of *Infinite Jest* to function as a status symbol on digital bookshelves, given its academic and critical acclaim; *Twilight*'s cultural notoriety, which has the effect of mandating that readers assert their own position with regards to its perceived quality or value; and the sheer length and complexity of *Infinite Jest*, which means that large numbers of readers may abandon it without feeling able to assess its worth. Such theories could, perhaps, be supported by using Goodreads' qualitative data (e.g. scanning the content of readers' reviews). It is not my business to conduct such an enquiry here, but I have briefly sketched it out in order to make the point that we must be careful and self-reflexive in constructing our interpretive approaches for the analysis of such data. The scale of Goodreads' data sets suggests that new kinds of questions can now be levelled at literary criticism in the twenty-first century, as the site serves to remove many of the logistical and financial obstacles previously inherent in conducting quantitative research. However, such data does not explain itself; instead, it requires informed interpretation to be of use. Unlike in previous decades of digital humanities scholarship, the problem is no longer one of data collection, but one of determining the nature of data, recognizing its limitations and determining its meanings.

Miéville's Reception on Goodreads

To return to our consideration of fantasy texts and the generic expectations of Miéville's readers: it is relatively easy to use Goodreads to gain a sense of the comparative popularity of the books in a given set. Table 2 provides the appropriate data for Miéville's books, sorted by number of ratings.

This table gives a clear indication of the relative readerships for each book from among the online community that constitutes Goodreads' self-selecting audience. As we can see, as of January 2013, *Perdido Street Station* was clearly the most frequently read of Miéville's novels, with *The City & The City* (2009) in second place, followed by *The Scar* and then by a fairly close grouping comprising *Kraken* (2010), *Un*

Table 2. Miéville's books: Sorted by number of Ratings

Book	Adds	Ratings	Reviews	Average Rating
Perdido Street Station (2000)	34006	18509	1904	3.95
The City & The City (2009)	22868	12631	2112	3.88
The Scar (2002)	16198	9863	706	4.15
Kraken (2010)	15058	7279	1388	3.57
Un Lun Dun (2007)	14199	7091	1001	3.79
Embassytown (2011)	14094	6408	1210	3.82
Iron Council (2004)	**8180**	**4791**	**374**	**3.66**
King Rat (1998)	5342	3130	260	3.50
Looking for Jake (2005)	4032	2036	152	3.80
Railsea (2012)	5997	1830	493	3.97

Lun Dun (2007) and Embassytown (2011). The position of Miéville's collection of short stories, Looking for Jake (2005), confirms the general difficulty of attracting audiences to short story collections. The position in this table of Miéville's then most recent novel, Railsea (2012), has likely changed since this data was collected, as at that time the paperback edition had yet to be released. The likelihood of its acquiring a larger readership can be inferred from the significantly higher ratio of adds to ratings when compared with Miéville's other books, indicating that many readers had marked it out for their attention as soon as it became available to buy in a cheaper form. If we were to present the data in an additional order according to the number of adds, Railsea would jump above Looking for Jake and King Rat, but otherwise the order would remain exactly the same. Significantly, Iron Council is fairly near the bottom of this table, while its two predecessors in the Bas-Lag trilogy are both in the top three.

Calculating the percentage of readers who have rated each book out of the available sample of those who have added it to their personalized Goodreads bookshelves gives the results shown in Table 3. For most of these books, this number is relatively close to fifty per cent. The glaring exception is *Railsea*; again, this is probably because only the hardback edition was available when this data was collected. It is also notable that the three other books with conversion rates of less than fifty per cent are Miéville's recent publications *Un Lun Dun*, *Kraken* and *Embassytown* (all of which were published after Goodreads was launched in January 2007). This would suggest that some of Goodreads' users work through quite long 'to-read' lists, but also that a significant number of them do so methodically, eventually reaching the books that they have marked out as interesting. The figures shown here for *The Scar* and *Iron Council* are relatively high, indicating that more readers who express an interest in reading the second two novels of the Bas-Lag trilogy go on to do so by comparison with Miéville's standalone works. I would like to read these figures as

Table 3. Miéville's books: Adds to Ratings

Book	Adds	Ratings	% of Adds to Ratings
The Scar (2002)	16198	9863	60.89
King Rat (1998)	5342	3130	58.59
Iron Council (2004)	**8180**	**4791**	**58.57**
The City & The City (2009)	22868	12631	55.23
Perdido Street Station (2000)	34006	18509	54.43
Looking for Jake (2005)	4032	2036	50.5
Un Lun Dun (2007)	14199	7091	49.94
Kraken (2010)	15058	7279	48.34
Embassytown (2011)	14094	6408	45.47
Railsea (2012)	5997	1830	30.52

indicative of the investment of Goodreads' readers in Miéville's Bas-Lag series, and to interpret the lower figures for *Perdido Street Station* as being in part caused by its position as the first novel in the series and by its role as a gateway into the world of Bas-Lag. However, readerly investment in an ongoing series will not serve to explain the high percentage of adds compared to ratings for *King Rat*, so other factors are doubtless also in play.

As Table 4 shows, the order of Miéville's books changes significantly if the data is sorted according to the number of reviews each has received. Perhaps unsurprisingly, the books published after the launch of Goodreads tend to have more reviews relative to their numbers of ratings than those published before the site was launched. *The City & The City*, *Kraken*, *Embassytown* and *Railsea* each have approximately one review for every five ratings, while the older books have one review for every ten or so. It is interesting, though, to compare *Perdido Street Station*, which has around 9.7 ratings for each review, with *The*

Table 4. Miéville's books: By number of Reviews

Book	Adds	Ratings	Reviews	Average Rating
The City & The City (2009)	22868	12631	2112	3.88
Perdido Street Station (2000)	34006	18509	1904	3.95
Kraken (2010)	15058	7279	1388	3.57
Embassytown (2011)	14094	6408	1210	3.82
Un Lun Dun (2007)	14199	7091	1001	3.79
The Scar (2002)	16198	9863	706	4.15
Railsea (2012)	5997	1830	493	3.97
Iron Council (2004)	**8180**	**4791**	**374**	**3.66**
King Rat (1998)	5342	3130	260	3.50
Looking for Jake (2005)	4032	2036	152	3.80

Table 5. Miéville's books: By Average Rating

Book	Adds	Ratings	Reviews	Average Rating
The Scar (2002)	16198	9863	706	4.15
Railsea (2012)	5997	1830	493	3.97
Perdido Street Station (2000)	34006	18509	1904	3.95
The City & The City (2009)	22868	12631	2112	3.88
Embassytown (2011)	14094	6408	1210	3.82
Looking for Jake (2005)	4032	2036	152	3.80
Un Lun Dun (2007)	14199	7091	1001	3.79
Iron Council (2004)	**8180**	**4791**	**374**	**3.66**
Kraken (2010)	15058	7279	1388	3.57
King Rat (1998)	5342	3130	260	3.50

Scar and *Iron Council*, which have around 13.9 ratings per review and 12.8 ratings per review respectively. As the tables later in this chapter demonstrate, readers of series commonly see the first volume as the most suitable location for analysis. The discrepancy between *Perdido Street Station* and its successors is in fact considerably less marked than for many other fantasy trilogies, indicating Miéville's success at differentiating the various perspectives that his books offer readers on the universe of Bas-Lag.

While *Iron Council* remains towards the bottom of Table 5, where the books are sorted by their average ratings, there is quite a lot of movement elsewhere. *Looking for Jake* leaps up the table, indicating that those who take a chance on the short story collection seem generally – and understandably – to enjoy it. At the very top of the table, though, is *The Scar*, with *Perdido Street Station* not far behind. The first two novels in the Bas-Lag trilogy thus provide an apparent benchmark for lay readers, representing two of Miéville's most suc-

Table 6. China Miéville's Bas-Lag books

Book	Adds	Ratings	Reviews	Average Rating
Perdido Street Station (2000)	34006	18509	1904	3.95
The Scar (2002)	16198	9863	706	4.15
Iron Council (2004)	8180	4791	374	3.66

cessful narratives. As in the other hierarchies we can discern in the Goodreads data, *Iron Council* can clearly be identified as less popular among the site's users, losing out to its predecessors in the trilogy.

If we remove the non-Bas-Lag books, as in Table 6, we can identify some fairly clear patterns within user adds, ratings and reviews. *Perdido Street Station* has around twice as many adds and ratings as *The Scar*, which in turn has almost twice as many as *Iron Council* does. There are also considerable discrepancies in the average ratings, which peak with *The Scar* before falling off for *Iron Council*. In isolation, it is difficult to interpret what these numbers might mean. However, Miéville's works do not exist in a vacuum on real or virtual bookshelves. Comparisons with other sequences will serve to provide some helpful indicators as to the reading habits which these numbers signify.

Situating the Bas-Lag Books

As I asserted at the beginning of this chapter, Miéville is most commonly identified as a writer of fantasies. To properly contextualize the Goodreads data on his works and to help to provide an explanation as to why *Iron Council* loses out to its predecessors, I will now examine four series of works which are commonly – although in some cases erroneously – perceived to be both fantasies and trilogies in order to determine the ways in which continuities and disjunctions within series and authorial oeuvres have been received by readers.

Table 7 gives Goodreads data for Robin Hobb's Farseer Trilogy (1995–7), a well-written and relatively conventional fantasy series. Hobb's trilogy tells the story of FitzChivalry Farseer, the bastard son of a prince who serves as an assassin in the household of his grandfather, the king. The kingdom faces both an external threat, in the form of Viking-like raiders who wield disturbing magics, and an internal threat – the King's third son, Regal, who is not content with his dynastic lot. The trilogy is stylistically and tonally consistent across its three volumes, following its first-person protagonist through a fairly grim *bildungsroman* narrative which peaks at the end of each book, but which reaches a fuller – though not terminal – conclusion at the end of the third. This is reflected in the fairly uniform average ratings given by Goodreads' reviewers, though it is notable that the first volume has the lowest rating by a whisker. Also notable are the fairly significant drop-offs in adds and ratings between the first volume and the second, and between the second volume and the third. This is a pattern repeated across all the series I have examined, and one which speaks to the importance of first volumes, which are seen as setting out series' rules and agendas. Readers overwhelmingly approach trilogies through their first volumes – if they do not enjoy the first book, they are unlikely to continue on to the later ones. It is clear from these figures, and from the fact that *Assassin's Apprentice* (1995) has the lion's share of the reviews, that it serves both as an entry point into a longer continuing narrative and as the point at which readers address and analyse that narrative. This is corroborated by a considerable number of its written reviews, which address the Farseer Trilogy as a holistic experience.[5] Similarly uniform ratings can be found for other trilo-

Table 7. Robin Hobb's Farseer Trilogy

Book	Adds	Ratings	Reviews	Average Rating
Assassin's Apprentice (1995)	58771	38410	1753	4.11
Royal Assassin (1996)	38193	30437	655	4.17
Assassin's Quest (1997)	28326	22505	679	4.16

Table 8. Jeff VanderMeer's Ambergris books

Book	Adds	Ratings	Reviews	Average Rating
City of Saints and Madmen (2001, 2002 and 2004)[7]	5157	1748	175	3.94
Shriek: An Afterword (2006)	1139	559	63	4.00
Finch (2009)	2312	965	158	3.98

gies within which styles and narrative strategies are consistent. For example, the ratings for the three books in Guy Gavriel Kay's Fionavar Tapestry slowly rise, but only from 4.01 to 4.16, and within any one of David Eddings' first four series (the Belgariad, the Malloreon, the Elenium and the Tamuli) the ratings differ by no more than 0.05. Within these relatively mainstream series, authorial consistency is seen as a merit, with ongoing plots carrying readers forward. As one Goodreads reviewer of Hobb's *Assassin's Quest* (1997) puts it, 'the big questions that have been hanging since Book 1 and 2 push the reader to just. Keep. Reading. More.'[6]

Jeff VanderMeer's stylistically complex Ambergris books – which give the history of the eponymous city and its inhabitants through pastiches, metanarratives, hallucinations, codes and cephalopods – are far more heterogeneous than a conventional series like Hobb's. Nevertheless, the average ratings given by Goodreads' users are approximately the same, as Table 8 shows. There are, however, large discrepancies in the other figures. *Shriek* (2006), the middle book in the sequence, only attracts about a quarter of the adds and a third of the ratings of its predecessor, while *Finch* (2009), the third book, has figures that are around double those of *Shriek*.

The experimental nature of the sequence as a whole is telegraphed pretty clearly by *City of Saints and Madmen* (2001), a collection of interconnected and often hallucinatory accounts of fungus-haunted Ambergris, including a story of love and a dangerous festival, a partial history of the city, a world-shift narrative and a memoir by a transforming squidologist. Of the three books, *Shriek* is the one that makes the most sustained use of a complex stylistic device. The book presents an account by Janice Shriek of the life of her brother, Duncan Shriek, the author of the early history of Ambergris included in *City of Saints and Madmen*, who has subsequently vanished. However, Janice's account is regularly interrupted, modified and contradicted by Duncan's later annotations. By contrast, *Finch* employs a more straightforward narrative voice inspired by noir thrillers.

The specificities of each book in VanderMeer's Ambergris sequence mean that as a series they deliberately shuck off many of the implications of the trilogy format. While *Shriek* is seemingly more imposing than the other two books, each has succeeded in attracting readers who are attuned to its merits. After the kaleidoscope of perspectives used in *City of Saints and Madmen*, readers who continue with the series are well prepared for the complex chronologies and voices that inhabit the subsequent two books. It is possible, though, as the rise in readers for *Finch* suggests, for the books to be enjoyed independently of one another – while the three books together offer solutions to a whole range of questions about Ambergris, knowledge of the earlier books is not absolutely presupposed by the later ones. The strange distinctiveness of each individual book therefore precludes their being read as operating within the rules of conventional trilogies, which build up through the use of a relatively uniform and consistent narrative voice (or set of voices) over the course of three books. That the Ambergris books are considered independently by readers is indicated by the high numbers of reviews for *Shriek* and *Finch*. Proportionally, there is no drop-off here, and no sense that the series as a whole can be addressed through any one of its parts.

Table 9. Neal Stephenson's Baroque Cycle

Book	Adds	Ratings	Reviews	Average Rating
Quicksilver (2003)	25061	15246	1116	3.87
The Confusion (2004)	14291	9365	387	4.18
The System of the World (2004)	13327	8434	346	4.25

Neal Stephenson's sprawling Baroque Cycle (2003–4) comprises a sequence of intertwined picaresque narratives set in late seventeenth- and early eighteenth-century Europe. These narratives offer pirates, slavery, wars, exploration, economics, politics and derring-do, but focus most powerfully on alchemy, natural philosophy and their clashing perspectives on the world. For this sequence, Goodreads' data records a significant drop-off in readers between the first and the second volumes, but not a particularly large difference between the readerships for the second and the third. Also apparent is a significant discrepancy between the average rating for *Quicksilver* (2003) and those for its two successors. I would read this as indicating that a relatively large number of readers found the distinctive style rehearsed in Stephenson's first volume off-putting. *Quicksilver's* one-star reviews seem to support this theory, opining that the book is 'bloated with details', 'completely plotless' and 'written in the present tense, which is jarring to read'.[8] Hobb and VanderMeer were both relatively unknown when they published the first books in the series discussed above (although Hobb had previously published a number of works under another pseudonym Megan Lindholm). Stephenson, by contrast, was established as an author of science fiction whose works were generally written in clean prose and set in relatively contemporary environments, whether the near future of *Snow Crash* (1992), the neo-Victorian world of *The Diamond Age* (1995) or the slightly deformed twentieth century of *Cryptonomicon* (1999). The Baroque Cycle thus represented a significant departure from Stephenson's earlier narrative style, which evidently left a number of his existing readers nonplussed. However, the drop in readers and the rise in average ratings for the later volumes both serve to indicate that these stylistically-affronted readers generally choose not to continue reading the series beyond *Quicksilver*. While Stephenson's faux-seventeenth-century grammar and spellings and his dense and allusive narration are potentially intimidating, it seems that those readers who persevered were able to master the sequence's particularities and idiosyncrasies and found that their initial efforts continued to pay dividends as they proceeded. While the series was a departure from Stephenson's previous work, its later volumes did not depart a great distance from the

Table 10. Mervyn Peake's Titus books

Book	Adds	Ratings	Reviews	Average Rating
Titus Groan (1946)	9641	4401	384	3.89
Gormenghast (1950)	7059	4248	136	3.92
Titus Alone (1959)	2714	1470	82	3.39
The Gormenghast Novels (compiled and collected editions)	8090	3507	346	4.00

patterns which its first volume established, and its readers navigated these patterns with increasing pleasure.

The ratings for Mervyn Peake's Titus books (1946–1959) provide a clear example of readerly discontent in response to a later book in a sequence making a significant shift away from the style established in earlier volumes (Table 10). There is only a very small drop-off in ratings between the first and the second book, indicating that most people read on. A more significant drop-off in the number of reviews between the two displays the pattern you would expect from a series with established conventions. Both of these drops are probably slighter than they appear, as the sequence is commonly read in various collected editions – the amalgamated numbers for these are given at the bottom of the table. As with many of the other trilogies I have examined, the individual rating for *Gormenghast* (1950) shows a slight increase from Peake's 1946 novel *Titus Groan*, as the readers put off by the first book refuse to continue on to the second. What is really striking, though, is the enormous drop in adds, ratings, and reviews from *Gormenghast* to *Titus Alone* (1959), and the even more significant drop in average rating.

Titus Alone is a very different beast to the two previous books, stripping back much of the richness and slow sinuousness that characterizes Peake's narrations within the many-halled castle of Gormenghast and instead employing brevity and disjunctions to create a hallucinatory and destabilizing cityscape. For many readers, this shift can only be explained pathologically. A number of Goodreads reviews attribute *Titus Alone*'s style to Peake's having suffered from Parkinson's Disease during the book's composition, seeing it as a pale substitute: 'a monument to what might have been had not illness intervened.'[9] The book's drafts do not bear out this conclusion – the Beckettian dialogue scenes that Peake sketched in his notebooks indicate that he was quite consciously searching for a new style to represent both his modernist, nightmarish city and Titus's condition within it.[10] Coming after two books with which it strikes such a marked contrast, though, *Titus Alone* is often read as aberrant, its readers considering the novel as being, in the words of one review, 'not really one of the *Gormenghast* novels'.[11] However, it is interesting that the most 'liked' review of *Titus Alone* on Goodreads is a highly allusive exploration of the ways that the book 'completes Peake's philosophical and literary journey as well as we could wish', contending that the book 'ends with beauty, with questions, with verve, and with a wink.'[12] Even though many reject *Titus Alone*, others admire it for the same differences and divergences that the novel's naysayers decry, and the space Goodreads provides allows for both reactions to be shared, analysed and responded to in turn.

Return to Bas-Lag

Bringing together the responses to these four three-book sequences (Robin Hobb's Farseer trilogy, Jeff VanderMeer's Ambergris books, Neal Stephenson's Baroque Cycle and Mervyn Peake's Titus books) can help to suggest some explanations for the patterns we have considered in the Goodreads ratings, adds and reviews for the Bas-Lag books (repeated in Table 11 for convenience).

Table 11. China Miéville's Bas-Lag books

Book	Adds	Ratings	Reviews	Average Rating
Perdido Street Station (2000)	34006	18509	1904	3.95
The Scar (2002)	16198	9863	706	4.15
Iron Council (2004)	8180	4791	374	3.66

Perdido Street Station serves as a relatively challenging entry point to the series, one which, like Stephenson's *Quicksilver*, puts off a number of Goodreads readers but which inspires others to continue reading Miéville's subsequent Bas-Log novels. Those readers who do continue feel rewarded by *The Scar* and are impressed by the ways in which that novel, as one reader puts it, 'expands on the world and the mythology originally set forth in *Perdido Street Station*'.[13] The numbers for *The Scar* indicate that it is being read more like a novel situated within a conventional series (such as Hobb's Farseer trilogy), than a novel from an experimental series (such as VanderMeer's Ambergris books). Most of the longer user reviews consider its narrative strategies exclusively in relation to those of its predecessor, *Perdido Street Station*, often characterizing it as being 'a smoother reading experience', although this may be because, as one reader notes, 'Once you get the hang of [Miéville's] writing style and become more accustomed to Bas-Lag, he is much easier to read.'[14] While reviewers are keen to draw thematic contrasts between the two books, such contrasts generally depict them as two sides of the same coin rather than as fundamentally opposed or stylistically discrete texts that happen to explore the same narrative world.

For many readers, the perceived consonances between *Perdido Street Station* and *The Scar* establish a set of conventions necessary to a novel in the Bas-Lag series. Having internalized these conventions, many readers approach the series' final instalment, *Iron Council*, with a clear set of criteria by which it will succeed for them, drawn from their enjoyment of, and admiration for, Miéville's two previous novels. Like Peake's *Titus Alone*, this puts the self-consciously experimental *Iron Council* in an awkward position. It can never match up to its Bas-Lag predecessors if the standard by which it is to be judged is a standard for which they are the best exemplars. The success of the two previous novels and the devotion they inspire thus militates against readers easily enjoying *Iron Council*'s stylistic differences. One reviewer writes that '*Iron Council* gives us the world, and it is too much. Miéville offers too many places in his third book, and he never lets us know one place with anything close to the depth or intimacy we come to know New Crobuzon and Armada.'[15] Similar responses are offered by readers who complain that the book, unlike Miéville's previous two in the Bas-Lag series, 'flip flop[s] between revolting factions' and who bemoan the lack of a clear central character to occupy, however awkwardly, the role of protagonist. One reader writes that, 'Unlike Isaac or Bellis, I never really connected with or identified with Cutter, Ori [or] Ann Hari'.[16] By failing to provide the stylistic continuities which they expect, *Iron Council* falls short for such readers. It does not meet their generic expectations, either as the final volume of a trilogy or as tale about Bas-Lag.

Iron Council, then, is a book that many readers approach with a highly-developed set of reading contexts in mind. It is not just a fantasy novel, or a western, or even what we might call 'a China Miéville novel', but specifically a Bas-Lag book: the sequel to two previous novels through which readers have traced particular conventions of style and plot which constrain their desires regarding its content. Ironically, having enjoyed the subversions in the previous two books can make readers less open to the rather different subversions offered by *Iron Council*, which, as a novel, fails to settle into a comfortable pattern but instead radically expands the possibilities of the world of Bas-Lag.

I would contend, though, that the disappointment some readers feel on reading *Iron Council* is in fact a good starting point for thinking about what the book does. While the book's general reception on Goodreads is more negative than those of the other two Bas-Lag books, the site does feature a number of very positive reviews, many of which ascribe their enjoyment to the same differences that put other readers off. Perhaps the best concise expression of this is given by the reader who calls it 'my favorite of Miéville's anti-trilogy'.[17] As Miéville contended in his interview with Haynes (2008), *Iron Council* is a self-consciously political book, and this extends from its subject matter to its narrative logic, which resists the easy and satisfying formulas which third books in standard trilogies employ and instead offers a more painful, provoking and realistically disappointing conclusion. The most developed positive responses on Goodreads take time to think through and appreciate *Iron Council's* differences and difficulties, considering why Miéville ends with a resolution suspended in stasis rather than one with all its potentialities rolled out. The following passages give a couple of thoughtful and engaged examples, clipped from longer reviews:

> I loved this book. It was not the insta-love like it was with "The Scar" but a long, careful, slow-to-build-up affair that by the end of the story fully blossomed. **This book is fascinating, passionate, brutal at times, thought-provoking and deliberately anger-inducing.** But at the same time, it's like Miéville deliberately made it not as easy to love as his other works.[18] (emphasis in original)
>
> It jumbles in places, it tosses about; it's not always a pleasant read, or an easy one. It's tougher, more political, more insistant [sic]. But it's so *good*. So rewarding. And even the end, that fat and unnatural anticlimactic-climax, that so-wrong final meeting of the Council and the City, even as you want to yell "that is *not* how it should have happened!" you cannot help but think "Yes, yes, *that* is how it was, how it is, how it should be."[19] (emphasis in original)

For these readers, the ways that Miéville deviates from the stylistic forms of his earlier Bas-Lag novels and subverts the shining climaxes of conventional trilogies serve aesthetic and ideological purposes. By presenting two seemingly viable alternatives to New Crobuzon's despotic government and depicting that government as far more vulnerable than in the previous two books, *Iron Council* deliberately raises a guilty hope in the reader that perhaps the pattern of the standard trilogy might play out, the book ending with the defeat of oppressive power. As the two responses demonstrate, the snatching-away of this hope is not a comfortable experience; it is, in fact, close to the opposite of the way that readers of trilogies are used to feeling when they finish a series. This is exacerbated by the fact that while *Perdido Street Station* and *The Scar* end with victories of sorts for the populaces of New Crobuzon and Armada respectively (even at the costs of large numbers of personal tragedies), *Iron Council* ends with abeyance, failure and only the smallest flicker of hope. The perpetual train is frozen in time, betrayed, in some senses, by one of its own. The regime it sought to overthrow remains in place. By the book's final paragraph, the train's potential has become narrative: 'we will tell the story of the

Iron Council and how it was made, how it made itself and went, and how it came back, and is coming, is still coming' (*IC*, 564). A story in which the train definitively changes the world, though, remains untold.

This downbeat conclusion functions as a provocation to think about the natures of power and genre. It is only through disappointing its readers that *Iron Council* can add to, deepen and reinflect the readerly experience of the previous two books in the Bas-Lag trilogy, rather than simply piling up more of the same. Its contrasts challenge its readers to question precisely why its divergences are both necessary and revealing. Just as Iron Council, the perpetual train, serves as an enduring challenge to the existing order of New Crobuzon, so the positioning of *Iron Council* at the end of the trilogy offers an enduring challenge to the readers approaching the Bas-Lag books as a reiterative generic sequence, calling on them to reconsider the nature of the world which they are experiencing, contemplate the realities of revolutionary action and awaken to the possibilities offered by confounding generic expectations.

Notes

1 From the description of the award on its website. URL (consulted September 2013): http://www.clarkeaward.com/the-arthur-c-clarke-award/what-is-the-arthur-c-clarke-award/

2 URL (consulted January 2013): http://www.goodreads.com/about/us. By September 2013, those numbers had grown to twenty million readers and five hundred and seventy million books added.

3 A good comparison would be the cumulative review scores published on the various Amazon sites, which tend to occupy the 3.5–4.5 range for books reviewed ten or more times.

4 I will not give detailed URLs for the pages from which the numerical data cited in the rest of this article is drawn, as the figures will inevitably have changed and as the page for any particular book can be easily located using Goodreads' own search function. I will, however, give links for the user reviews I refer to in these notes. Each review has a unique identifier which allows for easy reference.

5 URLs (consulted January 2013): http://www.goodreads.com/review/show/51014823; http://www.goodreads.com/review/show/1559383; http://www.goodreads.com/review/show/43853218

6 URL (consulted January 2013): http://www.goodreads.com/review/show/20050093

7 The publication history of *City of Saints and Madmen* is complex – it was first published in 2001 by Cosmos Books in the US, then republished in an expanded version by Prime Books in 2002 and expanded again for Tor Books' 2004 UK edition. Goodreads collates all these editions despite the considerable differences between them.

8 URLs (consulted January 2013): http://www.goodreads.com/review/show/28988965; http://www.goodreads.com/review/show/49455837; http://www.goodreads.com/review/show/57377912

9 URL (consulted January 2013): http://www.goodreads.com/review/show/432603404

10 See, for example, the sections written as playscripts in British Library Additional Manuscript 88931/1/3/24. Peake's illustrated manuscript notebooks are now fully catalogued and available for use by researchers.

11 URL (consulted January 2013): http://www.goodreads.com/review/show/106451856

12 URL (consulted January 2013): http://www.goodreads.com/review/show/46276484

13 URL (consulted January 2013): http://www.goodreads.com/review/show/304728929

14 URLs (consulted January 2013): http://www.goodreads.com/review/show/101948499; http://www.goodreads.com/review/show/72872878

15 URL (consulted January 2013): http://www.goodreads.com/review/show/18620369

16 URLs (consulted January 2013): http://www.goodreads.com/review/show/89779379; http://www.goodreads.com/review/show/24646301.

17 URL (consulted January 2013): http://www.goodreads.com/review/show/3914978

18 URL (consulted January 2013): http://www.goodreads.com/review/show/324964138

19 URL (consulted January 2013): http://www.goodreads.com/review/show/27088743

Works Cited

Anders, Lou (2005) 'China Miéville', *The Believer*, Spring 2005, URL (consulted September 2014), http://www.believermag.com/issues/200504/?read=interview_mieville

Birns, Nicholas (2009) 'From Cacotopias to Railroads: Rebellion and the Shaping of the Normal in the Bas-Lag Universe', *Extrapolation* 50(2): 200–11.

Freedman, Carl (2005) 'To the Perdido Street Station: The Representation of Revolution in China Miéville's *Iron Council*', *Extrapolation* 46(2): 235–48.

Goodreads, URL (consulted January 2013), http://www.goodreads.com/

Haynes, Steve (2008) 'Serious Fantastication: acclaimed novelist China Miéville in interview with Steve Haynes', *Horizon Review*, 1(1), URL (consulted January 2013), http://www.saltpublishing.com/horizon/issues/01/text/Miéville_china02.htm/

Hobb, Robin (1995) *Assassin's Apprentice*. London: Voyager.

Hobb, Robin (1996) *Royal Assassin*. London: Voyager.

Hobb, Robin (1997) *Assassin's Quest*. London: Voyager.

Joyce, James (1922) *Ulysses*. Paris: Sylvia Beach.

Killick, Ruth (2004) 'A Perpetual Train Journey', *Daily Telegraph*, 9 November, URL (consulted September 2014), http://www.telegraph.co.uk/culture/books/3626771/A-perpetual-train-journey.html

McKie, Andrew (2002) 'Artist of a Floating World', *Sunday Telegraph*, 12 May, URL (consulted September 2014), http://www.telegraph.co.uk/culture/books/3577305/Artist-of-a-floating-world.html

McNeill, Dougal (2015) 'Failing Better: Iron Council, Benjamin, Revolution', in Caroline Edwards and Antonio Venezia (eds) *China Miéville: Critical Essays*, pp. 97–126. Canterbury: Gylphi.

Martin, George R. R. (1996) *A Game of Thrones*. London: Voyager/HarperCollins.

Meyer, Stephanie (2005) *Twilight*. London and New York: Little, Brown.

Palmer, Christopher (2009) 'Saving the City in China Miéville's Bas-Lag Novels', *Extrapolation* 50(2): 224–38.

Peake, Mervyn (1999) *The Gormenghast Trilogy*. London: Vintage.

Poole, Steven (2004) 'Blood on the tracks', *Guardian*, 25 September, URL (consulted September 2014), http://www.theguardian.com/books/2004/sep/25/featuresreviews.guardianreview16

Rankin, Sandy (2009) 'AGASH AGASP AGAPE: The Weaver as Immanent Utopian Impulse in China Miéville's *Perdido Street Station* and *Iron Council*', *Extrapolation* 50(2): 239–57.

Reading Experience Database (RED), URL (consulted January 2013), http://www.open.ac.uk/Arts/RED/

Stephenson, Neal (2003) *Quicksilver*. London: William Heinemann.

Stephenson, Neal (2004) *The Confusion*. London: William Heinemann.

Stephenson, Neal (2004) *The System of the World*. London: William Heinemann.

VanderMeer, Jeff (2002) *City of Saints and Madmen*. Rockville, MD: Prime.

VanderMeer, Jeff (2006) *Shriek: An Afterword*. London: Macmillan.

VanderMeer, Jeff (2009) *Finch*. Portland, OR: Underland.

Wallace, David Foster (1996) *Infinite Jest*. New York and London: Little, Brown.

Woolf, Virginia (1927) *To the Lighthouse*. London: Hogarth Press.

9

BETWEEN
INTERNATIONAL LAW IN *THE CITY & THE CITY* AND *EMBASSYTOWN*

Anthony F. Lang, Jr.

International law can be understood in a wide variety of ways. One useful binary can be borrowed from the title of a famous work by Martti Koskenniemi, *From Apology to Utopia* (1989/2005). The term 'apology' refers to the era when international law formally emerged, roughly the late eighteenth and early nineteenth centuries. It embodies the idea that international law is a structure designed to reflect the interests and practices of states and, as a result, reinforces the power dynamics of the state system in which great powers can structure the international system in ways they see fit (Goldsmith and Posner, 2005). Utopia, on the other hand, reflects the ideas of liberal international lawyers and actors in the early twentieth century who saw in international law the potential to resolve conflict and create a more peaceful international order. This utopian tradition continues to this day in the way that human rights and international humanitarian law seek to create more a more peaceful and just international order (Casesse, 2012; Teitel, 2011).

These traditions of international law reflect different normative visions; the first reinforcing the value of order governed by powerful states and the second reflecting the ideal of justice found in demands for equal representation in the global political community. Both reflect an underlying normative idea of peace, of a sort, in that they allow for war but seek to moderate and structure it according to rules. It is somewhere between these two ideal types, however, that most international law functions. For instance, 'apology' exists in the current international order as a presumption in favour of the great powers or power structures, perhaps most clearly reflected in the United Nations Security Council (UNSC) but also in weighted voting in the European Union (EU) and in a variety of other international structures. The International Court of Justice, the only international 'supreme court' allows only states as parties before the Court and tends to reinforce the privileges of states and their representatives over the concerns of other actors in the international order, such as individual persons or NGOs.

At the same time, there is a strong utopian element in international law and its practices. Since the end of World War II and decolonization movements around the world, previously colonial subjects were able to move toward self-determination and increase their power. At the level of individuals, the appearance of the International Criminal Court in 2002 provides a context in which individuals whose rights have been violated can find an institutional framework through which they can seek to have their rights protected.[1] And, increasing NGO activity surrounding issues of human rights and other progressive causes has made an impact on broader international legal and political practices.

Between apology and utopia, then, is where international law resides. What happens in this space between these normative visions? How does international law actually work? What purpose does it serve in the current international order? In this chapter, I explore this space between apology and utopia. I do so not in the traditional manner, however, but through fiction, specifically the fiction of China Miéville. Miéville is an obvious choice for such a venture in that he is a scholar of international law as well as an accomplished novelist. In fact, his scholarly monograph on international law (2005) draws on Karl Marx's famous phrase about law, 'between equal rights, force decides' (Marx, 1867/1978: 364). Miéville's work on international law develops a Marxist critique of the legal form, drawing on the Soviet era international legal theorist, Evgeny B. Pashukanis (1929). Rather than this more technical work, however, this chapter will use two of Miéville's novels to explore the role of international law: *The City & The City* (2009) and *Embassytown* (2011). The novels provide a window into the two poles of international law identified above, although neither reflects a single normative vision in the way I have described them. Instead, the novels reveal how the two normative visions can be perverted and result in more violence and greater injustice rather than peace and equality in the global realm.

In *The City & The City*, the law allows two communities to relate to each other through protocols and rules that do not arise from a legislature but from practices and customs that have emerged through time – in the same way that international law has emerged through custom and the practice of states. As with international law, the resilience of the law in this novel allows the story to 'work', as the narrator on the final page notes that he wishes 'to maintain the skin that holds the law in place' (CC, 373). *Embassytown*, in contrast, also relies upon legal codes and protocols, but ones that have arisen from an imperial context. This context relies on knowledge and language, which when overturned, leads to the breakdown of the law and revolutionary violence. This novel demonstrates the fragility of international law precisely because it is constituted by this imperial context. The chapter uses Miéville's novels to explore the role of law in these 'between' spaces and probes the tensions to which international law is subject in the current international order. Specifically, it argues that law in *The City & The City* is what international law ought to do in international affairs, but *Embassytown* reflects how international law cannot escape its imperial past, a past which exposes its fragility in the modern world.

The purpose of this chapter is to use Miéville's oeuvre to uncover something about international law. Rather than simply impose an interpretative framework of Marxism or Marxist legal theory onto his fiction, I instead seek to put his international legal theory and fiction into conversation with each other. In so doing, I argue that his theoretical argument can be supplemented from the narratives of how law 'works' in the two novels. The point is not to 'trap' Miéville in a contradiction between his fiction and non-fiction writing; rather, it is to find in the fictional material a critical perspective on his international legal theory. It is precisely the fecundity in both his fiction and non-fiction that allows this kind of analysis.

In order to undertake this project, the chapter begins with a brief overview of Miéville's legal theory, which also puts into context his ideas about Marxism and international law. The following two sections explore the two novels under consideration, making links to his theoretical framework. The conclusion seeks to draw together the novels in order to think about the space 'between' apology and utopia, and create a critical dialogue with his non-fiction writing on international legal theory.

International Law from the Left

Miéville's work on international law derives from his theoretical engagement with the Soviet era legal theorist Evgeny Pashukanis. Pashukanis's most well-known book is *Law and Marxism: A General Theory* (1929) in which he argues that the very form of law can only be understood as a form of commodity exchange between subjects. Instead of the law being a species of norms (Kelsen, 1946) or rules (Hart, 1994), Pashukanis argues that law is a particular form of social relations, one in which legal subjects only come into existence as a result of their need to regulate their use of commodities. The legal form can be reduced to a contract, one in which conflicting private interests are somehow regulated:

> The legal subject is thus an abstract owner of commodities raised to the heavens. His will in the legal sense has its real basis in the desire

to alienate through acquisition and to profit through alienating. For this desire to be fulfilled, it is absolutely essential that the wishes of commodity owners meet each other halfway. This relationship is expressed in legal terms as a contract or an agreement concluded between autonomous wills. Hence, the contract is a concept central to law. To put it in a more high-flown way: the contract is an integral part of the idea of law. (Pashukanis, 1929/1978: 121)

Because his focus is on the form of the law, and the way in which the law mirrors the capitalist process of commodification of all it touches, Pashukanis did not subscribe to the dominant Soviet legal theory which saw law solely as a tool of the bourgeois state, one that could be altered when the proletariat took over the state. Instead, Pashukanis believed that not only the state would wither away but the legal form as well (Pashukanis, 1929/1978: 63).

Pashukanis was a legal theorist not an international legal theorist. He did write a few pieces on international law, though, one of which Miéville reproduces as an appendix in his own work on international law. In that article, a contribution to a Soviet encyclopaedia of law, Pashukanis extends his account of the legal form by exploring how relations between states at the international level mirror the relations between individuals at the domestic level. To make this point, he targets one of the 'fathers' of international law, the seventeenth-century Dutch theorist Hugo Grotius: '[Grotius's] whole system depends on the fact that he considers relations between states to be relations between owners of private property; he declares that the necessary conditions for the execution of exchange, i.e., equivalent exchange between private owners, are the conditions of legal interactions of states' (Pashukanis, 1927/2006: 329). This results in an international legal theory which, like his general legal theory, reduces law to the contractual relations among legal subjects – here states – in which social disagreements about commodity exchange are regulated.

Miéville offers one of the most thorough and sustained uses of Pashukanis's work to provide a wide ranging critique of international law, one that ends with the provocative sentence: 'The chaotic and bloody world around us is the rule of law' (Miéville, 2006: 319). Miéville sets out his understanding of international law in relation to the Critical Legal Studies (CLS) movement, an effort by a range of scholars from different theoretical traditions who have sought to challenge the dominant positivist and, for most of these critics, imperialist idea of international law. Miéville describes himself as a fellow traveller with these movements, though he astutely notes that 'The coagulation of these [strands of CLS] into an often rather nebulous "critical theory" can obscure the real philosophical differences between various of these strands, and lead to a sometimes internally contradictory body of thought' (Miéville, 2008: 93). Instead, Miéville draws directly on the theoretical framing of Pashukanis and, in so doing, provides a more precise and more thorough going critique of international law. Rather than rely just on Pashukanis's limited writings on international law, Miéville explores in more detail the nature of the international order as an instance of the kind of contractual based relations that the former finds in domestic social life.

Miéville locates Pashukanis in the 'capital logic' theory of Marxism which stresses that the state itself results from the nature of commodity relations under capitalism. While Pashukanis is writing about law, the centrality of the sovereign state for both domestic and international legal theory reinforces his relevance for international law; just as the individual person comes into existence as a legal subject as a result of his/her contractual relations with other subjects in the pursuit of commodity exchanges, so too does the sovereign state as an international legal subject only come into existence as a result of its interactions with other states in pursuit of its form of commodity exchange.

While indebted to the Marxist theorist for setting out his framework, Miéville diverges from Pashukanis on a central point. Pashukanis argued that while coercion exists, it is inimical to the commodity exchange that creates the contracts from which law derives. Miéville disagrees:

> I have argued that contrary to some of Pashukanis's claims, disputation and contestation is intrinsic to the commodity, in the fact that its private ownership implies the exclusion of others. Similarly, violence – coercion – is at the heart of the commodity form, and thus the con-

tract. For a contract to be 'mine-not-yours' – which is, after all, central to the fact that it is a commodity to be exchanged – some forceful capabilities are implied. (Miéville, 2006: 126)

Miéville continues with this crucial addition to Pashukanis's thought and links it directly to the international legal form. Unlike in the domestic context where the state removes the actual use of violence (though it may remain in the background), in international law and international relations violence and coercion become the central way in which the contract and commodity exchange are enacted.

This conclusion stands counter to the narratives of international law which posits it as a means to create more peaceful interactions among states. Indeed, the origins of positivist international law in the late 19th century were part of an effort to replace the rule of force with the rule of law. But Miéville's reading of international law undermines this narrative, proposing a form of law that is inherently violent. Even more importantly, Miéville argues that rather than searching for an authority structure by which a positivist theory can ensure that international law is 'real law', this conclusion links domestic and international law, but in a way that most legal theorists would resist; i.e. both forms of law are contractual in a way that requires coercion and violence to make them work. Miéville connects this conclusion to the imperial origins of international law, a genealogical link made by other theorists but not through the Marxist theory of form used here (Angie, 2005; Grovogui, 1996). Miéville explores how imperialism grew up alongside of international legal developments concerning the freedom of the seas and religious conflict. In so doing, he does not excoriate international law as a tool of capitalists, as simplistic Marxism might do; rather, he finds in the origins of international law violence and coercion operating in ways that instantiate the legal form.

Miéville ends his account of international law with his attack on the rule of law. Rather than a panacea to resolve violence and war in the international system, an international rule of law can only reinforce violence and conflict. One example of this is the way in which the US used legal arguments and justifications to launch its war on Iraq in 2003, a war many public international lawyers strongly critiqued.

But the reliance on Security Council resolutions and discourses of enforcement only reified international law as a means by which to ensure the position of the United States as the global hegemon (Lang, 2006).

One might assume that the path to this critical position on international law travels through dense thickets of Marxist theory. Miéville's theorization, however, cuts through those thickets and clarifies some difficult concepts. He also makes clear that international law is not the answer that many liberal theorists believe it to be. Instead, its imbrication with capitalist modes of production and contractual relations of property owners, whether they are people or states, produces the very violence that its publicists believe it can eliminate. We are left in a state of nihilistic abandon, a political system without justice, order or even peace.

Can we make life work without the legal form, either domestically or internationally? This question is not one Miéville answers or even poses in his theoretical work on international law, nor need he necessarily answer. But I do not think we need to end our investigations there. Instead, in the following sections, I turn to his fiction to find out whether or not international law can be made to work, even if imperfectly. For in his imaginative spaces, spaces that are in my reading inherently international, Miéville provides visions of law that both correspond to, and, at points, diverge from, the pessimistic conclusions found in his theoretical work on international law.

Law, Violence and Enforcement: Thinking in and Through Breach

The City & The City is a detective story set in the context of two cities which coexist in the same geographical space but are politically divided. The main character is a detective trying to solve the murder of a PhD student in archaeology who is exploring the origins of the two cities. Her research unsettles the delicate politics of the two cities, which are held together through a series of complicated cultural, political and legal structures. The detective ends up working with another detective from the opposite city, during which they have to negotiate a range of issues, such as jurisdiction and evidence gathering. The murdered student is from the United States and is doing research at a branch campus of a Canadian university, both of which allow the story to include observations by characters from outside the context of the two cities.

As with any good speculative fiction story, one of the most interesting elements of it is the setting. In this case, the setting of the two cities is the core of the story. The relationship between the two cities – Besźel and Ul Qoma – is a complex one. They exist in one physical space, but residents of each city learn to 'unsee' residents, buildings and even streets of the other city. For those native to the two cities, this process is something they learn from childhood, while visitors must go through a thorough training regime to learn how to unsee those not in their cities. Streets and even a few buildings are 'crosshatched', meaning they exist for residents of both cities, but they cannot 'see' each other. This idea takes to an extreme the complexities of real cities, with Jerusalem and Sarajevo (prior to the Balkan wars) being obvious examples. In Jerusalem, for instance, Palestinians and Israelis live side by side and often do not interact with each other even though they might be living on the same street. More interestingly, perhaps, is how similar relationships exist in more 'developed' cities such as London, Los Angeles or Paris, where wealth and poverty sit next to each other and a simple bus ride across town results in a graphic change in sociopolitical context.

More important than the physical setting, however, is the way in which the relationship between the residents of the two cities functions. The ability to unsee each other results, it would seem, from a set of cultural and pragmatic rules. These rules are not codified in any one place but rather depend on habit and training. Yet, despite this informality, there also exists a form of enforcement that is rather extreme. When a resident from one side or the other purposefully or even accidentally 'sees' someone from the other city, Breach steps in. Breach is an organization that is formally run by the Oversight Committee, a group of citizens from both cities that monitor the relationship between the two. Breach is a kind of police, although both cities have their own police departments. Instead of a formal police, Breach materializes only in situations when a violation of the rules keeping the two cities apart takes place. Throughout most of the novel, Breach does not seem even human, but when the main character is taken by Breach, he learns that they are indeed humans with a special ability to meld into the two cities and cross the boundaries between them. It is unclear what happens to those taken by Breach, although the reaction to a violation of the rules is swift and certain. Fear of Breach is inherent in the protocols that exist to keep the two cities in place.

This brief overview provides some parallels in the international legal order. First is the question of sources of law. Traditional international law arises from two main sources: treaties between, and among, states; and, customary law that arises from a range of sources, some of which stretch back quite far into history (d'Aspermont, 2011). Treaties and agreements reflect the interests of states, often times powerful states, who are able to set the agenda of the international order. Customary international law sometimes reinforces these treaties and sometimes challenges traditional international law by providing support for changes such as the development of stronger human rights regimes or international criminal law. What is absent in international law, however, is any kind of formal law making body, such as a parliament, that can pass law on the basis of representative government. Certain organs of the UN system have a representative nature (the General Assembly, for instance), but the resolutions that come out of this body do not have the force of law. There is some debate as to whether or not the UN Security Council is 'legislating', which would go beyond its original mandate to be an executive organ designed to enforce international peace and security as described in Article 24 of the UN Charter (Alvarez, 2005). Here, the problem is not so much its inability to pass binding legislation (which it does) but its lack of representative character.

In *The City & The City*, the nature of the law governing the two cities has a similar character. First, the only formal governing body is the Oversight Committee, which includes individuals from both cities. It governs rather than legislates, constructing rules that it sees fit to keep the peace between the two cities in a secretive and often informal way.

In fact, politicians are hardly part of the story; the only politician who actually appears in the story is at the conclusion, and he comes across as a venal and self-interested actor, one in collusion with business interests. But a law of sorts certainly exists, and it is one that arises, from two different sources: daily practices and history. Their ability to make the law work does not rely on legislators but on the cultural norms that seem to have arisen over the years.

As with international law, there is no need for a formal legislative body but only the need for the individuals in the two communities to follow the rules as they have developed over time. Toward the conclusion of the book, a member of Breach describes to the narrator how the law works:

> Nowhere else works like the cities…. It's not just us [Breach] keeping them apart. It's everyone in Beszel and everyone in Ul Qoma. Every minute, every day. We're only the last ditch: it's everyone in the cities who does most of the work. It works because you don't blink. That's why unseeing and unsensing are so vital. No one can admit it doesn't work. So if you don't admit it, it does. (CC, 370)

History is also central to the function of law in the two cities. In his investigation, the narrator discovers that the murdered girl had begun to explore an alternative historical narrative, one that suggests a past in which the two cities were not divided (CC, 140–1). This re-emphasizes that the law does not depend on some conception of representation for its legitimacy, and indeed often seems to be outside of the bounds of representative government. Rather, its status is based on a combination of history and necessity. The murdered woman challenges the narrative structure upon which the law's authority rests, and so cannot be allowed to live. So, while the law functions, we can see its fragility when its history is exposed. The woman and her supervisor might be read as representatives of a kind of postcolonial critique of international law, which has included genealogical efforts to mine international law for its failure to account for the fictive way in which it constructs a liberal vision of itself while relying on hidden and unspoken assumptions about the developing/third/uncivilized world (Anghie, 2005; Grovogui, 1996; Keene, 2002; van Ittersum, 2005).

It is not simply out of good will that the people in both communities follow the rules, however. Breach represents a background of enforcement that ensures compliance. The existence of Breach provides precisely that element of the law that is missing from international law. What makes Breach so interesting is that it takes to the extreme the notion of enforcement. International law has long been criticized for its lack of enforcement for those who break the law; indeed, some go so far as to say this means it is not real law at all. Others have made the case that there are forms of enforcement in the international order, ones that do not necessarily rely on a domestic legal analogy (Lang, 2008; O'Connell, 2008). Despite these efforts, however, enforcement remains a central problem in international legal theory. At one level, Breach solves the problem of enforcement. By making enforcement automatic, the law can be upheld even when the cultural norms that undergird it fail. We can see Breach, therefore, as the international lawyer's fantasy as a means to solve the bedevilling problem of enforcement.

At the same time, Breach reflects the reality of international legal enforcement as well. First, Breach does not function like a domestic police force as demonstrated by the fact that it does not involve itself in a case of murder that seems to have included individuals from both cities. Rather, Breach only appears when a border has been violated. In the same way, international law does not concern itself with killing. In fact, the laws of war are precisely that, laws of war. They enable war in the traditional formulation, and only seek to moderate its excesses. What international law, in this traditional sense, concerns itself with is the violation of borders, such as illegal immigrants or military interventions. That is, international law allows individuals to kill each other as long as they do so in their own polities or in the context of an official war. As the narrator of the novel states: 'No breach had occurred though a woman had been killed brazenly, across a border' (CC, 282).

Second, Breach's enforcement methods stand above any other law, in the same way that international law sometimes does. When the main character is taken by Breach, he is taken to what seems very much like a Guantanamo type location, where he is interrogated along with others. It is a 'no place', somewhere without any sense of time or space. He hears torture taking place, although he finds it to be a strangely bureaucratic location as well. There is no 'law' in this space, only efforts to extract information:

> The woman straddled my back and held me in some necklock. 'Borlú, you are in Breach. This is the room where you trial is taking place,' the older man said. 'This can be where it's finished. You're beyond law now; this is where the decision lives, and we are it.' (CC, 295)

The formalities of a legal trial are not part of Breach, in the same way that they are not part of the interrogations that have been undertaken in the war on terror. One response here might be that such interrogations are a violation of international law. But, a great power seeking to combat terrorism by arresting and detaining individuals without any formal legal status corresponds in some ways to more traditional conceptions of international law, ones in which powerful states use the law to promote their own agendas.

The City & The City provides one insight into the functioning of international law. My claim here is not that Miéville intended this as a portrayal of international law, only that law appears in a guise that maps onto traditional international law in some interesting ways. It is also, importantly, a story about how law 'works'. In the conclusion, the narrator moves from being a police detective in one city to a member of Breach. He describes his new role in the following: 'My task had changed; not to uphold the law or another law, but to maintain the skin that keeps law in place. Two laws in place, in fact' (CC, 373). The law here is an international one, that structure of law that keeps the other (domestic) laws functioning. It is the global legal and political system, kept in place by powerful economic and political interests that let most of us get on with our normal, law governed lives.

The Breakdown of the Law: Imperialism and Revolution

But international law does not always work. Those moments when it does not work often reveal its fragility, that structure of law that is only a 'skin' rather than a substantive structure. Miéville's novel, *Embassytown*, reveals how thin that skin really is and what happens when pressures build up and break through it. *Embassytown* is set in a future world, one in which humanity now engages with beings from a wide variety of planets. The story is set on the planet Arieka, colonized by humans from the country of Bremen on the planet Terre. The inhabitants of the world are called Hosts, their distinctive feature being their unique understanding and use of language. Rather than language – or 'Language' as it is called to differentiate it from normal language – serving a representative function, this mode of expression is instead a concrete expression of reality. That is, nothing can be said that is not true and everything said must reflect that reality. As one character explains:

> Their language is organized noise, like all of ours are, but for them each word is a funnel. Where to us each word *means* something, to the Hosts, each is an opening. A door through which the thought of that referent, the thought itself that reached for that word, can be seen. (*E*, 62, emphasis in original)

Moreover, Language is always spoken in a dual voice, one that the Hosts can employ because they have two mouths. Humans, however, are unable to speak Language as individuals for they need two mouths to speak the unique contrapuntal Language of the Hosts. Instead, they must have two people who are psychically linked in order to speak Language. These linked individuals, who are bred and raised separately from others, are called Ambassadors and are the only ones who can speak to the Hosts in a meaningful way. Even their names represent their unique relationship; they are referred to as a single person, but with a combined name, such as EzRa or HenRy.

The main character of the novel is a young woman, an astronaut of sorts, who travels on the 'Immer', an interdimensional pathway. She was raised on Arieka and, as a young girl, served as a metaphor by acting out a scene that allowed the Hosts to speak of doing something that they would not want to do otherwise – she became the 'girl who was hurt and ate what was given to her'. The narrator is not an Ambassador but is friendly with them and, as a result of her time off the planet travelling in the Immer and the fact that her husband is a professional academic linguist, can reflect upon Language and understand its complexities. She also learns of the existence of others who have served as metaphors for the Hosts, and who have regular meetings that eventually serve as a source for revolutionary activity.

The human colonizers of Arieka benefit from the Hosts' ability to create biological machines, 'biorigged' materials that both grow and provide transport and housing materials. These materials are farmed by the Hosts and then bartered with the human colonizers (what the Hosts receive in return is not quite clear). There are other alien species scattered throughout the planet, but the primary interactions are between the Hosts and humans. Relations between the two communities rely heavily on the highly-trained Ambassadors, whose ability to communicate with the Hosts makes possible the colonial relationship. The Ambassadors work with bureaucratic staff members, one of whom serves a kind of colonial governor. There are multiple Ambassadors with all of them having similar levels of authority in relation to the Hosts and their human community.

The plot relies on the appearance of a new pair of Ambassadors who have not been genetically bred in the way of the others. Instead, one of them, Ez, has a natural empathy that allows him to link with any other person rather than directly to a fellow Ambassador as is the norm. '[Ez] had a certainly facility, a predisposition for mental connection unachievable by most of us: but it was generalized, not directed' (*E*, 268). When he and his companion, Ra, first speak to the Hosts, the Hosts are suddenly addicted to their speech patterns, a process that turns the Hosts into mindless drug addicts, addicted to the Language of EzRa (the paired Ambassadors). When this happens, the entire Host community suddenly begins losing its ability to function in normal ways. They demand to hear EzRa and refuse to listen to any other Ambassadors. At first, this development is empowering for the human community, for they realize that they can control the Hosts through the Language of EzRa. But, the Hosts' addiction to EzRa soon becomes a problem as the community's social and political norms begin breaking down. Eventually, the Hosts turn to violence as they seek a way to ensure continued access to EzRa, violence that links up with their efforts to learn how to lie. This process, which had been more of a public game in which the Ambassadors had participated, soon becomes part of a revolutionary situation. Some of the Hosts try to lie on a regular basis, something they do in the public competitions (called 'Festivals of Lies') and also in private meetings, which sometimes include human 'similes' whom they have used to enable them to expand beyond their limited Language. When Ez kills Ra, the revolution breaks out in full force as the Ariekei can no longer fulfil their addiction.

The political and legal issues reveal themselves in the context of the Ariekei revolution, a result of both the existence of EzRa and the Hosts' efforts at lying. *Embassytown* does not have law at its fore as does *The City & The City*, but rather explores more of the relationship between politics and language. But, as recent scholars have argued, both language and politics are central to any legal system (Onuf, 1989, 2008). Perhaps more importantly, a revolution is a crucial moment for law. It is the moment when the old law breaks down but also when a new law must be created. Consider, for instance, the recent revolutions in the Middle East. In Tunisia, Egypt and Libya, efforts to create constitutions to replace the previous legal structures point to the intersection of law, politics, and revolution. Following these constitutional struggles demonstrates how creating new laws from revolutionary moments is a complex and highly politicized process (Lang, 2013).

The idea of the Hosts' Language has some interesting relations to legal theory. Law creates a general rule that applies to multiple situations. It must, of necessity be generalizable. Law requires a language that has referents. One could argue, then, that the Hosts could not have law because they cannot use language in the way that means something more general; their language expresses not general thoughts, and not even generalized meanings. If they cannot speak in general terms, in meanings that apply to more than one context, they could not have law. Instead, they would need a decision for each situation they faced rather than a rule that applies across a number of situations. While this is not part of the revolutionary process on Arieka, it does suggest that Miéville is positing a world in which law is absent. This is, at one level, a highly utopian world (or, of course, a dystopian world). It is utopian/dystopian because it is a world where there seems to be no need for law, no need for the regulation of conflicting interests through the creation of contractual relations (to bring us back to Pashukanis's and Miéville's legal theory). Rather, it is a world in which each agent somehow lives in and speaks of the now of the particular moment. There is no need, it would seem, for promising and contracting about the future. If there is no need for such commisive speech acts – speech acts which proclaim our intentions to do something in the future that will construct the world in a particular way, which is what law does – then there is no need or place for law (Onuf, 2008).

It is difficult for us to imagine a world without law, for this would be a world in which there were no rules and each decision resulted from the interest and power of those who make it. The life of the Ariekei Hosts without law takes the utopian vision of international law to an extreme. Avice, the narrator, notes that there was some violence that took place before the arrival of the colonists, but it was limited to small scale disputes, 'obscure internecine murders and feuds' (*E*, 131). Instead, it is the arrival of a colonizer – with its cultural, political and legal structures – that leads to violence. The creation of order, an imperial order, which the bureaucrat Wyatt represents in the narrative, requires violence, or the threat of violence. The bureaucrats who work for Wyatt 'must be armed ... The hidden silos were rumoured to contain firepower of a different magnitude from our own paltry guns. There for our benefit, of course, the claim was' (*E*, 131). The violence contained in the silos represents the violence Miéville describes in his legal theory, the violence necessary to keep contracts and laws in place. It is not the mysterious enforcement mechanism of Breach in *The City & The City*, but a more overt, though still hidden, violence. In the same way, the colonizer patrols the market with guns openly displayed in order to remind the colonized who remains in charge. In more civilized, domestic legal orders, the guns need not be displayed so openly, though they remain there, always ready to be used if necessary.

There is an alternative view of a world without law, one that perhaps corresponds in a different way to international law. One of the most famous articulations of this possibility comes from the legal theorist Carl Schmitt. Schmitt argued that law is really nothing other than decisions of the powerful, modelling his conception on a nominalist theological one in which God makes all decisions and we simply live under the fiction of an orderly legal system (Schmitt, 1922/2005, 1929/2007). Schmitt developed these ideas in the midst of the Weimar Republic in interwar Germany, where a utopian constitution failed to stop the rise of the Nazis. Schmitt associated himself with the Nazis, making many suspicious of his views. Moreover, one might argue that this account mirrors certain great power approaches to international law, wherein there is no set of generalizable rules but instead a realm in which powerful states can choose to follow the law or simply ignore it if they wish.[2] Returning to the sources of law noted above, the treaty-based nature of law means that law is only something that powerful states create by entering into treaties with each other. In so doing, they can decide not to obey the law when it suits their interests. A famous recent example of this attitude was the decision by the United States to ignore the International Court of Justice when it ruled that the US mining of the harbours in Nicaragua in the late 1970s and early 1980s was illegal.[3] By refusing to comply with such rulings, and suffering no consequence, we are left with a decision that ignores the need for generalizable claims.

Embassytown does not present such a picture of law, although one can see how it might result in a situation where it is impossible to generalize in language. If every act was the result of a decision that could not be expressed in any other way than a simple decision, one can see how a powerful actor might appear and control the situation. Indeed, the ability of EzRa, and through them the colonizers, to use the drug of his voice to control the Ariekei might have a loose correspondence to the Schmittian ideal as suggested here. Because each speech act from EzRa creates a new reality, the colonizers need merely parade them in public to create new realities. What soon becomes evident, however, is how reliant this makes the colonizers on the lives of these two Ambassadors. The narrator becomes enmeshed in stratagems to keep EzRa alive and functioning, and when this fails, chaos breaks out. In other words, the Schmittian decisionist system can create immense power, but that power rests on a very slim foundation, the life of two persons.

Language, and particularly deception through language, is also directly linked to diplomacy, a practice that sits at the heart of international law. Henry Wotten, a seventeeth-century English diplomat, famously stated that '[a]n ambassador is an honest gentleman sent to lie abroad for the good of his country.'[4] This saying captures one aspect of diplomatic practice: the ability to use language to advance the interests of a state. In so doing, diplomacy has been long understood as preferable to war and violence. In *Embassytown*, the Ambassadorial ranks are trained to speak in the same way the Hosts are – without lying. As such, Miéville turns on its head the idea that an Ambassador is trained to lie. And yet, the novel also reveals that Ambassadors are to 'speak for' their host state as they 'governed formally in Breman's name' (*E*, 51) The Ambassadors in the novel are slightly different from this role, in that there is not a single Ambassador but many. For this reason, they do not correspond exactly with the idea of traditional diplomacy (understood as a single representative who should speak in the name of his or her country and who acts in the name of that country rather than in the interests of the host state), although at one point we are reminded – by the chief bureaucrat, Wyatt – that the Ambassadors are speaking for Bremen and can be replaced at the will of the powerful (*E*, 271).

One might say *Embassytown* is more concerned with politics than with law. As the revolutionary feelings engendered by the emergence of EzRa increase, Avice discusses with the leading bureaucrat how cultural slips could lead to political upheaval. She notes that:

> Protocols between us were very firm, and for generations, there'd been trouble in relations. So it felt absurd to imagine the Ariekei, the

city, ever turning against Embassytown. But we were some thousands, and they were many, many times that, and they had weapons. (E, 131)

The idea that protocols and not laws kept relations in place is reflective of the quasi law that often governed colonial relations.[5] Rather than implement a fully-fledged legal order in a situation of dominance like this, colonial administrators would rather rely on social norms that had been in existence for some time in the colony. Of course, those norms were often slightly, but crucially, altered by the occupying power so that they would ensure the powerful would remain in place. The clearest manifestation of this is how the drug of EzRa's voice becomes the tool to control the Hosts. The voice becomes the currency through which the humans can continue to buy the biorigging they need, but in so doing, they spread the addiction to it outside the city and into the countryside (E, 208–9). Like the Western powers' use of opium in nineteenth-century China, the voice becomes both a source of wealth and a means of controlling the population, one that had been part of their culture but which is now beyond their control. When revolutionary moments begin, however, those norms begin to break down. The novel explores an extreme case of this; when EzRa's powerful voice creates drug addicts among all the Hosts, social norms collapse almost completely: 'There was a dangerous excitement, an amoralism manifesting in small cruelties and mass indulgence, that some let take them, while others struggled to make things work' (E, 203).

The city of Embassytown can itself be considered a character in the novel, in part because of the 'biorigging' or living buildings and machinery that result from the half biological and half mechanical structures created by the Hosts. As the revolutionary process increases, the city itself changes; 'Embassytown was violently dying' (E, 216). The manifestation of the city as a living and dying entity, one directly linked to the revolutionary politics of the city, evokes the idea of biopolitics, as articulated by the French social theorist Michel Foucault (2004). Foucault explored the ways in which governments exert control over populations through the regulation of health and reproductive policies. These efforts stretch from seemingly innocuous efforts to compile statistics about birth and death rates to using disciplinary practices to alter public health practices. Miéville's construction of a 'living' cityscape, which forms part of the trade relationship with the colonizers, combines Foucault's ideas with his Marxist inspired critical perspective.

Foucault argues that it is possible to resist such forms of disciplinary power, though resistance is often futile. Others, though, have pointed to the ways in which emerging forms of city life both demonstrate the truth of biopolitics yet also reveal sites of potential resistance to it. For instance, in their most recent collaborative work, *Commonwealth* (2009), Michael Hardt and Antonio Negri argue that the harnessing of the 'multitude' is part of a biopolitical revolutionary response to global capitalism. The 'multitude' is an alternative description of the people, one that highlights their unorganized, radical and revolutionary potential to constitute new political orders. It is simultaneously a source of great power and great danger for political life. In this work, and their previous collaborations, Hardt and Negri (2000, 2006) theorize the multitude as a global phenomenon rather than a purely domestic one (as it often appeared in the history of political thought in Machiavelli and Hobbes, for instance). In making their argument, they point directly to emerging forms of city life that do not correspond to traditional 'urban planning' models but arise from complicated social, political and legal norms that have arisen in African cities. Noting that in Marxism the city was a body without organs, today a different city is emerging:

> Today, finally, the biopolitical city is emerging. With passage to the hegemony of biopolitical production, the space of economic production and the space of the city tend to overlap. There is no longer a factory wall that divides the one from the other, and 'externalities' are no longer external to the site of production that valorises them. Workers produce throughout the metropolis, in its every crack and crevice. In fact, production of the common is becoming nothing but the life of the city itself. (Hardt and Negri, 2009: 251)

The authors are careful not to glamorize these new city forms, but they do point to the potential for a new form of revolutionary politics, one in which what seem to be random protests and practices result in new forms of political life, what they call 'a global commonwealth'. This is not a commonwealth based on a formal constitution, but one that exists in the economic and social practices of groups and peoples fighting against economic exploitation. In the same way, the revolt undertaken by those in Miéville's *Embassytown* is not a single, organized revolution in the traditional model. Its material power comes from the drug-addled hosts, who only want to hear the voice of EzRa. But it also comes from those Hosts who have been learning to lie over the past few years, some of whom resist the power of EzRa's voice. And, crucially, the revolution arises from the actions of some humans, such as the linguistic researcher Scile (Avice's husband), who wants to protect the linguistic innocence of the Hosts; '[Scile] wants to protect the Ariekei. From changing language' (*E*, 164). Through these uncoordinated actions and practices, a revolution arises that sweeps away the carefully constructed colonial legal order.

Embassytown, then, reveals the underside of the law, both international and domestic. Through its setting in the colonial context of Bremen's Ariekei outpost, the novel highlights how legal relations between the colonized and colonizer might seem, at one glance, to provide an order and economic relation of benefit to both. Yet in Miéville's exploration of language and its relation to the political context, the novel reveals a series of tensions that can easily snap when their fragility is exposed. Unlike *The City & The City*, where a kind of traditional international law 'works' and 'keeps the skin in place' (*CC*, 373), *Embassytown* explores the fragile nature of international legal relations and how quickly they can collapse.

Conclusion

It is interesting to note that in his work on international law, Miéville provides a full-scale critique of not only international law but law itself. In his critical use of Pashukanis, Miéville argues that it is the legal form which is intimately linked to violence. Widening his critical lens, Miéville argues that international law's form is linked to exploitation of various parts of the world, imbricating it with colonialism. Because of these overlaps, he argues that calls to use international law in a progressive sense will never succeed:

> To fundamentally change the dynamics of the system it would be necessary not to reform the institutions but to *eradicate the forms of law* – which means the fundamental reformulation of the political-economic system of which they are expressions. The project to achieve this is the best hope for global emancipation, and it would mean the end of law. (Miéville, 2006: 318, emphasis in original)

In *Embassytown*, the Hosts are depicted as simple victims of colonialism. Perhaps it is the absence of a legal form, either domestic or international, in their lives that contributes to their innocence. Yet, at the same time, when law breaks down, chaos results. Certainly, some forms of chaos can be productive and liberating, as any revolutionary moment will reveal. Others, though, are not so liberating and result in a simple reinscription of the previous power relations or ones that are even worse. *The City & The City* suggests a model of how international law can 'work'. It is a system in which two communities relate to each other and, as represented by Breach, provides an architecture in which they can function. Clearly, there are flaws in this model, as can be seen in the lack of trials for those accused and the fact that violence can take place within those communities, as long as it does not violate the borders between them. But, perhaps this is all that international law can provide.

Notes

1 To be clear, the ICC does not allow individuals to simply present a case before it. Rather, it allows various agents to bring cases against states which can support the rights of individuals in the international order.

2 Schmitt did write an important account of international law, one that traces the historical emergence of the current international legal order as a response to the age of discovery which ended in the early 20th century. This does not reflect in a direct way his wider legal theory, but draws on different intellectual resources (see Schmitt, 2006).

3 See Case Concerning the Military and Paramilitary Activities in and against Nicaragua (Nicaragua vs. the United States), 27 June 1986, available online at: http://www.icj-cij.org/docket/index.php?sum=367&p1 =3&p2=3&case=70&p3=5 (consulted 28 August 2012).

4 See the Wikipedia entry for 'Henry Wotten': http://en.wikipedia.org/ wiki/Henry_Wotton (consulted 28 August 2012).

5 For instance, law making in the British colonial context was made by means of 'legislative councils' that were composed of representatives from the centre along with business interests and some local interests. See Wight (1947/1952) and Lang (2013) for more on this institution and its relation to wider colonial aspects of the international legal order.

Works Cited

Alvarez, Jose (2006) *International Organizations as Lawmakers*. Oxford: Oxford University Press.

Anghie, Antony (2005) *Imperialism, Sovereignty and the Making of International Law*. Cambridge: Cambridge University Press.

d'Aspermont, Jean (2011) *Formalism and the Sources of International Law: A Theory of the Ascertainment of International Legal Rules*. Oxford: Oxford University Press.

Cassese, Antonio (ed.) (2012) *Realizing Utopia: The Future of International Law*. Cambridge: Cambridge University Press.

Foucault, Michel (2004) *Society Must be Defended: Lectures at the College de France, 1975–1976*, ed. Mauro Bertani and Alessandro Fontana, trans. David Macey. London: Penguin Publishers.

Goldsmith, Jack and Eric Posner (2005) *The Limits of International Law*. Oxford: Oxford University Press.

Grovugui, Siba (1996) *Sovereigns, Quasi-Sovereigns and Africans: Race and Self-Determination in International Law*. Minneapolis: University of Minnesota Press.

Hardt, Michael and Antonio Negri (2000) *Empire*. Cambridge MA: Harvard University Press.

Hardt, Michael and Antonio Negri (2006) *Multitude: War and Democracy in the Age of Empire*. London: Penguin Publishers.

Hardt, Michael and Antonio Negri (2009) *Commonwealth*. Cambridge, MA: Harvard University Press.

Hart, H. L. A. (1994) *The Concept of Law*, 2nd ed. Oxford: Oxford University Press.

Keene, Edward (2002) *Beyond the Anarchical Society: Grotius, Colonialism, and Order in World Politics*. Cambridge: Cambridge University Press.

Kelsen, Hans (1946) *General Theory of the Law and the State*, trans. Anders Wedberg. Cambridge, MA: Harvard University Press.

Koskenniemi, Martii (1989/2005) *From Apology to Utopia: The Structure of International Legal Argument*. Cambridge: Cambridge University Press.

Lang, Jr., Anthony F. (2006) 'Normative Causes and Consequences: Understanding and Evaluating the War with Iraq', in Raymond Hinnebusch and Rick Fawn (eds) *The Iraq War: Causes and Consequences*, pp. 269–82. Boulder, CO: Lynne Rienner Publishers.

Lang, Jr., Anthony F. (2008) *Punishment, Justice and International Relations: Ethics and Order after the Cold War*. London: Routledge.

Lang, Jr., Anthony F. (2013) 'From Revolutions to Constitutions: The Case of Egypt' *International Affairs* 89(2): 345–64.

Marx, Karl (1867/1978) *Capital, Volume I*, in Robert Tucker (ed.) *The Marx–Engels Reader*. New York: W. W. Norton.

Miéville, China (2006) *Between Equal Rights: A Marxist Theory of International Law*. London: Pluto Press.

Miéville, China (2008) 'The Commodity-Form Theory of International Law', in Susan Marks (ed.) *International Law on the Left: Re-examining Marxist Legacies*, pp. 92–132. Cambridge: Cambridge University Press.

O'Connell, Mary Ellen (2008) *The Power and Purpose of International Law: Insights from the Theory and Practice of Enforcement*. Oxford: Oxford University Press.

Onuf, Nicholas (1989) *World of Our Making: Rules and Rule in Social Theory and International Relations*. Columbia, SC: University of South Carolina Press.

Onuf, Nicholas (2008) *International Legal Theory*. London: Routledge.

Pashukanis, Evgeny (1929/1978) *Law and Marxism: A General Theory*, trans. Barbara Einhorn, ed. and intro. Chris Arthur. London: Pluto Press.

Pashukanis, Evgeny (1927/2006) *International Law*, reprinted in China Miéville, *Between Equal Rights: A Marxist Theory of International Law*. London: Pluto Press.

Schmitt, Carl (1929/2007) *The Concept of the Political*, trans. and notes George Schwab. Chicago, IL: University of Chicago Press.

Schmitt, Carl (1922/2005) *Political Theology*, trans. George Schwab, intro. Tracy Strong. Chicago, IL: University of Chicago Press.

Schmitt, Carl (1974/2006) *The Nomos of the Earth in the International Law of the Jus Publicum Europeaum*, trans. and ed. G. L. Ulmen. New York: Telos Press Publishing.
Teitel, Ruti (2011) *Humanity's Law*. Oxford: Oxford University Press.
Van Ittersum, Martine Julia (2005) *Profit and Principle: Hugo Grotius, Natural Rights Theories and the Rise of Dutch Power in the East Indies, 1595–1615*. Leiden: Brill Publishers.
Wight, Martin (1947/1952) *British Colonial Constitutions 1947*. Oxford: Clarendon Press.

10

ABNATURAL RESOURCES
COLLECTIVE EXPERIENCE, COMMUNITY AND COMMONALITY
FROM EMBASSYTOWN TO NEW CROBUZON

Mark P. Williams

In this chapter I will demonstrate why it is important to treat China Miéville's fantasy fictions as much closer to reality than they, at first, might appear. My argument has two main strands. First, by drawing together Miéville's theory of fantasy with the theories of immaterial and material labour under globalization put forward by Antonio Negri and Michael Hardt I will show how Miéville's conception of the fantastic is intimately engaged with debates about the status of contemporary everyday life under capital. Second, I will illustrate how the fantastic elements of his fictions are resolved by his characters developing a fantastic understanding of everyday activities. My analysis focuses on the term 'abnatural', a phrase Miéville develops in *Iron Council* and which although he uses rarely in his novels I argue is significant to his development of fantasy. In this chapter, I will relate the abnatural to comparative concepts in Miéville's novels that describe his protagonists' everyday activities as being invested with fantastic qualities. I am calling these activities 'abnatural resources', and the examples I will consider include: making music, writing and speaking creatively using metaphor, and forming communities which are organized around political or aesthetic pursuits.

As Miéville has indicated in various interviews, his primary interest in the forms of science fiction (SF) and fantasy is not because they offer 'political blueprints' to their readers. Rather, he is fascinated by the fundamental link between the estrangements afforded by genre fiction and those present in avant-garde literatures – such as the writings of the surrealists – which share with politically revolutionary projects their act of imagining a fundamentally different way of life. As he puts it, '[t]here's some shared soup somewhere in my head from which these two things are ladling' (Miéville, 2011). This chapter is concerned with finding and examining how one ingredient of the 'soup' of Miéville's interests flavours the others. My argument stems from the words of Miéville's own protagonists at those moments when they really grasp their worlds: this begins from understanding that when Miéville uses the prefix 'ab–' with natural it is not simply as a substitution for unnatural, or an intensifier. The abnatural is neither *natural* nor *unnatural*: it is its own thing, a whole term, departing from our conceptions of both natural (biological, inherent, intrinsic) and unnatural (social, artificial, extrinsic). I will show how this works with reference to the interaction of material and immaterial conditions of everyday life in the world of the reader as well as in Miéville's secondary worlds.

To establish a foundation for this reading, let me make clear that by *material* conditions I mean those which are underpinned by a reference to the actual social conditions of the real world; as a Marxist materialist, Miéville argues that without this basis in objective reality theories of ideas 'cannot give a sense of why those ideas at that time' (Miéville, 2005: 4). Miéville's fictions demonstrate this point in the social worlds they construct. For example, in New Crobuzon, Spatters is a tower block where the lifts 'never got put in' because it is housing for the bird-people known as Garuda, who can fly (*PSS*, 144). We are left to wonder: were no lifts ever put in *and then Garuda were encouraged to live there,* or were no lifts ever put in *to encourage Garuda-only to live there?* The social effect is ghettoization; only as Isaac and Lin arrive at 'the seventh floor, did the stairs look like they had ever been used', and then mostly for rubbish (*PSS*, 150). In Miéville's secondary worlds, as in our world, concrete social conditions may be produced by physical structures or institutions (tower blocks and town planning) but they also reproduce themselves by social habit, and internalized social habits (in the form of values, expectations or ideology) are an example of what I mean by *immaterial*. In their book *Commonwealth* (2009), Michael Hardt and Antonio Negri demonstrate the ways in which immaterial forces, such as community and social habits, are used to generate surplus value in property prices as an example of contemporary capital's capacity to exploit immaterial relationships for material gain (Hardt and Negri, 2009: 156). I argue that the things, people and activities which can be read as 'abnatural' in Miéville's texts are fantastic extensions of actual cultural practices which reveal shared or communal resources which are not instrumental to capitalism; as such they encourage Miéville's reader to reflect upon the use of the fantastic within fantasy narratives, and also reflect on real social relations in our own contemporary world. Hardt and Negri's trilogy *Empire* (2000), *Multitude* (2006), and *Commonwealth* (2009) argues that since the end of the 1990s we have been living in a world defined by a new form of global power called Empire that regulates itself across the whole planet. It does this by means of immaterial, information-based technologies which enable the migration of manufacturing industries to countries or regions where that material labour will cost least and produce the greatest surplus. Under this system, Hardt and Negri argue that non-material or immaterial labour has become the dominant form of labour, meaning labour which does not produce goods but, rather, *affects* (emotional experiences which appear to be invisible, or naturalized, and are essential to the services industries, healthcare and caring professions, and other areas of the contemporary workplace), and has come to dominate manufacturing and extractive industries.

The 'abnatural' is a concept that Miéville infrequently invokes across his fictions to suggest the rapaciousness of contemporary capitalism in exploiting the creative potential of his protagonists and their social worlds. In this chapter, I will develop Miéville's concept into the idea of what I am calling 'abnatural resources', as a useful formulation for grasping the contemporary critique of global capitalism that his fiction encourages. For clarity, I will refer throughout the chapter to Miéville's concept as 'abnatural' and my own reconsideration, and extension of this term, as 'abnatural resources'. First, I will briefly sketch Miéville's theory of the fantastic to show how the abnatural is essential to his secondary worlds and his political position on contemporary fantasy. In order to extend this reading of fantasy's political function I will draw on the work of Hardt and Negri – and explain how their concepts of 'the multitude' and 'the common' relate to immaterial and material labour – to consider the relationship between the immaterial realms of fantasy's world-building and the material contexts of its co-operative relationships of labour, creativity and work. Finally, I will show how Miéville's usage of the 'abnatural' can be extended further and explain why I term this potential use 'abnatural resources'.

From Miéville's Theory of Fantasy to the Multitude and the Common

The conceptualization of the 'abnatural' in Miéville's fictional universes is closely related to the theories of fantasy which he has put forward in interviews and articles (Miéville cited in Gordon, 2003; Miéville, 2009: 231–48; Newsinger, 2000). Miéville (2002b) writes that the fantastic (as employed in either SF or fantasy) provides a uniquely useful approach for incorporating the political critique of ideology into fiction.[1] As he explains, capitalism presents us with a 'reality' in which material relationships are determined by imaginary, immaterial forms: 'The lived reality of capitalism is commodity fetishism', he suggests, arguing that '[o]ur commodities control us, and our social relations are dictated by their relations and interactions' (Miéville,

2002b: 41). The fantastic, therefore, allows writers and readers to engage in a critical reflection of contemporary relations under capitalism:

> I am claiming that the fantastic, particularly because 'reality' is a grotesque 'fantastic form', is *good to think with*. Marx, whose theory is a haunted house of spectres and vampires, knew this. Why else does he open *Capital* not quite with an 'immense', as the modern English translation has it, but with a 'monstrous' (*ungeheure*) collection of commodities? (Miéville, 2002b: 46, emphasis in original)

Miéville connects the grotesqueness, the monstrousness, of commodity relations with Gothic metaphors from Marx, who famously writes: 'Capital is dead labour, that, vampire-like, only lives by sucking living labour, and lives the more the more labour it sucks' (Marx, 1885/2013: 146). Imaginary monsters are thus useful ways of conceptualizing capitalism because capital itself is imaginary and its extraction of surplus value from the creative work of the proletariat is analogous to the ingestion of human blood and flesh by vampires and other monsters.

Miéville extends his conception of the fantastic or immaterial conditions determining everyday life through his re-reading of the science fiction theorist and founding editor of *Science Fiction Studies*, Darko Suvin. In his seminal text *Metamorphoses of Science Fiction: On the Poetics and History of a Literary Genre* (1979), and the essays collected in *Positions and Presuppositions in Science Fiction* (1988), Suvin argues that SF is the most politically progressive mode of fiction because of its ability to negate present social conditions and its speculative orientation towards the future, which allows the SF text to enact a critical reflection on the present and demand social and political change. He differentiates the SF tradition from those fantasy texts with which it shares its genesis as a modern aesthetic response to industrialization and modernity. For Suvin fantasy is, at worst, backward-looking and engenders a longing for idealized versions of the past that should be considered actively reactionary; at best, it offers its readers an escapist mystification or distraction from present conditions, which is therefore a purely ideological gesture since it leaves the interests of capital unquestioned and unchallenged. Miéville (2009: 231–48) questions Suvin's distinction between SF and fantasy by asking to what extent any fictional representation can be considered *intrinsically* more or less ideological than any other.

This critique of Suvin's privileging of SF above fantasy is also developed by Mark Bould in 'The Dreadful Credibility of Absurd Things' (2002), in which he theorizes fantasy as a mode of critical thinking that possesses an inherently subversive potential: even when presented in its most commodified form (e.g. within a blockbuster film or the novelization of a Role Playing Game), fantasy always places a specific contradictory demand on its audience. He argues that when we read or watch fantasy narratives we are asked to accept the impossible *as if* it were real and judge it on its own terms, while *simultaneously* never forgetting (but rather embracing) its impossibility as well as its non-representational qualities. This process, which Bould (2002: 83–4) calls the 'fantasy of fantasy', develops in its readers and viewers a kind of in-built reflexiveness: it creates a moment of radical uncertainty, a crisis, which remains irresolvable at the root of even the most ideologically compromised and commercial fantastic fictions. For Bould it is the centrality and persistence of obvious contradiction that enables fantastic fictions to be resistant to the principles of global capitalism even when they are products owned, or published, by large corporations. They are narratives of an immaterial that demands to be read simultaneously as if it could potentially be material (somewhere) while also presenting itself in such a way as to undercut this implication. Bould uses the examples of novels written in established populist fantasy universes such as K. W. Jeter's *Star Wars* novels (*The Mandalorian Armour*, 1998; *Slave Ship*, 1998; *Hard Merchandise*, 1999) and Kim Newman's *Warhammer* fantasy novels written under the pseudonym 'Jack Yeovil' (*Drachenfels*, 1989; *Beasts in Velvet*, 1991; *Genevieve Undead*, 1993; *Silver Nails*, 2002; collected as *The Vampire Genevieve*, 2005), but to this we might add superheroes, a mode Miéville has taken on in rebooting DC's series *Dial H* (2012) – which was originally *Dial H for Hero* (1966–8, 1981) – where his characters Manteau and Nelson explicitly problematize their own superpowers. Miéville's interest in the critical and creative potential of fantasy lies in its contrary appeals to absolute freedom (fantasy as a narrative where literally anything could happen, in defiance of all rules) and at the same time their extreme codification and commodification; he explains this in terms of Surrealism on the one hand and on the other the 'superheroically banalifying impulse' of Role Playing Games that give numerical value to magic and mystery (see Gordon, 2003: 357).

Miéville's fantasy brings critical awareness of the immaterial in material conditions to the level of character and plot: his characters talk, speculate, and argue about the contradictions of immaterial forces that affect their worlds. Most importantly, they also use immaterial forces to effect changes within their respective worlds. The most significant manifestations of these forces are non-magical: music (*King Rat*), community (*Iron Council*), metaphor-making (*Kraken*) and linguistic play (*Embassytown*). This enables the reader to share Miéville's consciousness of the fantastic qualities of the everyday by presenting a world where the central contradictions of *thinking about fantasy* as if it were real are already present within everyday cultural activities that materially affect people's lives and wellbeing: these are abnatural resources. As a fictional mode of critical or oppositional imagination, fantasy can thus be understood as central to Miéville's political activism, his theoretical engagements as a Marxist, and his aesthetic interests as a novelist. Like the forces of capitalism, fantasy is concerned with the application of an imaginary system to the real world; like capitalism it is not always rational. Miéville argues that this politicized act of imagining the impossible is in fact part of the ordinary processes of labour in our everyday lives:

> Consider Marx's distinction of 'the worst of architects' from 'the best of bees': unlike for any bee 'At the end of every labour process a result emerges which had already been conceived by the worker at the beginning, hence already existed ideally.' For Marx, human productive activity, with its capacity to act on the world and to change it – the very mechanism by which people make history, though not in the circumstances of their choosing – is *predicated on a consciousness of the not-real*. The fantastic is there at the most prosaic moment of production. (Miéville, 2002b: 44, emphasis in original)

Miéville argues that in everyday life, the fantastic is present as consciousness of alterity, or of the not-(yet-)real. This process of uncovering the fantastic 'not-real' status of capitalist production becomes further complicated in those cultural activities that produce immaterial goods or ideas which also have material consequences – establishing the value of currency, for example, or the process of identifying within a specific community. In such activities as reading fantasy fiction or considering how to construct one's own cultural identity, the immaterial realm of imagination and subjective self-awareness becomes politically reflexive. One central example of such a reflexive cultural activity is the function of art in *Perdido Street Station*. The khepri artist Lin's sculpture is coloured and textured according to her unique perceptions as a khepri who is resistant to the collective sculptural practice of khepri traditional art. Her cultural rebelliousness includes dressing in 'human fashion, not the traditional blooming pantaloons of these ghetto-dwellers' (*PSS*, 20), as well as having a relationship with a human, Isaac Dan der Grimnebulin: 'her love-life was an avant-garde transgression, an art-happening' (*PSS*, 12). Her sculpture, like her clothing and relationship with Isaac, are thus expressions of the cultural hybridity of her everyday life.

In *Embassytown*, the Ariekene Festivals of Lies can only take place after the indigenous Ariekei Hosts have been subject to sufficient levels of contact with their human planetary co-inhabitants. The very designation of the planet's indigenous people as Hosts implies the presence of aliens (human/oids) in their culture; this evocation of a postcolonial culture has resonance with that of nations such as New Zealand where *tangata whenua* in te Reo Māori (the Māori language) means both 'people of the land' and 'hosts'.[2]

The Hosts in *Embassytown* use a language (capitalized in the novel as 'Language') that cannot express any untruth, and they are fascinated by the human ability to signify abstract ideas, express falsehoods, or speak metaphorically. As the novel's protagonist Avice reflects at the Festival of Lies: 'These eisteddfods of mendacity had not existed – how could they? – before we Terre came' but 'had occurred almost as long as Embassytown had existed' (*E*, 83). The ambiguities of language explored through the Festivals of Lies become crucial to the plot of *Embassytown*, ultimately providing a way of understanding how the Hosts can save themselves from the crisis EzRa unleashes through employing metaphor as a logical extension of lying. Similarly, in *Kraken* Billy realizes his own power to act when he recognizes the fantastic quality of 'knacking'. 'Knacking' is a peculiar skill which uses belief (personal and collective) and literalized metaphor, to power transformations that physically alter the world. The concept, like the term, combines vagueness and specificity: sometimes it operates like a separate thing, either an object or a power. In short, it operates in its physicality very like figurative language: '*it's all metaphor*, Billy remembered *it's persuasion*' (*K*, 460, emphasis in original).

Kraken and *Embassytown* in particular are centred on the abilities of immaterial processes to effect material change. Such cultural practices as the production of art, fiction, music, and co-operative labour all involve imagining commonality, which helps construct and (re)produce a social environment. Cultural practices such as these have both material and immaterial aspects which are never fully instrumentalized by capital; their excess is what makes them powerful. The immaterial investment of an individual's imagination in constructing a fiction allows anything which also involves fantasy to be analogically extended to other life activities, which also require immaterial (imaginative) investment to have material effects. That is, once you acknowledge the presence of imagination in one act it becomes easier to see it in other, dissimilar activities that also use the imagination – they become analogous. Thoughts, emotions, *phantasy* (to retain Freud's spelling and denote its connection to the unconscious), as well as fantasy in the more colloquial English sense of daydreaming (linked to the 'Fancy' of Coleridge), and language, faith in the 'character' of others, or of groups, faith in deistic or theistic systems of belief, philosophy, political movements, creative endeavours and their products, are thus all blends of material circumstance and immaterial construction. These combinations of the material and the immaterial appear throughout Miéville's fictions. Metaphor and belief, for instance, work powerfully in the London of *Kraken* because they operate outside of rational determination but are nevertheless lived experientially. Similarly, the strong correlation between music and community in *King Rat* reminds us of the collective ties that underpin such creative practices, and of those social, emotional, and affective experiences that lie outside of capitalist production yet which capitalism consistently attempts to incorporate into its own productive realm. This idea of the collective engagement involved in creative pursuits is extended into the directly political in *Iron Council*, where the Iron Councillors actively imagine themselves operating as a community and political movement; demonstrating that the imagination of social and political alternatives can lead to collective political transformation.

Miéville's various fictions are thus explorations of how we might understand the realm of the immaterial as fostering not just material social transformation at the level of the individual, but also enabling collective acts of self-determination. Mieville insists that music, creative language and co-operative labour be thought of as specifically social activities. In doing so, he emphasizes that they originate outside the reified relations of capitalist productivity, even if capitalism subsumes them. Hardt and Negri's conclusion to *Commonwealth* emphasizes the significance of activities which are based on, and develop, our capacities of conviviality and living together, aiming to 'affirm the autonomy and interaction of singularities in the common' (Hardt and Negri, 2009: 380). They call this 'love', and oppose it strongly to the individuation and separation of love into romantic and familial loves, asserting it instead as a social force that underpins and reinforces individual and collective drives. Similarly, Miéville's fictions show comparable social capacities at work in the climactic moments of *Embassytown*, *Iron Council* and *King Rat*; each novel reveals to his reader a means of transforming the irreducible differences of unique individual characters and species into a relationship of commonality.

In order to situate Miéville's political and theoretical investment in the relationship between the material and the immaterial, I would like to turn now to Hardt and Negri's concepts of 'the multitude' and 'the common' to explain the significance of the abnatural to this discussion. Antonio Negri comes from an Italian tradition of Autonomous Marxism, or Autonomism: a worker-orientated, anti-statist and anti-authoritarian set of groups emerging in Italy since the 1960s

(Garland, 2009: 322-5; Eden, 2012: 35-64). Negri's conception of the multitude as a political subject is constructed in opposition to the sovereign concept of 'the people'; it is drawn partly from Machiavelli, but primarily from Spinoza. Paolo Virno, an Autonomist thinker and contemporary of Negri's, summarizes Spinoza's multitude as follows:

> For Spinoza, *multitudo* indicates a *plurality which persists as such* in the public scene, in collective action, in the handling of communal affairs, without converging into a One [....] Multitude is the form of social and political existence for the many, seen as being many. (Virno, 2004: 21, emphasis in original)

Hardt and Negri's conception of the multitude draws upon Virno's text: for them, *multitude* denotes a collective, politically-charged identity which is not reduced to a unitary, homogeneous and singular identity such as 'the people', but neither is it an undifferentiated, uniform collective like 'the masses'.[3] Hardt and Negri's multitude is 'composed of innumerable internal differences that can never be reduced to a unity or single identity', including 'different cultures, races, ethnicities, genders and sexual orientations', and also 'different forms of labour' as well as 'different ways of living' (Hardt and Negri, 2004: 89). This insistence on collectiveness and singularity co-existing without reducing either quality makes Hardt and Negri's concept of the multitude useful for a comparative analysis of Miéville's diverse characters. Indeed, the above description of the multitude could be used to characterize the social composition of the Iron Councillors, reminding us of the diverse backgrounds and labouring experiences of the manual labourer Cutter, the technical worker and golemist Judah, the (f)Re(e)made Uzman, and the sex-worker Ann-Hari.

Hardt and Negri link the rise of the multitude to the hegemony of immaterial labour within contemporary production because immaterial labour dominates other class divisions within the industrial proletarian or rural peasant classes. Although the nature of the multitude's labour might be primarily extractive (mining, farming), infrastructural (maintenance, service), affective (child-rearing, aged-care), as well as informational (data entry and computing), all labour, they argue, is *determined* by the conditions of immaterial labour. In

Commonwealth, Hardt and Negri explain how they see the multitude as including peasant cultures and industrialized cultures, as well as information workers, and domestic and other insecure or precarious workers – because their labours are already linked and exploited by the networks of globalization (they adopt the term 'precariat' [Hardt and Negri, 2009: 290]), and, most importantly, because they are all controlled and managed by immaterial and networked conditions, even if they remain otherwise separate sectors. As a model for contemporary subjectivity, the multitude has the advantage of being flexible and inclusive towards differences of gender, economic class and cultural difference that other forms of solidarity, such as industrial unions, have struggled to accommodate historically.

This flexible and inclusive characteristic of the multitude, and its relationship with 'the common', can be linked directly with Miéville's construction of fantasy and, I suggest, his development of the idea of the abnatural. In the expression of the abnatural in Miéville's fiction we can recognize appeals to, and relationships with, 'the common' appearing as a result of social relationships; his heroes (and anti-heroes), particularly the Iron Councillors, but also Jack Half-a-Prayer, Saul, Isaac, Deeba and Avice, are not just diverse, they are *of the multitude*, insofar as these characters embody vital, irreducible characteristics (singularities) as well as inescapably belonging to particular social groups (which demonstrates their commonalities with other characters). Miéville's figuration of what I am calling 'abnatural resources' can therefore be identified as conceptualizing the common as something both fantastic and real – formed within specific cultural, expressive activities that demonstrate how immaterial ideas and socialities have tangible material consequences in shaping behaviours and fomenting change within the worlds of Miéville's protagonists.

Abnatural Resources and Cultural Activities: Building Music, Metaphor, and Community

Kraken is the novel that brings the concept of the abnatural explicitly into contact with contemporary London. The alterity of the novel takes place between and within the everyday London of Miéville's readers and the only two mentions of the term 'abnatural' are very specific. The first use of the term denotes the type of crime investigated by the 'Fundamentalist and Sect-Related Crime Unit' (*K*, 36), which is considered to be 'knacked and abnatural' (*K*, 135). This combination of 'knacked and abnatural' implies an intrinsic connection between knacking, the performance of magic(k) in the novel, and the other phenomena; it also implies that everything we encounter in this crime story is related to that paired conception. Miéville's second use of 'abnatural' in the novel confirms this impression: Professor Cole has a knack for pyrokenesis and has written a book titled *Abnatural Burnings* (*K*, 367). This book documents conceptual forms of pyrokenesis that he has researched and learned to practise: a knack is an ability to produce an abnatural effect. As the protagonist reminds us: knacking is '*all metaphor* [...] *it's persuasion*' (*K*, 460, emphasis in original), it is about affecting the world materially through immaterial means. It is a cultural practice that can (at least partly) be learned and which produces effects which are irreducible: not natural, not unnatural, but singular and common all at once.

To subjects engaged in diverse cultural practices – whether making revolution or making musical events – these affects are always surplus to the functioning of capitalism, and are therefore analogous to all other cultural activities which are *experienced as always expressing something more* by those subjects invested and involved in them. This surplus characterizes the abnatural resources we find in Miéville's fiction: in such activities, the mundane world of our own capitalist present reveals itself to harbour fantastic qualities manifested in community building and solidarity. Music, for instance, appears in *Iron Council* during the process of the Iron Councillors becoming conscious of their own irreducible collectivity:

> Demons of motion. [....] They eat the rhythm, the *ka ka ka* of turning iron on iron. After millennia of snapping up only the quickstep of plains hunters and prey, the demons are drunk on the heavy beat. They evanesce out of colours in the near-shapes of foxes and rockrats, the only animals they have seen. They learn the newcomers and as

hours pass the motion demons mimic humans and cactacae inexpertly, to the track-layers' delight. [....]

If councillors detrain, demons pullulate about their feet, eating the echoes of their steps. One woman dances and the air goes alive with the rapture of motion-demons now-seen-now-unseen gorging on her tempo. (*IC*, 296-7)

The concrete actions undertaken in making revolution in *Iron Council* thus echo the activities of club culture in *King Rat* because they are both about developing a sense of community for the disaffected and the disenfranchised. They are both also manifestations of a dialectic of natural/unnatural, material/immaterial because they have specific material conditions (electronic/mechanical reproduction of music, mechanical rhythm), yet they also produce affects which are not reducible to those elements.

In *Iron Council* the Iron Councillors are, from the beginning of the novel, already a collective expression given form by the train in which they journey, but when they physically pass through the Cacotopic Stain some Iron Councillors are trapped inside one of the train carriages when Torque energy transforms it into a 'vast membranous cell'; they become conscious nuclei 'still vaguely shaped like men and women afloat in cytoplasm' who wave their 'arm-flagella at their comrades' (*IC*, 462). Through this transformation the collective of people who make up the Iron Council becomes materially (familially) *related* to the train itself: in this sense the train defines them in immaterial terms, both in their own minds as well as in the popular imagination of New Crobuzon's revolutionaries as Iron Councillors – they are therefore 'becoming-train' at the same time that they are becoming Iron Councillors. Finally, both the rhythm demons and the concept of the abnatural are echoed by Judah's creation of the time golem at the end of the novel which preserves the Iron Councillors in their collectivity as the Iron Council: 'there was pulse-magic [...] a palimpsest tempo [...] each accented block of noise intervening in time, cutting time into shape', forming 'a golem of sound and time' (*IC*, 590). Judah's time golem '[stands] into its ablife', defining both itself and the collective of the Iron Council as abnatural and irreducible to the dimensions which determined it: *sound* and *time*, like an incarnation of rhythm and music (*IC*, 590). Like Saul in *King Rat*, Lin's position as a khepri outsider artist in *Perdido Street Station*, and the Ariekene Absurd in *Embassytown*, the Iron Council is more than the sum of its parts. Its immaterial qualities of musical and temporal revolution are made into a concrete artifact, that at once visualizes abstract ideas in substantive form whilst also bringing together different conceptual elements in the image of the Iron Council, which remain conceptually irreducible just as Hardt and Negri's multitude retains the various singularities of its constituent subjects.

For Miéville, the abnatural is a way of describing the immaterial part of fantasy which is always distinctly, singularly itself but also *always analogous to all other immaterial investments in material activities* (reading/writing, performing/listening) which partakes in what Hardt and Negri call the common: a non-reductive collective identity. As such, Miéville's abnatural is a fantasy-world analogue for those immaterial qualities of everyday (material) life which always emerge reflexively through social interaction (music as an example which connects his earlier and later fictions, *Iron Council* and *King Rat*). Abnatural resources are points where we can construct ways of talking about solidarities of experience across the differences that striate globalization and (apparently) separate us from those actions which the global networks of capital connect; such as, for example, the rhetoric of 'immigration and asylum' (see the discussion of the real profits made by the asylum and immigration detention industry versus the tabloid-led public rhetoric of social cost [Tyler, 2013: 75–103]). In Miéville's texts characters have moments of realization, where they see through or uncover ideological disconnections or facades, which occur alongside the more fantastical elements of the plot, adding to them. In other words, his fantastic narratives tell us that when we imagine ways of approaching each other's lived experiences, of understanding the commonalities that we share despite our many differences from one another, through cultural activities which can never be fully reduced to market standards or 'competitive' wage levels, *those are our abnatural resources*. In what follows, I will identify examples of abnatural resources in order to open up a discussion which asks: what can we accomplish if we think about our everyday lives in this way?

In a 2003 interview with Joan Gordon for *Science Fiction Studies* (Gordon, 2003) Miéville comments on his interest in the paradoxical quality of fantasy as a literary mode. As he explains, 'fantasy' encompasses some of the most commodified narrative forms such as fantasy Role Playing Games (RPGs), where magical and mythical creatures of the most incredible powers find their strengths and weaknesses reduced to numerical values (the common), but also such utterly irreducible (singular) enunciations as Surrealist collage and form-defying experiment (Miéville cited in Gordon, 2003: 357). His fictions constantly play with this central paradox of fantasy, in which the genre is capable of reducing the irreducible or expanding the banal beyond apparent limits. Miéville's fictions place his reader in a position to observe the shared characteristics of the materialist, real-social, and the immaterial, fantastic-social. In this way, all of his fictions are devoted to developing a sense of those abnatural resources to which we already have social access. The two clearest examples of this at work are the function of metaphor in *Kraken* and *Embassytown*.

In *Embassytown* (2011) Miéville begins to develop the term 'alt-reality' to describe the hyper spatial realm of 'the Immer' (from the German for 'always', in contradistinction to 'the Manchmal' from the German for 'sometimes'), a clear analogue for the abnatural (*E*, 22). Similarly, the technology of the Ariekene 'bioriggery' is 'molded from fecund plasms by the Hosts with techniques we could not merely not mimic, but that were impossible according to our sciences' implying that to human-based epistemology they are abnatural (*E*, 87). However, if the Ariekene Host technology is as baffling, as abnatural, as their Language, it is only through the singularity of Language that Miéville's most intriguing abnatural emerges: the Absurd Hosts. The absolute relationship between the Hosts' Language and their concept of truth makes them vulnerable to becoming addicted to the errant speech patterns of the new Ambassador EzRa, whose name suggestively recalls Ezra Pound as both Modernist and politically dangerous propagandist. Here again, 'ab–' returns to mark a subjective but social transformation and an incommensurable difference: the Ariekene who attempt to purge themselves of the malicious influence of EzRa's Language-drug are called the 'Absurd'. The name invokes imaginary numbers since the 'surd' is a sum containing multiple roots of irrational numbers, but the surd also linguistically refers to sounds pronounced without the larynx: voiceless sounds.[4] Both are apt, but I want to draw extra attention to the 'Ab–' prefix: in this novel it refers to Ariekene who *choose* to de-voice themselves and become a mass movement. Like the differentiation between Remade and fReemade in *Perdido Street Station*, choice, that is agency, effects an imaginary transformation with material consequences. The Ariekene Absurd *have become abnatural to Ariekene society*, but in the process they have found an abnatural resource beyond their 'natural' resources of Language and the artificial one of their technology, a shared, immaterial but social resource: the resource of metaphor, of the un-like and the 'what-if' which Ariekene Language cannot make explicit in speech until they transform their social being (*E*, 56). Borrowing from Mark Bould's readings of Miéville's fictions, we can suggest that *Embassytown* inverts the plot and thematic trajectories Bould identifies at work in *Perdido Street* Station (the intrusion of SF into a fantasy secondary world). Bould (2003: 408) argues that Isaac's creation of the crisis engine, and use of it to combine the mental resources of the Construct Council and the Weaver, constitutes the introduction of science fictional devices and concepts into a fantasy world because they rationalize magic, thaumaturgy, as a parallel logic to physics. Contrastingly, the disruption of the Absurd in *Embassytown* marks the discovery of the fantastic, in the form of lies and the irrational/ untrue as metaphor, within a science fictional secondary world which enriches Ariekene society, enabling it to survive. The Ariekei Absurd survive because they find a common resource in their abnatural state; that is an abnatural resource because it is the moment when they discover the power of metaphor.

In *Kraken*, Billy's understanding of the relationship that belief and metaphor have with magic comes to a head with his realization of his own impact on the stolen giant squid around which the plot has revolved:

"It's not an animal or a god," Billy said. "It didn't exist until I curated it. That's my specimen."
[...] He had birthed it into consciousness. It was *Architeuthis dux*. Specimen, pining for preservative. Squid-shaped paradox but not the animal of the ocean. *Architeuthis*, Billy understood for the first time, was not that undefined thing in deep water, which was only ever itself. *Architeuthis* was a human term. (*K*, 460–1)

Metaphor here is social: it relates the material (the body of the 'undefined thing') to the immaterial (the 'human term'). Persuasive metaphor is a shared power, a socially concrete manipulation of the immaterial which has a concrete material effect. It is an abnatural quality, transforming immaterial *affect* into material *effect*. Hardt and Negri identify this transformation as central to the interaction of the multitude in contemporary postmodernity: immaterial affects, such as networks of communication and cooperation, produce effects which generate surplus value.[5] Similarly, in *Kraken* when Billy observes 'it's all metaphor [...] it's persuasion' (*K*, 460) he realizes that belief, in the form of the diverse faiths and cults he has encountered, and magic (knacking) are immaterial things with concrete social effects, i.e. metaphor and beliefs are primarily immaterial but have discernible material effects in producing certain ways of life. As Billy observes, '[y]ou have to persuade the universe that things make sense a certain way. That's what knacking is' (*K*, 98); the magick of *Kraken* is an effort to demonstrate perspective through estrangement.

Representing the Complexity of the World; Or, 'It Is What It Is' (*IC*, 462)

An important dimension of Miéville's writing which underpins my argument is an assertion of non-reducible values; this is partly a response to his Marxist perspective, an opposition to capital's reduction of life to instrumental functions in networks of finance and commodities, but it also has aesthetic implications for the representation of other forms of value which go beyond this: it is philosophical. He introduces a conception of excess which is evident at the micro-level of sentences and description in texts such as *The Scar*, where the mysterious Avanc is known variously as '[t]he mountain-that-swims, the godwhale, the greatest beast ever to visit our world' (*TS*, 190), and moves using 'fins or filaments or paws or gods knew what' (*TS*, 397). This attention to excesses of possibilities is present in the comparatively minimalist techniques of Miéville's shorter fictions. For example, the protagonist of 'Go Between', a man named Morley receives his anonymous object to pass on and imagines the multiple, contradictory outcomes it might produce:

> Morley saw the little bullet or bullet-shaped thing or tightly folded instructions in a bulletlike case held in the hand of the horse rider or the doctor whose test discredited him, in the pocket of the African general who took power promising peace, in the gun belt of the mercenary whose forces invaded the capital. (*LFJ*, 131)

In each instance, the object or creature described has three possible similarities, which produce quite different chains of association. Morley never discovers what the object was and the reader of *The Scar* similarly never finds out what the Avanc might really resemble or what limbs it uses to move, except through a potentially unreliable character (a storyteller). This refusal of closure is central to the plots of all of Miéville's fictions and it is the key to understanding what critical and creative resources the concept of the abnatural offers to Miéville's reader; presenting multiple, simultaneous metaphorical comparisons without implied hierarchy or synthesis.

In *Perdido Street Station*, Isaac's defeat of the Slake-moths depends upon a radically irresolvable comparison between three minds. The engine compares the mind of the collective machine consciousness of The Construct Council (x), and the singular dream-like consciousness of the Weaver (y), with one human mind, Andrej (z). The implication is that the three minds form a dialectical progression of thesis, antithesis and synthesis but Miéville refuses this reduction and it is the irreducibility of the problem which defeats the Slake-moths by giving them an excess of their food. The crisis engine is forced to recognize that all three are complete wholes $x + y \neq z$ while being expected to still be able to compare them as $x + y = z$:

y and *x* were unified bounded wholes. And most crucially, so was *x*, Andrej's mind, the reference point for the whole model. *It was integral to the form of each that they were totalities.* (*PSS*, 772; emphasis in original)

No-one is reducible by being comparable: they are all *singular* but clearly have access to a *common* that literally exceeds restraint (here in the form of too much energy, too much Slake-moth food). This emphasis on plenitude is a similar point that is reached by the Ariekei at the conclusion of *Embassytown*: '$\frac{embassy}{town}$, they say, or $\frac{town}{embassy}$, or $\frac{embassytown}{embassytown}$' (*E*, 345). In the Language of the Hosts, in its new formulation, the three linguistic formulations are all similar and all refer to the same object, but are also all different and not reducible to each other; the fact that all three can be used has an additive effect similar to the conception of music as a representation of subjectivity in the conclusion of *King Rat*: 'one plus one equals one' (*KR*, 398). These formulations indicate the excessiveness of the world being described, the complexity of which cannot simply be reduced to signification and exceeds language. Most significantly, these formulations work to represent both the fantasy form in which Miéville is writing and also a perspective on the real world of contemporary capitalism. Mark Bould has effectively argued that the contrary equations of *Perdido Street Station* and the hybrid subjectivity of Saul in *King Rat* suggest that the genre of fantasy always exceeds the sum of its parts (techniques, conventions, devices). We can take this further if we apply the same principle to the objects, concepts and skills Miéville's characters actually use to effect the conclusions of their plots, if we take them *at strict face value*: these stories are literally about the irreducibility of music, community, and metaphor because these things all concern the meeting and interaction of the material and immaterial.

In drawing my argument to a close I want to return to Miéville's fictional debut in *King Rat* (1998), in which club culture and club music act as a reflection of the dyad of subjective experience (fantasy) and collective experience (cultural activity), as both material and immaterial. The sub-plots of the novel present individual subjectivity and collective practice in an uneasy dialogue through the perspectives of Natasha the DJ and the artist Fabian. According to Carl Freedman (2003), this dialogue is ultimately resolved through the central character Saul, who unites the urban aesthetics of the Drum and Bass scene with what Freedman identifies as a Marxist sublime. In contrast, I want to concentrate on the emergent qualities of music culture in the novel. The power of the Piper to manipulate both people and animals comes through his music and King Rat's fathering of Saul is an attempt to create a being who will not be governable by the Piper's logic – Saul is a singularity, being both human and rat and so not purely susceptible to any one of the Piper's tunes. In a structural echo of this underlying plot, Natasha's approach to the act of DJing is a subject-orientated way of viewing the singularity of sample music as a cultural activity which explains this logic; when she makes her tracks, the whole is always something more than the elements of its composition:

> When she finished a track she did not feel any purgation of relief, only a slight unease. Natasha would cast around, ransacking her friends' record collections in an attempt to find the sounds she wanted to steal, or would make her own on her keyboard, but they never touched her like the bass. [....]
>
> The track was nearing a crescendo now: *Gwan,* exhorted a sampled voice, *Gwan gyal.* Natasha broke the beat, teasing the rhythm out, paring it down. She stripped flesh from the tune's bones and the samples echoed in the cavernous ribcage, in the belly of the beat. (*KR*, 68)

Natasha's relationship to sampling and to the bass operates here as a metaphor for club culture, in that no single element (music, artwork, dancers, DJs) fully defines the whole experience just as no sample fully defines the whole track and no single track the whole mix, even though the bass determines them all. Her 'unease' is symbolic: nothing is ever complete as a track, or as a mix, because these are only dimensions of the experience of the DJ; the totality emerges in performance within club culture: 'It was the bass that united the Junglists, that cemented their community' which is contrasted to the 'hive mind' the Piper creates (*KR*, 397). The passage above satirizes the process: Miéville's reader is being walked through the subjective experiences of the concrete activities of a DJ, being made conscious in the process that this also metonymically stands-in for the concrete activities of the writer; *whilst still being irreducibly itself*. It prepares the way for Saul's ultimate realization of his own subjective status when he confronts the Piper: 'one plus one equals one, motherfucker [....] I'm bigger than either one and I'm bigger than the two. I'm a new thing' (*KR*, 398).

Music and art are thus presented in *King Rat* as abnatural resources within club culture: each directly analogous to the work of fantasy (writing/reading). More importantly, the *combination* of the individual and subjective dimensions of club culture with the interactive, community aspects that music requires, is *also* directly analogous to fantasy. In this sense, we might read this bringing together of subjective experience and collective encounter as enacting 'the common' in the way in which Hardt and Negri propose. It functions as an immaterial resource of continuous potential complexity. It is here that we arrive at Miéville's social dialectic: cultural activities are irreducible, their subjective experience is beyond measurement in material terms. Such experiences can only be expressed in terms of immaterial qualities – this is the social power of fantasy, which can render these abnatural resources, found in the everyday, visible and comprehensible. Using different cultural activities which have material and immaterial aspects, i.e. abnatural resources – including the making of revolution Miéville explores how we can reconceive the individual within social networks, and social networks within our own individuality, away from the overweening demand to produce surplus value for use by capital, and towards something beneficial to the ordinary processes of actually living.

Conclusion

Miéville's 'abnatural' is sometimes presented as a rupture in the rules of his secondary world but it retains an intimate proximity to the conditions of our real world, as in the instance of The Scar itself or the Cacotopic Stain, where each of these (similarly and/or singularly) unknowable forces serves to make concrete the social moments of transformation. 'Hedrigall's extraordinary, improbable story', we are told, 'has set [the citizens] free' to stand up to the Lovers' drive to take the whole of Armada into The Scar: it is a possible future that affects the decisions of the Armadans to avoid it, an unverifiable story that gives 'them the certainty they needed' and takes on the social effects of supporting a mutiny (*TS*, 765). As a sort of mirror to this, the transformation in *Iron Council* of part of the Iron Council train and those Iron Councillors within it into a giant cell makes physical, or literalizes, what was implied by their collectivity and solidarity (*IC*, 462). Miéville's abnatural can be found in those forces which affect us daily and can thus be understood to be already immanent in our everyday lives. By exploring the fantastic power of subjective choice and communal interaction to create transformative changes between alien cultures on alternate worlds – from New Crobuzon in *Perdido Street Station* to the colonial outpost of Embassytown on the Ariekene world – Miéville is highlighting these existing powers as already within our grasp. He achieves this by their *comparison* with the impossible-to-us powers manifested within his fictions, which rupture space and time. Analogically, we can read these powers in Miéville's fiction as creatively bridging our actually existing social divisions in ways that recognize both the singularity of our selves within our multicultural frames of reference, and simultaneously the commonality that emerges from that recognition.

Miéville's abnatural shows cultural activities to be possessed of irreducibly subjective, yet common, qualities that are analogous to all other irreducible parts of everyday life – allowing us to forge solidarities of experience across apparent divisions in the manner of Hardt and Negri's multitude. I have suggested in this chapter that we read the parts of Miéville's fiction concerned with social practices literally. Experiencing live music events and DJ sets, dancing and singing, storytelling and reading, are worthwhile activities which encapsulate radical, fantastical experiences, which can *also* be understood as metaphors, but *in themselves* enunciate the abnatural resources of social activities. Those are the abnatural resources we can find in Miéville's fiction; let's see what we can make with them.

Notes

1 I suggest Miéville follows John Clute and Peter Nicholl in defining SF as a subset of Fantasy. They write: 'There is no definition of SF that excludes fantasy' because 'all sf is fantasy, but not all fantasy is sf' (Clute and Nicholl, 1993: 407–8).

2 Public documents in New Zealand, such as governmental papers, and public sector contracts, recognize Maori as 'Treaty Partners and Tangata Whenua', embedding this use of 'host' and 'indigenous people' in public discourse. For definitions of *tangata whenua*, see: http://www.maoridictionary.co.nz/search?keywords=tangata+whenua (consulted 30 July 2015).

3 For discussion of the emergence of political collective subjects such as 'the masses' and 'the people' see Neocleous (2003).

4 '*Absurd*: from *ab*, away [...] and *surdus*, deaf, inaudible, insufferable to the ear [....] A surd in mathematics is a sum containing one or more irrational roots of numbers. The square root of two is an irrational number. There is a square root of two but it is not any number that can be said, rationally. A *surd* in phonetics is a voiceless sound, that is to say, a sound with no base in the vibration of the vocal chords' (Miller, 1985: 394, emphasis in original).

5 Hardt and Negri (2004: 110) use examples such as air steward roles which increase a sense of well-being, satisfaction or happiness in airline passengers which then benefit the airline. They also discuss the immaterial relationships of agriculturalists to traditional knowledge and present climatic conditions, and the affective labour of homemaking: 'domestic labour does require such repetitive material tasks as cleaning and cooking, but it also involves producing affects, relationships, and forms of communication and cooperation among children, in the family, and in the community' (Hardt and Negri, 2006: 110).

Works Cited

Bould, Mark (2002) 'The Dreadful Credibility of Absurd Things: A Tendency in Fantasy Theory', *Historical Materialism* 10(4): pp. 51–88.

Bould, Mark (2003) 'What Kind of Monster Are You?: Situating the Boom', *Science Fiction Studies* 30(3): 394–413.

Clute, John and Nicholl, Peter (1993) *The Encyclopaedia of Science Fiction*. London: Orbit.

Eden, David (2012) *Autonomy: Capitalism, Class, and Politics*. Farnham and Burlington, VT: Ashgate Publishing.

Freedman, Carl (2003) 'Towards a Marxist Urban Sublime: Reading China Miéville's *King Rat*', *Extrapolation* 44(4): 395–408.

Garland, Christian (2009) 'Autonomism' in *International Encyclopaedia of Revolution and Protest*, ed. Immanuel Ness, pp. 322–5. Oxford: Blackwell.

Gordon, Joan (2003) 'Revelling in Genre: An Interview with China Miéville', *Science Fiction Studies* 30(3): 355–75, URL (consulted 30 July 2015), http://www.depauw.edu/sfs/interviews/mievilleinterview.htm

Hardt, Michael and Negri, Antonio (2000) *Empire*. Cambridge, MA: Harvard University Press.

Hardt, Michael and Negri, Antonio (2004) *Multitude: War and Democracy in the Age of Empire*, Kindle Edition. New York: Penguin.

Hardt, Michael and Negri, Antonio (2009) *Commonwealth*, Kindle Edition. Cambridge, MA: The Belknap Press of Harvard University Press.

Marx, Karl (1867, 1885/2013) *Capital: Volumes One and Two*, ed. Mark G. Spencer. Ware: Wordsworth Classics.

Miéville, China (2002b) 'Marxism and Fantasy: Editorial Introduction', *Historical Materialism* 10(4): 39–49.

Miéville, China (2003) 'Fifty Fantasy & Science Fiction Books That Socialists Should Read', in *Breaking Windows: The Fantastic Metropolis Reader*, ed. Luis Rodrigues, pp. 187–96. Canton, OH: Prime Books.

Miéville, China (2005) *Between Equal Rights: A Marxist Theory of International Law*. London: Pluto Press.

Miéville, China (2009) 'Cognition as Ideology: A Dialectic of SF Theory', in Mark Bould and China Miéville (eds) *Red Planets: Marxism and Science Fiction*, pp. 231–248. London: Pluto Press.

Miéville, China (2011) 'A Life in Writing', *Guardian*, 14 May 2011 URL (consulted 30 July 2015), http://www.theguardian.com/books/2011/may/14/china-mieville-life-writing-genre

Miller, J. Hillis (1985) *The Linguistic Moment*. Princeton, NJ: Princeton University Press.

Neocleous, Mark (2003) *Imagining the State*. Maidenhead: Open University Press.

Newsinger, John (2000) 'Fantasy and Revolution: An Interview with China Miéville', *International Socialism* 88: 153–63.

Tyler, Imogen (2013) *Revolting Subjects: Social Abjection and Resistance in Neoliberal Britain*. London and New York: Zed Books.

Virno, Paolo (2004) *A Grammar of the Multitude*, trans. Isabella Bertoletti, James Cascaito and Andrea Casson. Los Angeles and New York: Semiotext(e).

11

Afterweird
Konvolut n + 1: City/Slither

Roger Luckhurst

Explanatory Note

As you may have heard on the grapevine, the research team I have constructed has been built up from experts across many disciplines, with members coming from across the University of London, but also numerous abquotidian operatives from the Diffuse College, from the International Necronautical Society, from members of the White Visitation (that counter-intelligence wing of PISCES), and some graduate students borrowed from Doctor Nathaniel Wingate Peaslee of Miskatonic University, of course well known for his skill at interpreting complex figures. This team has been assembled in emergency conditions due to the nature of our discovery, and I thank all of these colleagues, alive and undead, for their hard work, even though we are only just at the beginning of a long process.

As most readers of this convocation of papers are cultural critics and theoreticians, you will know the story of the remnants of the archive of Walter Benjamin, which is now mainly held in Berlin. Benjamin was an obsessive archivist and collator of his own works and projected works, leaving papers, notebooks, stashes of postcards and portions of his library among friends dotted across Europe as he sought safety from persecution in his stateless state. The reconstitution of his library in Paris after his permanent exile from Berlin in 1933 was all too brief. His friends and intellectual allies, Adorno, Horkheimer and others worked obsessively to bring these papers together and into print after the war and in the wake of Benjamin's desperate suicide and misburial in the village of Port Bou in 1940 on the French/Spanish border. For many scholars, the most triumphant victory against the attempt of Fascists to erase the traces of Benjamin's thought was no doubt the transcription and publication of the hundreds of pages of his unfinished *Passagen–Werk*, a complete edition of which was finally published, with full scholarly apparatus, in German in 1982 and in English translation as *The Arcades Project* in 1999.

As my colleague, Propheseer Esther Leslie has noted, there is a certain fetishism attached to the material traces of Benjamin's archive. The recent exhibition and book, *The Archive of Walter Benjamin*, pours over these remnants, the brute materiality of these convolutes or bundles of paper, the photographs, the postcards, the gnomic systems of annotation used by Benjamin. The scholars of the archive lovingly detail the tiny handwriting, the spatial distribution of his notes, the types of notebooks Benjamin used, the paper he requested especially from Berlin after his exile in order to ensure the pages of the Arcades manuscript be kept uniform. These texts are therefore some of the most over-fetishized archival materials of modern times.

Given that quality of attention, what we announce is rather astounding. **There is another, previously overlooked Konvolut amongst these papers**. It has rested there, not quite in plain sight, it is true, but rather in what we might call an odd, cross-hatched space between other bundles. It has been curiously overlooked, or perhaps been actively unseen, by all previous Benjamin scholars. Indeed, it took an expert in the geometry of infolding and weightomancy, an abmathematician, to see that there was something obtruded in these papers, inserted at an angle impossible in conventional Euclidean geometry. It was only when Propheseer Johann Zöllner of Leipzig examined the archive that the konvolut was discovered. Zöllner remains, after all, even 130 years after his death, the world's leading expert in fourth-dimensional space.

So, between Konvolut N, 'On the Theory of Knowledge, Theory of Progress' and Konvolut O, 'Prostitution, Gambling', is this extra text, abmathematically inserted and seemingly invisible except to those who have expertise in extreme librarianism or a training in non-Euclidean archivism. For obvious reasons, we have chosen to name this text, Konvolut n + 1.

This document only came to light in January of this year and has been kept secret until now. I have to acknowledge here that the status of this document is controversial, even to those who have been working so closely with it. The Konvolut appears to be consistent with the structure of Benjamin's note-taking, the text being built up largely from citations from elsewhere, some sourced and some not, and with the occasional gnomic utterance from the compositor himself. It appears to be in Benjamin's handwriting, and we know how much importance Benjamin invested in graphology (handwriting was a *mystical* matter for him). Yet because these texts and images appear to be an accumulation of citations and images from the early years of the 21st century, many from the year 2012 and many about London, a city Benjamin never visited, the majority view of the research team is that this must either be a later, alien insertion into the manuscripts, which of course travelled from Georges Bataille in Paris to New York in 1947 and then back to Berlin after the war, or else a hoax perpetrated perhaps by disgruntled postgraduates to mock their elders and betters. This is of course possible.

There is a more radical interpretation, nevertheless. If Benjamin had himself mastered infolding and the manipulation of abspace to insert this secret annex, might he not also have mastered the ability to manipulate time too? Would this explain the obscure and controversial references to *time golemetry* in the letters between Gershom Scholem and Benjamin? Could this document be the trace of Benjamin's first and only visit to London, not in his lifetime, but somehow beyond or beside it? Had he unlocked the secret that the Parisian passages, the arcades with which he was so obsessed, were also Viae Ferrae or *rue sauvages*, those fugitive and mercurial urban pathways that allow one, so it is said, to worm so unpredictably through space and time? After all, remember what Esther Leslie affirms: 'Benjamin wrote consciously for the future, constructing from early on archives of his writings.' Perhaps soon we can add: Benjamin wrote consciously *from* the future. But I am not able to assert this with confidence yet. I therefore bow to the wisdom of my colleagues (and my referees for promotion) and will not presume the compositor of these texts is actually Walter Benjamin.

Well, here I am. Amid the salvage. What I must now do is lay this text before you, and open the discussion of the status of this text and what it might mean, to this convocation, this weird council.

Konvolut n + 1: City/Slither

(1) 'Method of this project: literary montage. I needn't *say* anything. Merely show. I shall purloin no valuables, appropriate no ingenious formulations. But the rags, the refuse – these I will not inventory but allow, in the only way possible, to come into their own: by making use of them.' (Benjamin, Konvolut N, p. 460)

(2) 'The ideal of shock-engendered experience is the catastrophe. This becomes very clear in gambling: by constantly raising the stakes, in hopes of getting back what is lost, the gambler steers towards absolute ruin.' (Benjamin, Konvolut O, p. 515)

(3) *'In an unremarkable room, in a nondescript building, a man sat working on very non-descript theories. The man was surrounded by .... piles of books like battlements around him. He propped them open on each other. He cross-referred them, seeming to read several at the same time.'* (unsourced quotation)

I Higher Space: n+1 dimensional geometry

1 'Our present conception of space, familiar to us from habit, has been derived from experience, i.e. from empirical facts by means of the causal principle existing *a priori* in our intellect. This in particular is said to be of the three dimensions of our present conception of space. If from our childhood phenomena had been of daily occurrence, requiring a space of four or more dimensions for an explanation which should be free from contradiction, i.e., comfortable to reason, we should be able to form a conception of space of four or more dimensions. It follows that the *real* existence of a four-dimensional space can only be decided by *experience*.' (Johann Zöllner, 'On the Space of Four Dimensions', 1878).

2 'In pursuing it ... the mind passes from one kind of intuition to a higher one, and with that transition the horizon of thought is altered. It becomes clear that there is a physical existence transcending the ordinary physical existence; and one becomes inclined to think that the right direction to look is, not away from matter to spiritual existence, but towards the discovery of conceptions of higher matter, and thereby of those material existences whose definite relations to us are apprehended as spiritual intuitions ... I can now lay it down as verifiable fact, that by taking the proper steps we can feel four-dimensional existence, that the human being somehow, and in some way, is not simply a three-dimensional being' (Charles Howard Hinton, *A New Era of Thought*, 1888)

3 'The possible law of which I speak is the Interpenetration of Worlds ... The limitations of time and space – three-dimensional space – furl up and disappear' (W. T. Stead, 'Throughth' [sic], 1893). Exemplary hauntological space. Read Blacklock.

4 'There was once a polemic about the right angle and the straight line; now the 90th degree has become one among many. In fact, remnants of former geometries create ever new havoc, offering forlorn nodes of resistance that create unstable eddies in newly opportunistic flows ...Who would dare claim responsibility for this sequence?' (Rem Koolhaas, 'Junkspace', 2013)

5 Hyperbolic Space. Margaret and Christine Wertheim, The Institute for Figuring, California. 'The Institute's interests are twofold: the manifestation of figures in the world around us and the figurative technologies that humans have developed through the ages. From the physics of snowflakes and the hyperbolic geometry of sea slugs, to the mathematics of paper folding, the tiling patterns of Islamic mosaics and graphical models

of the human mind, the Institute takes as its purview a complex ecology of figuring.' Can it be true, what they say, that the negative curvature of hyperbolic space, the Riemann space, was considered impossible, purely theoretical, but was solved by a woman scientist crocheting it into existence, while the men argued?

6 Early that summer, the newpapers reported that experts had tried to stage how Gareth Williams folded himself into a bag in Pimlico, only to suffocate there, at the mercy of his fetish for claustrophilia. Better reach for a narrative of conspiracy in the intelligence services, amongst the clichés of shadows and spooks, than to conceive the possibility of abmathematics. 'There are ways of folding into forgettable space' (Miéville, *Kraken*, 2010).

7 Lovecraft's doggerel:

> Some complex Fruit of multiple Dimensions,
> With modern Outlines and remote Pretensions,
> Which, scorning Euclid and the pedant Race,
> Revolts from time, and flings a sneer at Space

'Old Keziah, he reflected, might have had excellent reasons for living in a room with peculiar angles; for was it not through certain angles that she claimed to have gone outside the boundaries of the world of space we know? ... For some time, apparently, the curious angles of Gilman's room had been having a strange, almost hypnotic effect on him ... and he had found himself staring more and more intently at the corner where the down-slanting ceiling met the inward-slanting wall.' (Lovecraft, 'Dreams in the Witch-House', 1933)

8 For him, everything is encapsulated in Lovecraft's phrase 'an angle which was acute but behaved as if it were obtuse.' Reality skewed with the pure chutzpah of language. See in the London book: 'London's growing fake public space abjures the backstreet-and-alleyway gestalt of the city. It and its planners have little room for any urban contingency where railway bridges cut low over streets, on their own business, at angles that make no sense from below, forming strange obliques and acutes with the houses they meet.' (China Miéville, *London's Overthrow*, 2012, p. 71)

II City

'Don't fucking tell me about secret cities. Don't.'

'The old man Fitch maundered about back streets and hidden histories, described pentacles in the banalities of town planning.'

(Miéville, *Kraken*)

Lead us not into psychogeographical temptation.

1 'In Lovecraft, space is most profoundly altered by his oneiric vision of the world. The disordering of perspective is a phenomenon that affects the *surface*, an anomaly which above all concerns the art of the etcher or painter. When the space of the dreamer breaks down, it becomes far more alarming; its very substance is broken, its profound reality affected.

'The city, insofar as it is one of the places where space is most strongly condensed and structured, is in this regard the fantastic space par excellence. The more space is organized, the more it incites dream and calls for the compensations of the irrational. If there is a favourite motif in fantasy, it is that of the *ville double*: the real city, the diurnal city with its streets, its bridges, its churches – the city of the maps and charts – which suddenly blurs, dissolves in an opaque mist. On its site is left a dream city – certainly as real, but black, malefic.' (Maurice Lévy, *Lovecraft: A Study in the Fantastic*, 1988, p. 46)

Sometimes, novels are actually footnotes to pre-existent scholarship, reversing the usual order of things.

2 'It is exceedingly thoughtless to send a young boy out on an urgent and important errand into a night like that, because in its semiobscurity the streets multiply, becoming confused and interchanged. There open up, deep inside a city, reflected streets, streets which are doubles, make-believe streets. One's imagination, bewitched and misled, creates illusory maps of the apparently familiar districts, maps in which streets have their proper places and usual names but are provided with new and fictitious configurations by the inexhaustible inventiveness of the night. The temptations of such winter nights begin usually with the innocent desire to take a shortcut, to use a quicker but less familiar way. Attractive possibilities arise of shortening a complicated walk by taking some never-used side street. But on that occasion things began differently.' (Bruno Schulz, 'Cinnamon Shops', 1934/2008)

3 'Not to find one's way around a city does not mean much. But to lose one's way in a city, as one loses one's way in a forest, requires some schooling. Street names must speak to the urban wanderer like the snapping of dry twigs, and little streets in the heart of the city must reflect the times of

day, for him, as clearly as a mountain valley. This art I acquired rather late in life; it fulfilled a dream, of which the first traces were labyrinths on the blotting papers in my school notebooks.' (Benjamin, 'Tiergarten', *Berlin Childhood*)

4 'Crooked Street. Fairy tales sometimes speak of arcades and galleries that are lined on both sides with small establishments full of excitement and danger. In my youth I was acquainted with such a byway: it was called Krumme Strasse – that is, Crooked Street... In winter, the gaslight was already burning when I left the swimming pool to return home. That could not prevent me from taking a detour, which brought me round to my corner from the back way, as though I were looking to catch it red-handed' (Benjamin, *Berlin Childhood*).

5 Part from your friends at the station
Enter the city in the morning with your coat buttoned up
Look for a room, and when your friend knocks:
Do not, o do not, open the door
But
Cover your tracks!

If you meet your parents in Hamburg or elsewhere
Pass them like strangers, turn the corner, don't recognize them
Pull the hat they gave you over your face, and
Do not, o do not, show your face
But
Cover your tracks.

Eat the meat that's there.
Don't stint yourself.
Go into any house when it rains and sit on any chair that's in it
But don't sit long. And don't forget your hat.
I tell you:
Cover your tracks.

Whatever you say, don't say it twice
If you find your ideas in anyone else, disown them.
The man who hasn't signed anything, who has left no picture
Who was not there, who said nothing:
How can they catch him?
Cover your tracks.

See when you come to think of dying

That no gravestone stands and betrays where you lie
With a clear inscription to denounce you
And the year of your death to give you away.
Once again:
Cover your tracks.

(That is what they taught me).
                    (from Bertolt Brecht, 'Ten Poems from *A Reader for Those Who Live in Cities*')

6 'It wasn't even real, the Flâneur – it was just some folklore nightmare, some hallucination generated by the city. Why would you dream of seeking it out? That ancient, lonely thing wandering the city forever in search of someone who could speak its tale. No one knew what that story was, or what happened to those who heard it, but everyone knew that if you listened you were lost. You would never be the same again… Gradually he came to understand that hidden in some fold of every scene was the Flâneur, always moving on just around the next corner, and sometimes he felt on the brink of understanding why he wanted so much to follow; sometimes he felt sure that real mysteries do not conceal themselves but live beside us in plain view.' (Sam Thompson, *Communion Town*, 2012)

7 'The Bay. Marseilles, a dazzling amphitheatre, rises around the rectangle of the old harbour. The three shores of the square paved with sea, whose depth cuts into the city, are lined with rows of facades, each one like the next… In the spongy depths of the harbour quarter the fauna of humanity is teeming, and in the puddles the sky is pristine… The mass of humanity in which the peoples of different nations blend together is flushed through avenues and bazaar streets. These define the borders of the districts into which the human tide disperses. In the shell-like windings of one of those districts rages the eternal mass of small-time tradespeople.

'The Quadrangle. Whoever the place finds did not seek it. The alleys, crumpled paper streamers, are laced together without knots. Crossbeams traverse the soil wrinkles, rubbing against plaster, plummeting into the depths of basements, then ricocheting back to their starting point. A backstairs quarter, it lacks the magnificent ascending entrances. Grayish green smells of sea waste come smoldering out of open doors; little red lamps lead the way. In the spaces that afford a view, one finds improvised backdrops: rows of flying buttresses, Arabic signs, stair windings. If once leaves them behind, they are torn down and reconstructed at a different site. Their order is familiar to the dreamer.

'A wall heralds the square. It stands sleeplessly erect, sealing off the labyrinth... It is a quadrangle which has been stamped into the urban tangle with a giant template... In this tangle of pictorial alleys, no one seeks the quadrangle. After painstaking reflection, one would have to describe its size as moderate. But once its observers have settled into their chairs, it expands towards the four sides of the world, overpowering the pitiful, soft, private parts of the dream: it is a square without mercy.' (Siegfried Kracauer, 'Two Planes', 1926, after visit to Marseilles with Walter Benjamin, *The Mass Ornament*, 1995, pp. 37–9).

8   'Word got around. It does that. A city like London was always going to be a paradox, the best of it so very riddled with the opposite, so Swiss-cheesed with moral holes. There'd be all those alternative pathways to the official ones and to those that made Londoners proud: there'd be quite contrary tendencies.' (China Miéville, *Kraken*, p. 170)

'There are many millions of Londoners, and the very great majority know nothing of the other mapland, the city of knacks and heresies. Those people's magicians. The scale of the visible city dwarfs that of the mostly-unseen, and that unseen is not the only place where there are amazing things.' (China Miéville, *Kraken*, p. 180)

9   'How can the abstract forces shaping urban life be rendered artistically, spatially and informatively in the form of alternative "maps" which represent the urban invisibles, and are not usually accessible to routine professional expertise (such as the urban designer or architect) or the ordinary urban dweller? In what ways do the new visualizations provide deeper insights into the city than conventional maps are capable of revealing? We will examine mapping representations and methods that reveal the "unacknowledged of the city", reviewing the contemporary history and theory of mapping explorations in terms of exposing the "invisible" forces that shape our urban environment.' (Nadia Amoroso's Preface to *The Exposed City: Mapping the Urban Invisibles*, p. xi)

~~III Junkspace~~

~~III The Kefahuchi Tractatus~~

III Weird Space

1. ~~As I was walking, one hot summer afternoon, through the deserted streets of a provincial town in Italy, which was unknown to me, I found myself in a quarter of whose character I could not long remain in doubt. Nothing but painted women were to be seen at the windows of the small houses, and I hastened to leave the narrow street at the next turning. But after having wandered about for a time without inquiring my way, I suddenly found myself back in the same street, where my presence was now beginning to excite attention. I hurried away once more, only to arrive by another detour at the same place yet a third time. Now, however, a feeling overcame me which I can only describe as uncanny, and I was glad enough to find myself back at the piazza I had left a short while before, without any further voyages of discovery. (Sigmund Freud, 'The Uncanny', 1919, p. 359)~~ Precisely not this

2. ~~'In Saudade City, topology itself is the crime… SiteCrime — the frail human attempt to bring order to a zone which cannot be understood — must deal with boundary-shifts, abrupt fogs of hallucination, a daily illegal traffic in and out of the event site — people, memes and artefacts no one can quite describe.' (M. John Harrison, *Empty Space*, p. 74)~~

'When the Kefahuchi Tract expanded, in what came to be known as "the Event", parts of it fell to earth on planets all along the Beach. Event sites appeared everywhere, sometimes in deserts or polar icefields or at the bottom of the sea: but often alongside the cities.

'They were assembly-yards of the abnormal – zones where physics seemed to have forgotten its own rules – expanding into the real world via a perimeter of fogs, hallucinations, half-glimpsed movements. From inside could be heard confused laughter, big music, the sound of machinery. Something was being produced in there. Obsolete objects came fountaining out. They were highly energetic and abnormally scaled: rains of enamel badges, cheap rings, windup plastic toys; nuts & bolts, cups & saucers, horses & carts; feathers, doves and black-lacquered boxes, conjuror's props the size of houses. They burst into the air above the roofline then toppled back and vanished. A blueprint unfolded itself across the sky then folded itself up again and faded away. No one minded these illusions, if illusions they were. But artefacts and inexplicable new technologies came out of the Event site too, and sought a foothold on our side of things. Some of them were conscious and looked human. They wandered into the cities and tried to become a part of life. That was when things went wrong.' (M. John Harrison, *Empty Space*, p. 155)

'Back at the beginning it had been a fracturing, disconnective experience, a space flickering with bad light and worse topology. The tunnels, small-bore and intricately turned one moment, would become huge and simple the next; as full of generated sounds as they were echoes, with no way of telling which was which. "Worse," Gaines told the assistant as he led her along, "they changed their nature." One moment they were tiled with shiny ceramics, next some sort of organic-looking fibre was matted over everything. You could be in a blood vessel or waiting for a train, or feel yourself running like a fluid between glass plates: it was an archaeology from which anything could be intuited and of which nothing was true. ... "These are the safe parts," he said. "Back in the day, entire sections would go missing. They'd be one thing when you lost them, another when you found them again. In circumstances like that, you have to understand that your perception is what's fragmentary, not the space itself. At some level an organising principle exists, but you will never have any confirmation of it. It will always be unavailable to you."' (M. John Harrison, *Empty Space*, p. 259)

3 ~~Junkspace vs. Salvagepunk~~

Not really this:

'If space-junk is the human debris that litters the universe, junk-space is the residue that man leaves on the planet. The built product of modernization is not modern architecture but Junkspace. Junkspace is what remains after modernization has run its course or, more precisely, what coagulates while modernization is in progress, its fallout. Modernization had a rational program: to share the blessings of science, universally. Junkspace is its apotheosis, or meltdown

'Junkspace for children ... : sections of sudden miniaturization – often underneath staircases, always near dead ends – assemblies of under-dimensioned plastic structures – slides, seesaws, swings – shunned by their intended audience – kids – turned into junkniche for the old, the lost, the forgotten, the insane.

'Restore, rearrange, reassemble, revamp, renovate, revise, recover, redesign, return – the Parthenon marbles – redo, respect, rent: verbs that start with *re-* produce Junkspace' (Rem Koolhaas, 'Junkspace')

But this:

'Salvagepunk is the post-apocalyptic vision of a broken and dead world: the rubble, but also the work of salvaging, repurposing.

'Salvagepunk represents an attempt to think lost social relations via relations to discarded objects.' (Evan Calder Williams, *Combined and Uneven Apocalypse*)

Or this:

'montaging, for Benjamin, cannot be disassociated from the act of rescuing, the efforts to recycle rubbish, detritus, scraps that appear to have no value … Benjamin's procedure involved less a rescue of tradition that the rescue of experiences unacknowledged, experiences under threat, rejectamenta, materials on the point of disappearance' (Esther Leslie, *Walter Benjamin*, p. 62–3)

Salvage. Read on for recalcitrant matter.

IV Slither

1   Examples:

'Above the waist it was semi-anthropomorphic; though its chest, where the dog's rending paws still rested watchfully, had the leathery, reticulated hide of a crocodile or alligator. The back was piebald with yellow and black, and dimly suggested the squamous covering of certain snakes. Below the waist, though, it was the worst; for here all human resemblance left off and sheer phantasy began. The skin was thickly covered with coarse black fur, and from the abdomen a score of long greenish-grey tentacles with red sucking mouths protruded limply. Their arrangement was odd, and seemed to follow the symmetries of some cosmic geometry unknown to earth or the solar system. On each of the hips, deep set in a kind of pinkish, ciliated orbit, was what seemed to be a rudimentary eye; whilst in lieu of a tail there depended a kind of trunk or feeler with purple annular markings, and with many evidences of being an undeveloped mouth or throat. The limbs, save for their black fur, roughly resembled the hind legs of prehistoric earth's giant saurians, and terminated in ridgy-veined pads that were neither hooves nor claws. When the thing breathed, its tail and tentacles rhythmically changed colour, as if from some circulatory cause normal to the non-human greenish tinge, whilst in the tail it was manifest as a yellowish appearance which alternated with a sickly greyish-white in the spaces between the purple rings. Of genuine blood there was none; only the foetid greenish-yellow ichor which trickled along the painted floor beyond the radius of the stickiness, and left curious discoloration behind it.' (Lovecraft, 'The Dunwich Horror').

'A smoglodytic tentacled squid-goat thing'

'a mongrel of whale-shark distended by bio-thaumaturgy to be cathedral-sized, varicellate shelled, metal pipework thicker than a man in ganglia protuberant like prolapsed veins, boat-sized fins swinging on oiled hinges, a dorsal row of chimneys smoking whitely'

How to transform the Kantian abolition of disgust from aesthetics for these new urban creatures?

2 INSERT OBLIGATORY QUOTE FROM BRUNO LATOUR ON HYBRID OBJECTS and HETEROGENEOUS ASSEMBLAGES.

3 Alfred Tennyson, 'The Kraken' (1830)
   Below the thunders of the upper deep;
   Far, far beneath in the abysmal sea,
   His ancient, dreamless, uninvaded sleep
   The Kraken sleepeth: faintest sunlights flee
   About his shadowy sides: above him swell
   Huge sponges of millennial growth and height;
   And far away into the sickly light,
   From many a wondrous grot and secret cell
   Unnumbered and enormous polypi
   Winnow with giant arms the slumbering green.
   There hath he lain for ages and will lie
   Battening upon huge sea-worms in his sleep,
   Until the latter fire shall heat the deep;
   Then once by man and angels to be seen,
   In roaring he shall rise and on the surface die.

4 'But it may be fancied, that from the naked skeleton of the stranded whale, accurate hints may be derived touching his true form. Not at all.

For it is one of the more curious things about this Leviathan, that his skeleton gives very little idea of his general shape. Though Jeremy Bentham's skeleton, which hangs for candelabra in the library of one of his executors, correctly conveys the idea of a burly-browed utilitarian old gentleman, with all Jeremy's other leading personal characteristics; yet nothing of this kind could be inferred from any leviathan's articulated bones. In fact, as the great Hunter says, the mere skeleton of the whale bears the same relation to the fully invested and padded animal as the insect does to the chrysalis that so roundingly envelopes it.' (Herman Melville, 'Of the Monstrous Pictures of Whales', *Moby Dick*).

5 'Highly developed cephalopods live in the abysses of the sea, and the most developed species of them all is *Vampyroteuthis infernalis giovanni*. Should we care to recognize something of ourselves in this animal, we will have to plunge into its abyss.

'Humans and vampyroteuthes inhabit planet Earth, and yet the assertion that both of us occupy the same earth, as this chapter has attempted to show, is nonsense... At the moment when these embraces do come together, two earths will somehow converge: our bland and veneered world of appearances with its – energy-laden, orgasmic, and brutal as it is. Our *Daseins* will intertwine. The following considerations can be regarded as invitations to harrow this hell.' (Vilem Flusser and Louis Bec, *Vampyroteuthis Infernalis: A Treastise*, pp. 21 and 43).

6 Pynchon's Pavlovian octopus: '"Octopi", Spectro wheedles, "are docile under surgery. They can survive massive removals of brain tissue. Their unconditioned response to prey is *very* reliable – show them a crab, WHAM! out wiv the old tentacle, home to poisoning and supper. And, Pointsman, they don't *bark*.' (Thomas Pynchon, *Gravity's Rainbow*, p. 52).

V Seven Weird Theses

I The uncanny *always* goes home; the weird *has no home to start with*. No *oikos*, no pure originary state. Only non-Euclidean folds and refolds. With no origin, no death drive either, that exhausted geometry. Freudianism disabled.

II The old weird is premised on terror; the new weird on the possibilities inherent in boundary rupture. In Lovecraft, coupling and collapse leads to pathology, the panic of purification. After Lovecraft, a renegotiation with the legacies of history. Hopeful monsters: regenerative politics: new urban species. The weird bursts out of the chest of the old carcase in liberation, not horror. Read Vint.

III The weird *couples* inappropriate things, tangles objects. Hence the obsession with the copula and the ampersand. Hence also the love of puns and linguistic games, the insistent collapse or literalization of metaphors. Knuckleheads. Marge. 'We've got feelers out.' 'Spare me the littoral-minded.' Read Easterbrook.

IV Gloss the phrase: 'radicalised sublime backwash' (Miéville, 'Weird Fiction', p. 511). The stub of the numinous, torn out, like a rotting tooth, and flung back at the riot police.

V The weird builds its own archive. It is a tissue of texts and citations. Fake grimoires remixing older, faker grimoires. Remember Sorensen's question about the *Necromonicon* that writes itself into being: 'What are we to make of an archive of texts that point toward their own possible future composition?' (Leif Sorensen, p. 518). Then Lovecraft: 'Meant to last as long as the race, and to withstand the fiercest of earth's convulsions, this titan repository surpassed all other buildings in the massive, mountain-like firmness of its construction' (Lovecraft, 'The Shadow Out of Time', p. 360)

VI The weird builds worlds precisely to breach them. *It is* (in) *Breach*. This is profane illumination, *not* Clute's metaphysic of vastation. Vastation is 'an emotion linked to the story of the world at those moments when that story threatens to overwhelm us, or when its incoherence or coherence becomes mercilessly visible' (Clute, *The Darkening Garden*, 2006). My starry speculative arse.

VII A painting by Klee's lesser known brother named 'Tentaculex Novus' shows an octopus looking as though he is about to move away from something he is fixedly contemplating. His eyes are staring, his mouth is open, his tentacles are spread. This is how one pictures the octopus of history. His face is turned toward the past. Where we perceive a chain of events, he sees one single catastrophe which keeps piling wreckage upon wreckage and hurls it in front of his tentacles. The octopus would like to stay, awaken the dead, and make whole what has been smashed. But a storm is blowing; it has got caught in his tentacles with such violence that the octopus can no longer close them. This storm irresistibly propels him into the future to which his back is turned, while the pile of debris before him grows skyward. This storm is what we call progress.

Works Cited

Amoroso, Nadia (2010) *The Exposed City: Mapping the Urban Invisibles*. New York: Routledge.
Benjamin, Walter (1968) 'Theses on the Philosophy of History', in *Illuminations*, ed. Hannah Arendt, pp. 253–63. New York: Harcourt.
Benjamin, Walter (2002) *The Arcades Project*, trans. Howard Eiland and Kevin McLaughlin. Cambridge, MA: Harvard University Press.
Benjamin, Walter (2006) *Berlin Childhood Around 1900: Hope in the Past*, trans. Howard Eiland and Michael W. Jennings. Cambridge, MA: Harvard University Press.
Blacklock, Mark (2012) 'On the Eve of the Fourth Dimension: Utopian Higher Space', in R. Gregory and B. Kohlmann(eds) *Utopian Spaces of Modernism: Literature and Culture, 1885–1945*, pp. 35–51. Basingstoke: Palgrave.
Brecht, Bertolt (1976) 'Ten Poems from *A Reader for Those Who Live in Cities*', in *Bertolt Brecht, Poems*, ed. John Willett and Ralph Mannheim, pp. 131–50. London: Methuen.
Clute, John (2006) 'Vastation', in *The Darkening Garden: A Short Lexicon of Horror*, pp. 147–51. Cauheegan: Payseur and Schmidt.
Easterbook, Neil (2009) 'Alterity and Ethics', in Mark Bould, Andrew M. Butler and Adam Roberts and Sherryl Vint (eds) *The Routledge Companion to Science Fiction*, pp. 382–92. London: Routledge.
Easterbook, Neil (2011) 'Languages and Monsters (a review of *Embassytown*)', *Los Angeles Review of Books*, 26 August 2011 (consulted 14 July 2015), http://lareviewofbooks.org/review/language-and-monsters
Flusser, Vilem and Louis Bec (2012) *Vampyroteuthis Infernalis: A Treatise, with a Report by the Institut Scientifique de Recherche Paranaturaliste*, trans. Valentine Pakis. Minneapolis: University of Minnesota Press.
Freud, Sigmund (1919/2001) 'The Uncanny', in *The Standard Edition of the Complete Psychological Works of Sigmund Freud, Vol. XVII: An Infantile Neurosis and Other Works*, trans. James Strachey and Anna Freud, pp. 217–56. London: Vintage.
Haraway, Donna (1992) 'The Promises of Monsters: A Regenerative Politics for In/Appropriate(d) Others', in Lawrence Grossberg, Cary Nelson and Paula Treichler (eds) *Cultural Studies*, pp. 295–337. London: Routledge.
Harrison, M. John (2012) *Empty Space: A Haunting*. London: Gollancz.
Hinton, Charles Howard (1888) *A New Era of Thought: Scientific Romances*. London: Swan Sonnenschein and Company.

Koolhaas, Rem (2013) *Junkspace*, ed. Hal Foster. London: Notting Hill Editions.
Kracauer, Siegfried (1963/1995) 'Two Planes' in *The Mass Ornament: Weimar Essays*, trans. and ed. Thomas Y. Levin, pp. 37–9. Cambridge, MA: Harvard University Press.
Latour, Bruno (2004) *Politics of Nature: How to Bring Sciences into Society*, trans. Catherine Porter. Cambridge, MA: Harvard University Press.
Leslie, Esther (2007) *Walter Benjamin*. London: Reaktion Books.
Lévy, Maurice (1988) *Lovecraft: A Study in the Fantastic*, trans. S. T. Joshi. Detroit, MI: Wayne State University Press.
Lovecraft, H. P. (2013) *Classic Horror Stories*, ed. Roger Luckhurst. Oxford: Oxford University Press.
Marx, Ursula et al. (eds) (2007) *Walter Benjamin's Archive: Images, Texts, Signs*, trans. Esther Leslie. London: Verso.
McCarthy, Tom et al. (2012) *The Mattering of Matter: Documents from the Archive of the International Necronautical Society*. Berlin: Sternberg Press.
Miéville, China (2009) 'Weird Fiction', in Mark Bould, Andrew M. Butler and Adam Roberts and Sherryl Vint (eds) *The Routledge Companion to Science Fiction*, pp. 510–15. London: Routledge.
Miéville, China (2012a) 'Alien Invasion', *Arc Infinity* 1(1): 32–9.
Miéville, China (2012b) *London's Overthrow*. London: The Westbourne Press.
Melville, Herman (1851/1983) *Moby Dick, or, The Whale*. Berkeley: University of California Press.
Pynchon, Thomas (1973/2013) *Gravity's Rainbow*. London: Vintage.
Schulz, Bruno (2008) *The Street of Crocodiles and Other Stories*, trans. Celina Wieniewska, London: Penguin.
Sorensen, Leif (2010) 'A Weird Modernist Archive: Pulp Fiction, Pseudobiblia, H. P. Lovecraft', *Modernism/Modernity* 17(3): 501–22.
Stead, W. T. (1893) 'Throughth: Or, on the Eve of the Fourth Dimension: A Record of Experiments in Telepathic Automatic Handwriting', *Review of Reviews* 7: 426–32.
Thacker, Eugene (2015) *Starry Speculative Corpse: Horror of Philosophy*, Vol. 2, Alresford: Zero Books.
Thompson, Sam (2012) *Communion Town*. London: Fourth Estate.
Vint, Sherryl (2012) *Animal Alterity: Science Fiction and the Question of the Animal*. Liverpool: Liverpool University Press.
Williams, Evan Calder (2011) *Combined and Uneven Apocalypse: Luciferian Marxism*. Alresford: Zero Books.

Zöllner, Johann (1878) 'On the Space of Four Dimensions', *Quarterly Journal of Science* 8: 227–37.

Notes on Contributors

Ben de Bruyn is an Assistant Professor at Maastricht University and an active member of the research groups BASCE, MDRN and CERES. He is the author of the first book-length study of Wolfgang Iser's reception theory (De Gruyter, 2012) and has published articles on ecology, posthumanism, book history and the (non)circulation of objects in journals like *English Studies*, *Oxford Literary Review* and *Neohelicon*. His current book project deals with the representation of animals in the twenty-first century novel.

Caroline Edwards is Lecturer in Modern & Contemporary Literature at Birkbeck, University of London. She is completing a monograph entitled *Fictions of the Not Yet: Time and the Contemporary British Novel*, which explores the representation of time and utopia in twenty-first-century British fiction. She is co-editor of *Maggie Gee: Critical Essays* (Gylphi, 2015) and the *Reader's Guide to Contemporary Literary Theory*, 6th edition (Routledge, 2017). Caroline is also Editorial Director of the *Open Library of Humanities* and is Founding and Commissioning Editor of *Alluvium*, an open-access journal of twenty-first-century literary criticism.

Anthony F. Lang, Jr. holds a Chair in International Political Theory in the School of International Relations at the University of St Andrews, where he is the founder and Director of the Centre for Global Constitutionalism. He is an editor of *Global Constitutionalism*, and is on the editorial board of the *Journal of International Political Theory* and *Ethics & International Affairs*. His research and teaching focus on international political theory, particularly the intersection of law, ethics, and politics at the global level, with an occasional regional focus on the Middle East. His most recent book is *International Political Theory: An Introduction* (Palgrave, 2014).

Roger Luckhurst is Professor of Modern Literature at Birkbeck, University of London.

Dougal McNeill teaches in the School of English, Film, Theatre, and Media Studies, Victoria University of Wellington. He is the author, with Charles Ferrall, of *Writing the 1926 General Strike: Literature, Culture, Politics* (Cambridge University Press, 2015).

Paul March-Russell teaches Comparative Literature at the University of Kent. He is editor of *Foundation: The International Review of Science Fiction*, commissioning editor for SF Storyworlds (Gylphi), and an editorial advisor to the journal, *Short Fiction in Theory and Practice*. He is also a member of the European Research Network for Short Fiction and a founding member of the May Sinclair Society. His most recent book, *Modernism and Science Fiction*, is published by Palgrave Macmillan in 2015. He is currently writing chapters for both *The Cambridge Companion to the English Short Story* (ed. Ann-Marie Einhaus) and *The Cambridge History of the English Short Story* (ed. Dominic Head).

Joe Sutliff Sanders is an Associate Professor at Kansas State University, where he teaches in the children's literature graduate track of the English Department. He is the author of *Disciplining Girls: Understanding the Origins of the Classic Orphan Girl Novel* (Johns Hopkins University Press, 2011), the co-editor of a collection of new essays on *The Secret Garden* (Scarecrow, 2011), and the editor of the forthcoming *The Comics of Hergé: When the Lines Are not so Clear* (University Press of Mississippi, forthcoming).

Matthew Sangster is Lecturer in English Literature at the University of Birmingham. Prior to this, he completed a PhD at Royal Holloway, University of London, taught in London and Oxford, and conducted research using the library records held at the University of St Andrews. His work principally focuses on authorship in the Romantic period, but he is also interested in fantasy writing and contemporary fiction. In 2011, he co-curated (with Zoë Wilcox) 'The Worlds of Mervyn Peake', a centenary exhibition held at the British Library. He is currently thinking about literary institutions, digital communication, and how genres can best be used.

Sherryl Vint is Professor of Science Fiction Media Studies at the University of California, Riverside, where she co-directs the Science Fiction and Technoculture Studies program. An editor of the journals *Science Fiction Studies* and *Science Fiction Film and Television*, she is the author of a number of books, most recently *Science Fiction: A Guide for the Perplexed* (Bloomsbury, 2014).

Tony Venezia has taught contemporary literature, culture, and cultural theory at Birkbeck, University of London, London South Bank University, and Middlesex University. He is currently transforming his doctoral thesis into a monograph entitled *Alan Moore and the Historical Imagination*. He is founder and co-organizer of the annual Transitions Comica Symposium at Birkbeck and is on the editorial board of the journal *Studies in Comics*. He has also been involved with conferences and publications on twenty-first century British fiction, on US author David Foster Wallace, and on British comics writer Warren Ellis. He is co-convenor of the Contemporary Fiction Seminar at the Institute of English Studies at Senate House. For more details see http://researchingthecontemporary.net/

Mark P. Williams is currently a Teaching Fellow (Wissenschaftlicher Mitarbeiter) in the Department of English and Linguistics at Johannes Gutenberg University of Mainz. He has previously taught at Victoria University of Wellington (New Zealand) and the University of East Anglia (UK), and has also worked as a political reporter in the New Zealand Parliamentary Press Gallery. His research focuses on literature and politics; crossovers between Science Fiction and Fantasy modes and avant-garde writing are of particular interest, especially the cultural innovations of the SF 'New Wave' and the New Weird. Recent publications include a literary history for *The 1970s: A Decade of Contemporary Fiction* (Bloomsbury, 2014), and a forthcoming critical survey of experimental fiction for *The 1990s: A Decade of Contemporary Fiction* (Bloomsbury, 2015). In 2014 he organized a conference on 'The Science Fiction "New

Wave" At Fifty' at the University of East Anglia and will be co-editing a special edition of *Foundation* on New Wave SF.

Raphael Zähringer is a research assistant in English literature and cultural studies at the University of Tübingen. His major interests are in the field of dystopian fiction, graphic narrative, and spatial-turn approaches to literature. He has recently finished his dissertation (title: 'Hidden Topographies: Traces of Urban Reality in Dystopian Fiction'), in which he discusses spatial concepts of recent dystopian novels by bringing together the literary history of the dystopian tradition, concepts of reality and fictionality, and systems-theoretical lines of thought.

Index

abnatural 30–31, 239–264
ab-realism 24, 30, 39–60
Actor-Network Theory (ANT) 16
American Library Association
    (ALA)
  Caldecott medal 130
  Newbery medal 130–132
Amis, Martin
  Invasion of the Space Invaders xv
anti-capitalism 25, 91, 93–95,
       98–99, 100–104, 112–113,
       114n.2, 114n.4, 115n.9,
       115n.11. *See also* capitalism
author-function xiv
authorial intent xiv

Badiou, Alain
  the Event 14
Balchin, Nigel
  No Sky xv
Ballard, J. G. 3, 167
  Drowned World, The 19
  Wind from Nowhere, The xiv
Banks, Iain M. 2
Barker, Clive
  Books of Blood 3
Barthes, Roland
  Empire of Signs 72–73, 74
Baum, L. Frank
  Oz 123
Baxter, Stephen 2
Beeck, Nathalie op de 132

Bellmer, Hans 15
Benjamin, Walter 15, 26, 89–118,
    266
  One-Way Street 112
Beringer, Johann
  Lithographiæ Wirceburgensis xv
Berlin Wall
  collapse of (November 1989) 99
Birns, Nicholas 189
Bishop, K. J.
  Etched City, The 3
Blake, William 21
Bloch, Ernst 14, 57n.4, 58n.8
  utopian formulation of the 'Not
    Yet' 48
  'utopian trace' 45
Bloom, Harold
  Flight to Lucifer, The xv
Bloom, Nora
  Promise Me Tomorrow xv
Blyton, Enid
  Faraway Tree 122
Borges, Jorge Luis 140, 155
  Book of Imaginary Beings, The 19
Brecht, Bertolt 110
Breton, André
  'Gothic Marxism' 15
  Les Vases communicants 15
Brod, Max xvi
Brooke-Rose, Christine
  Dear Deceit, The xv
  Language of Love, The xv

Middlemen, The xv
Sycamore Tree, The xv
Brothers Grimm
   'The Twelve Dancing Princesses' 143
Burial (DJ/musician) 22
Butler, Octavia 163
   Survivor xiii

Calvino, Italo 143
campus novels 159–161
capitalism 12, 23–24, 40–41, 90, 101, 105, 106, 114, 218, 233, 241–245, 248, 251. *See also* ant-capitalism
   forces of 245
   real within 41
capitalist realism 24
Carey, Mike 6
Carpenter, Edward 95
Carroll, Lewis
   Alice's Adventures in Wonderland 120
cartography 20, 61–88. *See also* maps
Chandler, Raymond 139
children's literature 18, 26, 130–132, 134, 136
Chu, Seo-Young 43
   Do Metaphors Dream of Literal Sleep 39–40
'science-fictioneme' 40, 43
cognitive estrangement 34n.9, 39–41
Cold War 99
commodification xv, 217, 245
Conrad, Joseph 27–29
   Heart of Darkness 154
creative writing 28, 159–184
Critical Legal Studies (CLS) 218

Crush Design 14

Dash, Mike
   Borderlands xiv
DC Comics 6
Debord, Guy 20
de Certeau, Michel 68, 71–88, 79–80, 82–83
   Practice of Everyday Life, The 62–88
   'urban space' 62
   voyeur 72–81
Delano, Jamie 6
Delany, Samuel R. 3, 153
Deleuze, Gilles
   and Félix Guattari
      rhizome 57n.5, 78
      'virtual' 45
Delvaux, Paul 15
De Quincey, Thomas 21
Derrida, Jacques 5
Dickens, Charles
   Dombey and Son 107
Dick, Philip K. 3
doppelgänger 11

Egypt 228
Engels, Friedrich
   Socialism: Utopian and Scientific 95
Ernst, Max 15
Eugenides, Jeffrey
   Marriage Plot, The 160
European Union (EU) 214
Extrapolation 189

fantasy 6, 9, 16, 24–30, 34n.9, 40–41, 46, 48, 56, 61, 91–96, 101–107, 109, 111, 114n.5, 119–138, 144, 180n.1, 186, 188, 193, 197, 199,

206, 239, 242, 244–250,
253–255, 258, 260
Faulkner, William
As I Lay Dying 155
Filippo, Paul Di 3
Fleming, Ian
Spy who Loved Me, The xv
Ford, Laura Oldfield 22
Foundation 152
Fourier, Charles 95
Freedman, Carl 7, 95–96, 115n.11,
189, 259
Fukuyama, Francis
'end of History' 99

Gaiman, Neil 128–130, 133
Graveyard Book, The 26, 127
Gaskell, Jane
Shiny Narrow Grin, The xiii
General Strike, 1926 107
'generic overdetermination' 7
Genette, Gérard 64
Godwin, William
Caleb Williams 147
Gogol, Nikolai
'The Overcoat' 143
golemetry 47–48, 54, 58n.9,
96–98, 100, 110, 267
Goodreads 189–208
Gothic 105
fiction 21, 147
London 21
Marxism 94
metaphors 243
science fiction 16
urban 6, 11
Griffith, Nicola 2
Guardian 188

Hardt, Michael

and Antonio Negri 239, 242, 249
Commonwealth 233, 241, 248
Empire 241
Multitude 241
Harley, J. B. 70
Harrison, M. John 2
Third Alternative 3
Viriconium 3
hauntology 21
'Haute Weird' 2
historical materialism 15, 94
Hobb, Robin
Assassin's Apprentice 199–200
Hodgson, William Hope 2
Hopkins, Gerard Manley xv
Hutton, May Arkwright
*Coeur d' Alenes: or, A Tale of the
Modern Inquisition in Idaho,
The* xv
'hybrid' cultures 9

imperialism 225–234
International Court of Justice 214
international law 213–238

Jakobson, Roman 153, 154
James, M. R. 2, 21
Japanese culture 74
Jefferies, Richard
After London; or, Wild England 19
Jeter, K. W.
Star Wars 244
Jones, Gwyneth 2
Joyce, James
Ulysses 192
Juster, Norton
Phantom Tollbooth, The 120

Kafka, Franz xvi, 90, 139, 143
Kincaid, James R. 132
King, Stephen

Rage xv
Koskenniemi, Martti
  From Apology to Utopia 213
Kubin, Alfred 139

Lacan, Jacques
  the 'Real' 13
language 8–9, 62, 80, 104, 143, 145, 161, 173–179, 215, 226–228, 230–231, 246–247, 254–255, 258
  fractal 39–60
  persuasive power to shape the experience of reality 42
Latour, Bruno 16–17
Le Guin, Ursula 180n.1
Lem, Stanislaw
  Astronauts, The xv
L'Engle, Madeleine
  A Wrinkle in Time 130–131
Lenin 107
Lewis, C. S. 133
  Narnia Chronicles 26, 124–129
  Lion, The Witch and the Wardrobe, The 125
  Prince Caspian 124–125, 136n.1
Libya 228
linguistic philosophies 5
literary realism 109
Littell, Jonathan
  Bad Voltage xiv
  Kindly Ones, The xiv
Lodge, David
  Modes of Modern Writing, The 154
London 17–23, 32, 71, 83, 119–138, 160, 221, 247, 250–251, 267, 268, 270, 274
  Psychogeographical Society 21
Lovecraft, H. P. 21

'The Call of Cthulhu' 2
Weird Tales 2
Luxemburg, Rosa
  account of the Russian Revolution 92
  'Order Reigns in Berlin' 113

Machen, Arthur 2, 21
MacIntyre, Alastair xvi
MacLeod, Ken 2
Manichean binaries 14
maps 61–88. *See also* cartography
  as a narrative device 64
  double function of 25
  implicit narrativity of 70
  intra-textual 72–81
  map-making 25
  tendency towards desocialization 70–88
Martin, George R. R.
  A Game of Thrones 192
Marxism xvi, 8–10, 12–13, 16, 90–118, 215–216, 218–220, 232–233, 240, 245, 256
  and fantasy 40
Marxist
  dialectic 9
  historiography 10
Marx, Karl 215
  German Ideology, The 9
  materialist historiography 92
McCarthy, Cormac 163
McGurl, Mark
  Program Era, The 161–162
Mead, Margaret 180n.1
Melville, Herman
  Moby Dick 9, 42, 160
metafiction 164
metaphor 43, 44, 54, 55, 105, 256
  capacities of 40

Index

fractal power of 43, 49, 53, 56
 function of 254
 literalized 43, 47, 52
 polysemy of 43
 power of 51, 52
 theory of 50
Meyer, Stephanie
 Twilight 190, 191, 193
Miéville, China
 awards
  Arthur C. Clarke 2, 186
  British Fantasy 2
  Hugo Awards, The 2
  Locus 2, 186
  Nebula Awards, The 2
  World Fantasy 186
 Bas-Lag (trilogy) 6, 8, 46, 61–88, 66–88, 78–79, 90, 93, 102, 106, 169, 185, 195, 197
 essays
  London's Overthrow 23
  'M. R. James and the Quantum Vampire: Weird; Hauntological: Versus and/or and an/or or?' 14
 film scripts
  Deep State 7
 interviews
  with Stephen Shapiro 43
  with Steve Haynes 187
 non-fiction
  Between Equal Rights: A Marxist Theory of International Law 12
 novels
  City & The City, The 2, 6, 11, 48, 53, 139–158, 160, 168, 179, 193, 196, 213–238
  Embassytown 5, 6, 9, 12, 13, 14, 40, 55, 145, 159–184, 194, 195, 196, 213–238, 247, 248, 253, 254
  Iron Council 3, 4, 6, 9, 10, 42, 54, 89–118, 185–212, 239, 248, 252, 261
  58n.9
  King Rat 1, 6, 9, 17, 21, 170, 171, 196, 248, 252, 258
  Kraken 6, 12, 13, 14, 22, 49, 56, 168, 169, 179, 193, 195, 196, 247, 254, 255, 256
  Perdido Street Station 2, 3, 4, 12, 13, 14, 25, 43, 46, 61–88, 159–184, 186, 193, 196, 197, 198, 205, 246, 253, 255, 257, 258
  Railsea 6, 9, 10, 12, 15, 42, 160, 168, 173, 194, 195, 196
  Scar, The 2, 3, 6, 12, 13, 14, 42, 46, 57n.1, 57n.5, 186, 188, 193, 195, 197, 198, 205, 257
  Un Lun Dun 2, 6, 18, 26, 119–138, 159–160, 193, 195
 PhD in International Relations at the London School of Economics 12, 166, 170
 short fiction
  Looking for Jake and Other Stories 6, 194, 197
  'An End to Hunger' 19
  'Go Between' 18, 257
  'Looking for Jake' 6, 18
  'Reports of Certain Events in London' 21
  'The Tain' 9, 18, 19
  ''Tis the Season' 19
  Three Moments of an Explosion: Stories 6

'Polynia' 20
'The Bastard Prompt' 14
'Watching God' 6
mimesis
  SF 43
mimetic realism 24
modernity
  material experiences of 39
Moll, Herman
  A New & Correct Map of the Whole World 83n.2
Moore, Alan
  Swamp Thing 6
Morris, Jan 139
Morris, William
  News From Nowhere 18
Munroe, Randall
  xkcd 123

Nabokov, Vladimir 163
narration 112, 169, 202
  first-person 147
  third-person 147
Nazism xiv, 103
neoliberalism 102
Nesbit, E.
  Five Children and It 122, 144
New Wave fabulism 3
New Weird 4
  aesthetic strangeness of 2
nonrealist fiction 3
novum 7, 14

objectivity 83n.1
Observer 119
October Revolution 107
O'Hara, Frank 141
Oulipo 165
Owen, Robert 95

Palmer, Christopher 189
Pashukanis, Evgeny 234
  Law and Marxism: A General Theory 216–218
Pasternak, Boris 141
Pathfinder Chronicles: A Guide to the River Kingdoms (fantasy role-play game) 7
Peake, Mervyn 203
  Gormenghast 203
  Titus Alone 204, 205
  Titus Groan 203
Plato
  Republic, The 142
  ring of Gyges 142
political activism 104
postgrenre fiction 3
postmodern fantasy 3
Pound, Ezra 254
Priest, Christopher
  Glamour, The 139–158
Prynne, J. H.
  Force of Circumstance xiv, xviii
psychogeography 20–21
  contemporary psychogeographers 22
Pullman, Philip 128–130, 133
  His Dark Materials 26, 125–127, 128–129

Rankin, Ian 6
Rankin, Sandy 189
Reading Experience Database (RED) 190
realism 39
  capitalist 41
  limitations of 40
  mimetic 43, 45, 53, 54
reality 53
revolution 89–118, 225–234

China 102
Germany 112
Russia 102, 106
Ricoeur, Paul 5
Robson, Justina 2
Role Playing Games (RPGs) 254
Romantic Sublime 14
Roth, Philip 163
Rowling, J. K. 142

Saint-Simon, Henri de 95
Santolouco, Mateus 7
Saussure, Ferdinand de 5
Schmitt, Carl 230
Schulz, Bruno 139, 143, 155
  Cinnamon Shops, The (*The Street of Crocodiles*) 11
Science and Technology Studies (STS) 16
science fiction 2–4, 6–7, 8, 16–17, 39–41, 44, 56, 91–92, 92, 95, 102, 109, 111, 135, 140, 152–153, 153–154, 165, 167, 170, 172, 180n.1, 186, 202, 240, 242
Science Fiction Studies 154, 243
Scott, Sir Walter 143
Second World War 214
sexuality 131
SFReviews.net 119
Shakespeare
  Henry V 12
Sinclair, Iain 22
Situationists 20, 22
slipstream 3
Smith, Clark Ashton 2
Socialism 8, 89, 103
Soviet Union
  collapse of 150
Spearman, Frank H.

Whispering Smith 106
Stalinism 101–102
steampunk 3
Stephenson, Neal
  Cryptonomicon 202
  Diamond Age, The 202
  Quicksilver 202, 205
  Snow Crash 202
Stevenson, Robert Louis 21
  Treasure Island 64
storyworlds 61, 63, 66, 69, 81, 107, 112
Strugatsky, Boris
  Roadside Picnic 149
  Second Invasion from Mars, The 148, 149
Surrealism 15, 254
surrealist aesthetic 15
Suvin, Darko 17, 39, 46, 102, 153, 243
  critique of Fantasy 96
  Metamorphoses of Science Fiction: On the Poetics and History of a Literary Genre 16, 114n.5, 243
  Positions and Presuppositions in Science Fiction 243
  privileging of science fiction 9, 244
Swainston, Steph
  Year of Our War, The 3
Swift, Jonathan
  Gulliver's Travels 5, 25, 64

Tanguy, Yves 15
Tertz, Abram (Andrei Sinyavsky)
  'Pkhentz' 148
Thatcherism 94
Tokyo 72

Tolkienesque conservatism 9
Tolkien, J. R. R. 142
Tor UK 14
transrealism 3
Trotsky, Leon 92, 107
Tunisia 228

United Nations Security Council (UNSC) 214
utopia 99–100, 107, 213

vagrancy 71
VanderMeer, Jeff 4, 200
  and Ann VanderMeer
    New Weird, The 3
  City of Saints & Madmen 3, 200
  Finch 200
  Shriek 200
ventriloquizing xiv
Virgil
  Aeneid xvi
voyeur 62

Wallace, David Foster
  Infinite Jest 191, 192–193
Weinstock, Nathan
  Salon des Abandonnés xvi
  Zionism: False Messiah xvi
Weird 6, 21, 103, 104, 155, 175, 280
  fiction 159, 167, 171, 172, 180n.1
  literary 2, 4, 14, 23
  New Weird 3, 4, 17
  space 275
Wells, H. G.
  Invisible Man, The 142
White, T. H.
  Sword in the Stone, The 144
Winterson, Jeanette
  Boating for Beginners xiv

Wolfe, Gary K. 3
Woolf, Virginia
  To The Lighthouse 155, 192
World Trade Organization (WTO) 93
World War II. *See* Second World War
Wyndham, John
  Kraken Wakes, The 20

www.ingramcontent.com/pod-product-compliance
Lightning Source LLC
Chambersburg PA
CBHW052013290426
44112CB00014B/2220